Studio 1

Teacher's Guide

www.pearsonschools.co.uk
✓ Free online support
✓ Useful weblinks
✓ 24 hour online ordering

0845 630 33 33

Tracy Traynor

Heinemann
Part of Pearson

Heinemann is an imprint of Pearson Education Limited, a company incorporated in England and Wales, having its registered office at Edinburgh Gate, Harlow, Essex, CM20 2JE. Registered company number: 872828

www.pearsonschoolsandfecolleges.co.uk

Heinemann is a registered trademark of Pearson Education Limited

Text © Pearson Education Limited 2010

First published 2010

14 13 12
10 9 8 7 6 5 4

British Library Cataloguing in Publication Data
A catalogue record for this book is available from the British Library

ISBN 978 0 435 02776 6

Copyright notice
All rights reserved. No part of this publication may be reproduced in any form or by any means (including photocopying or storing it in any medium by electronic means and whether or not transiently or incidentally to some other use of this publication) without the written permission of the copyright owner, except in accordance with the provisions of the Copyright, Designs and Patents Act 1988 or under the terms of a licence issued by the Copyright Licensing Agency, Saffron House, 6–10 Kirby Street, London EC1N 8TS (www.cla.co.uk). Applications for the copyright owner's written permission should be addressed to the publisher.

Edited by Melanie Birdsall
Designed by Emily Hunter-Higgins
Typeset by HL studios
Original illustrations © Pearson Education Limited 2010
Illustrated by Caron at KJA Artists
Cover design by Emily Hunter-Higgins
Cover photo © Pearson Education Ltd / Sophie Bluy
Printed in the UK by Ashford Colour Press

Acknowledgements
We would like to thank Harriette Lanzer and Isabelle Retailleau for their invaluable help in the development of this course.

Every effort has been made to contact copyright holders of material reproduced in this book. Any omissions will be rectified in subsequent printings if notice is given to the publishers.

Scheme of Work CD-ROM
Important notice
This software is suitable for use on PCs only. It will not run on a Mac.
If the CD is loaded into a CD drive on a PC it should autorun automatically. If it does not, please click on 'RB.exe' which can be found in the root of this CD ('D:\RB.exe', where D is the letter associated to your CD drive).

Active content
Your browser security may initially try to block elements of this product. If this problem occurs, please refer to the Troubleshooting document which can be found in the root of this CD ('D:\Troubleshooting.doc', where D is the letter associated to your CD drive).

Installation instructions
This product may be installed to your local hard drive or to the network. Further instructions on how to do this are available from the main menu.

VLE pack
The root of this CD contains the content from this product as a zipped SCORM 1.2 Content Pack to allow for convenient uploading to your VLE.
Please follow the usual instructions specific to your VLE system to upload this content pack.

Contents

Introduction 4

Module 1 **C'est perso** 14
Module 2 **Mon collège** 41
Module 3 **Mes passetemps** 74
Module 4 **Ma zone** 102
Module 5 **3 ... 2 ... 1 Partez!** 132
Module 6 **Studio découverte** 163

Introduction

Course description

Studio is a fully differentiated 11–14 French course in three stages – *Studio 1* for Year 7, *Studio 2* for Year 8 and *Studio 3* for Year 9. The Year 7 resources also include a separate short book, *Accès Studio*, which enables flexibility in teaching the language according to pupils' prior experience of learning French at Key Stage 2. In Year 7 pupils can be assessed at National Curriculum Levels 1 to 5.

Studio 1 and *Studio 2* are suitable for use on their own as a two-year Key Stage 3 course.

The course has been written to reflect the world pupils live in, using contexts familiar to them in their everyday lives and teaching them the vocabulary that they need to communicate with young French people of their own age on topics that interest and stimulate them. They are introduced to young French people and given insight into the everyday life and culture of France and other French-speaking countries, encouraging intercultural understanding.

At the same time, *Studio* ensures that pupils are taught the language learning skills and strategies that they need to become independent language learners. The four elements of the Key Stage 3 Programmes of Study (Key concepts, Key processes, Range and content and Curriculum opportunities) and the five strands of progression in the Key Stage 3 Framework for languages are fully integrated into the course. In addition, pupils have the chance to experience cross-curricular studies and are given regular opportunities to develop and practise the personal, learning and thinking skills required to operate as independent enquirers, creative thinkers, reflective learners, team workers, self-managers and effective participators.

The *ActiveTeach* DVD (see details on pp. 6–7) provides easy-to-use and exciting technology designed to add dynamism and fun to whole-class teaching, together with a wealth of interactive activities for pupils to enjoy and learn from both in class and independently.

Differentiation

Studio 1 provides one book for the whole ability range. Pupil requirements are catered for in the following ways:
- There are differentiated activities at a range of NC Levels in all four Attainment Targets throughout the Pupil Book.
- Ideas are given in the Teacher's Guide for simplifying and extending the Pupil Book activities.
- *En plus* units at the end of every module contain longer reading and listening passages to provide opportunities for extension work.
- The *À toi* section at the back of the Pupil Book provides extra reading and writing activities at reinforcement and extension levels.
- The workbooks are differentiated at two levels: reinforcement (*Cahier d'exercices A*) and extension (*Cahier d'exercices B*).

Studio 2 and *Studio 3* are differentiated by means of parallel books:

Studio 2 Rouge	NC Levels 3–6
Studio 2 Vert	NC Levels 1–5
Studio 3 Rouge	NC Levels 4–7
Studio 3 Vert	NC Levels 1–5

Using *Studio 1* and *Accès Studio* together

Studio 1 and *Accès Studio* have been carefully planned to give you maximum flexibility in catering for pupils who arrive from primary schools with different experiences of learning French.

- **Pupils who have no prior knowledge:**
  With *Studio*, just like any French course, you can start from scratch, using *Accès Studio* and working through to the *Studio 1* Pupil Book.

- **Pupils who have some prior knowledge:**
  If some of your pupils have already learned French basics, you can go straight to *Studio 1* and use *Accès Studio* when you need to pause and revise topics with the class.

- **Pupils who are confident with French basics:**
  If you have a confident class that has covered the French basics listed in the table on p. 5, you can go straight to *Studio 1*. If necessary, you can use *Accès Studio* as a quick recap.

This symbol in the *Studio 1* Pupil Book tells you that at this point some prior knowledge is assumed and you are directed to the appropriate unit in *Accès Studio* should you need to teach or revise the language required to complete the unit.

Accès Studio Contents

Unit	Title	Topics
1	Bonjour!	Meeting and greeting people Spelling in French
2	Quel âge as-tu?	Counting to 21 Saying how old you are
3	Joyeux anniversaire!	Days and months Saying when your birthday is
4	Dans mon sac	Saying what there is in your school bag Using *un, une, des* – the indefinite articles 'a', 'some' Using plurals
5	Ma salle de classe	Describing your classroom Using *le, la, les* – the definite article 'the'
6	J'adore le judo	Saying what you like and dislike Talking about hobbies
7	Les goûts et les couleurs	Saying what colours things are Using adjectives
8	Tu as un animal?	Talking about animals Using a dictionary
9	Ma grand-mère est une hippie!	Talking about your family Using *mon, ma* and *mes*
10	J'habite dans un château!	Saying where you live Using *petit* and *grand*
11	À table!	Saying what you eat and drink Ordering in a café
12	Mon pays	Talking about nationalities and countries Using the verb *être* (to be)
13	La météo	Talking about the weather Exploring rhyming and syllables
	Grammaire	Gender and singular/plural, articles, adjectives, *mon/ma/mes*, verbs in the present tense (singular forms)
	Language Learning Skills	Learning vocabulary, listening strategies, reading strategies, study skills

Studio 1
Pupil Book
- One book for the whole ability range in Year 7
- Full coverage of the Programmes of Study and updated Key Stage 3 Framework for languages
- Assessment right from the start at National Curriculum Level 4
- Exciting video introducing pupils to the lives of young people in France
- Fully integrated grammar explanations and practice ensuring logical and rigorous progression
- Opportunities for cross-curricular topics and emphasis on language learning skills
- Fully integrated opportunities for PLTS

The Pupil Book consists of five core modules and a sixth optional module (see below). Modules 1 to 5 are subdivided as follows:
- Five double-page core units (three in Module 6) – these contain the core material that must be taught to ensure that all the key language and grammar is covered in Year 7.
- *Bilan* – this is a checklist of 'I can' statements, allowing pupils to check their progress as part of Assessment for Learning.
- *Révisions* – optional revision activities that can be used as a 'mock' test preceding the end of module *Contrôle* in the Assessment Pack.
- *En plus* – an optional unit in which no new core language is introduced. The unit can therefore be missed out if you are short of time. However, these units contain lots of useful activities and tips for developing language learning skills, including longer reading and listening passages and opportunities for oral presentations.
- *Studio Grammaire* – two pages where the key grammar points introduced in the module are explained fully and accompanied by practice activities.
- *Vocabulaire* – two pages of module word lists for vocabulary learning and revision, plus a *Stratégie* tip box to help pupils acquire the skills they need to learn vocabulary more effectively.

Module 6, *Studio découverte*, is an optional module with a more cross-curricular focus. The module consists of three units, each one dealing with a particular theme – animals, poetry and painting. These units can be taught as regular units or developed as project work for more individual study. Since Module 6 is the last in the book, it is ideal for less directed work in the final half-term or term of the school year. You can choose to work through all three units in the usual way, or to focus on one particular theme. Each of the units can be taught on its own earlier in the school year if you prefer. Module 6 contains an introduction to the perfect tense, allowing higher-ability pupils to reach NC Level 6 if appropriate.

At the back of the Pupil Book there are four further sections:
- *À toi* – self-access differentiated reading and writing activities. *À toi A* contains reinforcement activities for lower-ability pupils, and *À toi B* contains extension activities for higher-ability pupils. These are ideal for use as homework.
- Verb tables – two pages showing the present tense conjugation of regular –*er* verbs, reflexive verbs and the four most common irregular verbs: *avoir, être, faire* and *aller*, as well as the near future and perfect tenses.

- Dictionary skills – one page explaining to pupils how to use a bilingual dictionary.
- *Mini-dictionnaire* – a comprehensive French-English glossary, organised alphabetically and containing all the vocabulary encountered in *Studio 1*. There is also a list of the French rubrics used in the Pupil Book.

Teacher's Guide

The Teacher's Guide contains all the support required to help you use *Studio 1* effectively in the classroom:

- Clear and concise teaching notes, including lesson starters, plenaries and PLTS references for every unit
- Full cross-referencing to the National Curriculum Programmes of Study and the updated Key Stage 3 Framework for languages
- Overview grids for each module highlighting grammar content and skills coverage
- Answers to all the activities
- The complete audioscript for all the listening activities in the *Studio 1* Pupil Book
- Guidance on using the course with the full ability range

The accompanying CD-Rom contains a customisable scheme of work offering complete help with planning, and showing how the course covers the National Curriculum Programmes of Study and Key Stage 3 Framework for languages.

Audio CDs

The audio CDs contain all the recorded material for the listening activities in the Pupil Book. The different types of activities can be used for presentation of new language, comprehension and pronunciation practice. The material includes dialogues, interviews and songs recorded by native speakers.

This material is also contained on the *ActiveTeach* DVD. Therefore, if you buy *ActiveTeach* and can play audio using your computer, you can play all the listening activities from there.

Please note: the audio CDs and *ActiveTeach* do not contain the listening material for the end of module tests and end of year test. This material can be found in the Assessment Pack (see right).

Workbooks

There are two parallel workbooks to accompany *Studio 1*: one for reinforcement (*Cahier d'exercices A*) and one for extension (*Cahier d'exercices B*). There is one page of activities for each double-page unit in the Pupil Book. The workbooks fulfil a number of functions:

- They provide self-access reading and writing activities designed to offer the pupils enjoyable ways of consolidating and practising the language they have learned in each unit.
- They give extra practice in grammar and thinking skills, with integrated activities throughout the workbooks.
- Revision pages at the end of each module (*Révisions*) help pupils revise what they have learned during the module.
- Module word lists (*Vocabulaire*) with English translations are invaluable for language learning homework.
- The *J'avance!* pages at the end of each module allow pupils to record their NC level in each Attainment Target and set themselves improvement targets for the next module.
- NC level descriptors in pupil-friendly language at the back of the workbooks allow pupils to see what they must do to progress through the NC levels in all four Attainment Targets.

Assessment Pack

The Assessment Pack is a CD-Rom containing all the assessment material required to assess pupils in Year 7 against the National Curriculum Attainment Targets, as well as self-assessment sheets.

- 'Show what you can do' test
- End of module tests in all four Attainment Targets – listening, speaking, reading and writing
- End of year test in all four Attainment Targets
- Covers National Curriculum Levels 1 to 5
- Optional Level 6 test
- Target setting sheets

The audio CD contains the recordings of the listening tests. The CD-Rom contains all the sheets for the tests in PDF format and as Word files. The Word files can be customised to suit your individual needs.

ActiveTeach

ActiveTeach is a powerful and motivating resource combining the 'book on screen' and a wealth of supporting materials – providing you with the perfect tool for whole-class teaching and individual practice and revision on a PC.

- Use the on-screen Pupil Book with all the listening activities included.
- Zoom in on areas of text and activities to facilitate whole-class teaching.
- Build your own lessons and add in your own resources to help personalise learning.
- Use fun and motivating electronic flashcards to teach new vocabulary.
- Consolidate language using the whole-class interactive games.

- Use the video clips in Modules 1 to 5 to introduce your pupils to the lives of young French people.
- Teach and revise grammar using PowerPoint® presentations.
- Download and print off a variety of extra worksheets for consolidation of grammar, thinking skills and learning skills – ideal for follow-up work, cover lessons and homework.

Plus *Le Studio* pupil environment for:
- **Practice** using games and flashcards
- **Revision** of grammar and vocabulary
- **Self-assessment** of reading, listening and grammar skills

A Quick Tour in *ActiveTeach* provides you with an overview of the most common features. Fuller instructions can be accessed by clicking on the question mark icon in the top righthand corner of the book on screen.

In addition to the interactive activities in *ActiveTeach*, there is a wide variety of extra worksheets that can be used to consolidate and extend pupils' learning as follows:

Module 1
Thinking skills	Inventing categories
Thinking skills	Odd one out!
Learning skills	Using a dictionary (i)
Grammar skills	Accents
Thinking skills	Making comments
Assignment	Ma star préférée et moi (with NC assessment)

Module 2
Learning skills	Learning new words
Thinking skills	Nonsense! (spotting illogicalities in text)
Learning skills	New words (working out meanings)
Grammar skills	Parts of speech
Grammar skills	Questions
Assignment	Mon blog (with NC assessment)
Thinking skills	Joyeux Noël!

Module 3
Thinking skills	High-frequency words
Grammar skills	Regular –er verbs
Thinking skills	Logic puzzle
Grammar skills	*Faire*
Learning skills	Building your vocabulary
Assignment	Les graphiques vivants (with NC assessment)

Module 4
Thinking skills	Mnemonics
Learning skills	Using a dictionary (ii)
Grammar skills	*Aller*
Grammar skills	Negatives
Learning skills	Summarising
Assignment	Mon royaume à moi (with NC assessment)

Module 5
Thinking skills	Sound patterns
Learning skills	Improving sentences
Grammar skills	Reflexive verbs
Thinking skills	Logic puzzle
Grammar skills	Using two tenses together
Assignment	Chanson pour l'Europe! (with NC assessment)

Module 6
Thinking skills	Les animaux
Learning skills	Les poèmes
Learning skills	La peinture
Grammar skills	The perfect tense

Assignment (*Défi*)
The worksheets for Modules 1 to 5 include a collaborative assignment or challenge (*Défi*) to be carried out in pairs or groups.

The assignments consist generally of two worksheets, one containing the instructions for the task, the other providing preparation tasks and language to help the pupils.

The focus of the assignments is to help the pupils develop further their extended speaking and writing skills in cross-curricular contexts whilst fostering PLTS.

Incorporating ICT
Appropriate use of Information and Communication Technology (ICT) to support modern languages is a requirement of the National Curriculum. Suggestions for ICT activities (word-processing, using e-mail, videoconferencing, researching on the Internet, etc.) have been included in the Teacher's Guide and are identified by this symbol.

Grammar coverage
Grammar is fully integrated into the teaching sequence in *Studio* to ensure that pupils have the opportunity to learn thoroughly the underlying structures of the French language. All units have a grammar objective so that pupils can see clearly which grammar structures they are learning. The key grammar points are presented in the *Studio Grammaire* boxes on the Pupil Book pages and fuller explanations and practice are provided in the *Studio Grammaire* pages at the end of each module. In addition, there are grammar PowerPoint® presentations in *ActiveTeach* for presenting new grammar concepts to classes, followed by interactive practice activities that can be used with whole classes or for individual practice. Worksheets

focusing on the key grammar topics taught in *Studio 1* are also provided in *ActiveTeach* and can be printed off for individual pupil use.

Grammar points explained and practised in *Studio 1*:
- present tense of regular *-er* verbs
- present tense of *avoir, être, faire, aller*
- present tense of reflexive verbs
- *aimer* + infinitive
- *vouloir* + infinitive
- *pouvoir* + infinitive
- *je voudrais* + infinitive
- the near future (*aller* + infinitive)
- the perfect tense (optional in Module 6)
- the imperative
- the use of *tu* and *vous*
- using *jouer à*
- negatives (*ne … pas, pas du tout*)
- adjective agreement
- position of adjectives
- possessive adjectives
- asking questions
- question words
- connectives
- intensifiers/adverbs
- prepositions
- the partitive article
- *il y a/il n'y a pas de …*
- *à* + definite article
- accents

Coverage of the Programmes of Study in *Studio 1*

In *Studio 1* the four elements of the Programmes of Study – 1 Key concepts, 2 Key processes, 3 Range and content and 4 Curriculum opportunities – are comprehensively covered, as follows:

1 Key concepts
Pupils need to understand the key concepts that underpin the study of languages in order to deepen and broaden their knowledge, skills and understanding. Since these are implemented in all modules of *Studio 1*, they are not listed in the module grids but simply summarised here for reference.

1.1 Linguistic competence
a developing the skills of listening, speaking, reading and writing in a range of situations and contexts
b applying linguistic knowledge and skills to understand and communicate effectively

1.2 Knowledge about language
a understanding how a language works and how to manipulate it
b recognising that languages differ but may share common grammatical, syntactic or lexical features

1.3 Creativity
a using familiar language for new purposes and in new contexts
b using imagination to express thoughts, ideas, experiences and feelings

1.4 Intercultural understanding
a appreciating the richness and diversity of other cultures
b recognising that there are different ways of seeing the world, and developing an international outlook

Activities specifically designed to give pupils the opportunity to develop in the other Programmes of Study areas appear throughout *Studio 1*. The tables which follow show examples of these. Further details are given in the module grids throughout the Teacher's Guide.

2 Key processes	
2.1 Developing language learning strategies Pupils should be able to:	**Module and unit**
a identify patterns in the target language	M1 U3, M3 U5, M5 U2
b develop techniques for memorising words, phrases and spellings	M1 U5, M2 U4, M4 U5
c use their knowledge of English or another language when learning the target language	M1 U1, M2 *En plus* 1, M4 U2
d use previous knowledge, context and other clues to work out the meaning of what they hear or read	M1 U2, M4 U1, M5 U2
e use reference materials such as dictionaries appropriately and effectively	M1 U2, M4 U5, M6 U1
2.2 Developing language skills Pupils should be able to:	
a listen for gist or detail	M1 U4, M2 U3, M4 U3
b skim and scan written texts for the main points or details	M1 *En plus*, M2 *En plus* 1, M3 U5
c respond appropriately to spoken and written language	M3 U1, M4 U2, M5 U4
d use correct pronunciation and intonation	M1 U1, M2 U4, M4 U4
e ask and answer questions	M1 U1, M2 U1, M4 U2
f initiate and sustain conversations	M2 U3, M4 U1, M5 U3

g	write clearly and coherently, including an appropriate level of detail	M2 U2, M4 U4, M5 U1
h	redraft their writing to improve accuracy and quality	M1 U5, M4 U1, M5 U4
i	reuse language that they have heard or read in their own speaking and writing	M3 U2, M4 U5, M6 U1
j	adapt language they already know in new contexts for different purposes	M2 U5, M4 U3, M6 U2
k	deal with unfamiliar language, unexpected responses and unpredictable situations	all video episodes, M2 *En plus 2*, M3 U5, M5 U3

3	**Range and content** The study of language should include:	**Module and unit**
a	the spoken and written forms of the target language	M1 U4, M2 U5, M5 U5
b	the interrelationship between sounds and writing in the target language	M3 U1, M3 U5, M5 U5
c	the grammar of the target language and how to apply it	all *Studio Grammaire* sections, M2 U5, M4 U4, M5 U4
d	a range of vocabulary and structures	M2 U4, M5 U5, M6 U2
e	learning about different countries and cultures	all module introductions, M2 *En plus 1*, M3 U2, M4 *En plus*
f	comparing pupils' own experiences and perspectives with those of people in countries and communities where the target language is spoken	M2 module introduction, M3 U4, M5 *En plus*

4	**Curriculum opportunities** Pupils should have the opportunity to:	**Module and unit**
a	hear, speak, read and write in the target language regularly and frequently within the classroom and beyond	M2 U2, M3 U4, M6 U1
b	communicate in the target language individually, in pairs, in groups and with speakers of the target language, including native speakers, where possible, for a variety of purposes	M1 U3, M3 U2, M5 U1

c	use an increasing range of more complex language	M3 U3, M4 *En plus*, M6 U3
d	make links with English at word, sentence and text level	M1 U1, M2 U3, M3 U3
e	use a range of resources, including ICT, for accessing and communicating information in the target language	M2 U1, M5 U2, M6 U1
f	listen to, read or view a range of materials, including authentic materials in the target language, both to support learning and for personal interest and enjoyment	all video episodes, M2 U5, M4 U2, M6 U2
g	use the target language in connection with topics and issues that are engaging and may be related to other areas of the curriculum	M4 U2, M6 U1, M6 U3

Coverage of the Revised Framework for languages (2009)

Studio ensures full coverage of the five strands of progression in the Key Stage 3 Framework for languages (2009):
1. Listening and speaking
2. Reading and writing
3. Intercultural understanding
4. Knowledge about language
5. Language learning strategies

To help you with your **long-term planning**, the framework overview grid on p. 10 gives two examples of where each learning objective is met in the Pupil Book.

To help you with your **medium-term planning**, the overview grids at the start of each module in this Teacher's Guide indicate the particular objectives that are met in that module.

To help you with your **short-term (lesson) planning**, the overview boxes at the start of each unit indicate the particular objectives that are met in that unit.

Learning objective	Module and unit
1.1/Y7 Listening – gist and detail	M1 U4, M2 U1
1.2/Y7 Listening – unfamiliar language	M3 U5, M4 U5
1.3/Y7 Listening – (a) interpreting intonation and tone	M2 U2, M4 U4
1.3/Y7 Speaking – (b) using intonation and tone	M2 U2, M4 U4
1.4/Y7 Speaking – (a) social and classroom language	M1 U1, M2 U5
1.4/Y7 Speaking – (b) using prompts	M3 U3, M4 U5
1.5/Y7 Speaking – (a) presenting	M2 U4, M3 U2
1.5/Y7 Speaking – (b) expression/non-verbal techniques	M3 U4, M4 U2
2.1/Y7 Reading – main points and detail	M3 U1, M4 U1
2.2/Y7 Reading – (a) unfamiliar language	M3 U5, M5 U1
2.2/Y7 Reading – (b) text selection	M5 *En plus*
2.3/Y7 Reading – text features	M3 U3, M4 U4
2.4/Y7 Writing – (a) sentences and texts as models	M1 U1, M3 U2
2.4/Y7 Writing – (b) building text	M1 U4, M4 U1
2.5/Y7 Writing – different text types	M1 U5, M4 U4
3.1/Y7 Culture – aspects of everyday life	M2 U3, M3 U3
3.2/Y7 Culture – (a) young people: interests/opinions	M1 U1, M2 U4
3.2/Y7 Culture – (b) challenging stereotypes	M1 U1, M4 *En plus*
4.1/Y7 Language – letters and sounds	M1 U5, M2 U4,
4.2/Y7 Language – high-frequency words	M1 U3, M5 U2
4.3/Y7 Language – gender and plurals	M2 U1, M2 U5
4.4/Y7 Language – sentence formation	M2 U2, M4 U3
4.5/Y7 Language – (a) present tense verbs	M1 U3, M3 U1
4.5/Y7 Language – (a) set phrases about the future	M5 U4, M5 U5
4.5/Y7 Language – (a) set phrases about the past	M3 U5, M5 U1
4.5/Y7 Language – (b) modal verbs	M4 U4, M4 U5
4.6/Y7 Language – (a) questions	M1 U2, M2 U1
4.6/Y7 Language – (b) negatives	M1 U1, M1 U2
5.1 Strategies – patterns	M2 U1, M3 U1
5.2 Strategies – memorising	M1 U5, M4 U5
5.3 Strategies – English/other languages	M1 U4, M2 *En plus 1*
5.4 Strategies – working out meaning	M2 U3, M3 U3
5.5 Strategies – reference materials	M1 *En plus*, M5 *En plus*
5.6 Strategies – reading aloud	M1 U4, M5 U2
5.7 Strategies – planning and preparing	M2 *En plus 1*
5.8 Strategies – evaluating and improving	M1 U5, M4 U5

Coverage of Personal Learning and Thinking Skills in *Studio 1*

Activities supporting PLTS development are included throughout the course. Key examples are highlighted in the Teacher's Guide using the PLTS icon **PLTS**: one PLTS is identified in each unit, with Modules 1–5 all featuring the full range of PLTS. Each PLTS is given in the table below, with a selection of examples and details of how they meet the curriculum requirements.

Personal Learning and Thinking Skills	
I Independent enquirers	Pupil Book activities throughout the course (e.g. M5 U1 ex. 3, M6 U3 ex. 7); ICT-based activities (e.g. M3 U2 ex. 7)
C Creative thinkers	Regular activities developing skills strategies (how to improve listening/speaking, etc.) (e.g. M1 U1 ex. 2); Starters requiring pupils to apply logic and make connections (e.g. M4 U4 Starter 2); regular activities encouraging pupils to identify patterns and work out rules (e.g. M5 U3 ex. 1); activities requiring creative production of language (e.g. M6 U2 ex. 5)
R Reflective learners	Ongoing opportunities to assess work and identify areas for improvement (e.g. M2 U4 ex. 7, M5 U4 extension suggestion after ex. 6), including all *Bilans* and Plenaries (e.g. M4 U1 Plenary)
T Team workers	Regular pairwork activities (e.g. M3 U1 ex. 6), including many Starters; regular peer assessment (e.g. M1 U5 ex. 8); links with partner schools (e.g. M5 *En plus* ex. 7)
S Self-managers	Ongoing advice on managing learning (e.g. M3 *En plus* ex. 5), including strategies to improve learning (e.g. M4 U5 extension suggestion after ex. 6)
E Effective participators	Opportunities throughout the course for pupils to contribute (e.g. M3 U4 ex. 7), including presentations (e.g. M6 U1 ex. 7) and all Plenaries (e.g. M5 U2 Plenary)

Pupils may find the following short forms useful as a reference in class:

I am a/an ...		Today I ...
Independent enquirer	**PLTS** **I**	worked on my own to find out something new
Creative thinker	**PLTS** **C**	used what I know to work out or create something new
Reflective learner	**PLTS** **R**	thought about what I've learned and how I can improve
Team worker	**PLTS** **T**	worked well with other people
Self-manager	**PLTS** **S**	took responsibility for improving my learning
Effective participator	**PLTS** **E**	took part in the lesson in a positive way

Games and other teaching suggestions
Reading aloud
There are many reading activities in the Pupil Book which give scope for further activities.
1. You can use the texts to practise reading aloud. As an incentive, award five points to a pupil who can read a text without any errors. Points could also be given to teams, depending on seating arrangements – tables, rows, sides of the room.
2. Set a challenge – 'I bet no one can read this without a single mistake' or ask a volunteer pupil to predict how many mistakes he/she will make before having a go, then seeing if he/she can do better than predicted.
3. Texts could be read round the class with pupils simply reading up to a full stop and then passing it on to someone else in the room. They enjoy this activity if it is fast. Alternatively, pupils can read as much or as little as they want before passing it on.
4. You can also read a text, pause and have the pupils say the next word.

Reading follow-up
Motivation and participation can be enhanced by dividing the class into two teams and awarding points. Once they know a text very well, pupils should be able to complete a sentence from memory, hearing just the beginning. Move from a word to a phrase to a sentence: i.e. you say a word, the pupils give the word in a short context and then in a longer context.
1. You read aloud and stop (or insert the word 'beep') for pupils to complete the word or sentence.
2. You read aloud and make a deliberate mistake (either pronunciation or saying the wrong word). Pupils put up their hand as soon as they spot a mistake.
3. *Hot potato*: Pupils read a bit and pass it on quickly to someone who may not be expecting it.
4. *Marathon*: A pupil reads aloud until he/she makes a mistake. Pupils have to put up their hand as soon as they hear a mistake. A second pupil then takes over, starting at the beginning again and trying to get further than the previous pupil.
5. *Random reading:* You read a phrase at random and the pupils have to say the next bit.
6. You can play music and get the pupils to pass an object round the class. When the music stops, the person with the object has a turn. Let a pupil control the music, facing away from the class.

Mime activities
Mimes are a motivating way to help pupils to learn words.
1. You say a word, for example a job, sport or hobby, or an adjective, and the pupils mime it. This can be done silently with the whole class responding. Alternatively, it can be done as a knock out game starting with six volunteers at the front who mime to the class as you say each word. Any pupil who does the wrong mime or who is slow to react is knocked out. Impose a two-minute time limit.
2. Pupils say a word or phrase and you mime it – but only if the pupils say it correctly. This really puts you on the spot and gets the pupils trying very hard. You could also insist that the pupils say it from memory.
3. You mime and pupils say the word or phrase.
4. Send five or six pupils out of the room. They each have to decide on an adjective which sums up their character. They return to the room individually or together, each one miming their character adjective. The remaining pupils then guess the adjective. Get them to use a sentence, e.g. *Daniel est intelligent*.
5. *Envoyé spécial*: One person goes out of the room. The rest of the class decides on a character adjective to mime. The volunteer comes back into the room and has to guess the adjective that the class is miming. Again, encourage the use of whole sentences.
6. *Class knock-down*: As *Envoyé spécial*, but this time everyone in the class can choose different qualities to mime. The volunteer returns to the room with everyone doing his/her own mime. The volunteer points to each pupil and names the character adjective. If the volunteer is correct, the pupil sits down. This works well as a timed or team activity. The aim is to sit your team down as quickly as possible.
7. A version of charades is a good activity at the end of the lesson. Organise two teams, A and B. Have all the adjectives written down on separate cards, masculine forms only. Put the cards in a pile at the front. A volunteer from Team A comes to the front, picks up the first card and mimes it. The rest of the team must not see the word on the card. Anyone from Team A can put up his/her hand and is then invited by the volunteer to say the word. If correct, the volunteer picks up the next card and mimes it. The aim is to get through the whole list as quickly as possible. Note down the time for Team A. Team B then tries to beat that time.

Exploiting the songs
1. Pupils sing along. Fade out certain bits while they continue. When most of them know the song quite well you can pause the audio to let them give you the next line by heart. Then try the whole chorus, followed by a few verses completely from memory.
2. You could try the 'pick up a song' game: you fade the song after a few lines, the pupils continue singing, and then you fade the song up again

towards the end and they see whether they have kept pace with the recording.

Translation follow-up

Motivation and participation can be enhanced by dividing the class into two teams and awarding points. Once they know the text very well, you should be able to say any word, phrase or sentence from the text at random for the pupils to translate into English without viewing the text.

1. You translate the text and stop (or insert the word 'beep') for pupils to complete the word or sentence.
2. You translate, making a deliberate mistake. Pupils put up their hand as soon as they spot a mistake.
3. *Hot potato*: A pupil translates a bit and passes it on quickly to someone who may not be expecting it.
4. *Marathon*: A pupil translates until he/she makes a mistake. Pupils have to put up their hand as soon as they hear a mistake. A second pupil then takes over, starting from the beginning again and trying to get further than the previous pupil.
5. *Random translation*: You read a phrase in French at random and the pupils have to translate it.
6. One half of the class has their books open, the other half has them closed. The half with their books open reads a sentence in French at random. The other side has to translate. Do about five then swap round.
7. You can play music and get the pupils to pass an object round. When the music stops, the person with the object has a turn. Let a pupil control the music, facing away from the class.

Writing follow-up (text dissection)

Whiteboards are a useful tool. They do not need to be issued to every pupil. Pupils can work in pairs or groups or they can pass the whiteboards on. You could also divide the class into teams, with one whiteboard per team.

After reading a text in some detail:
1. Display some anagrams of key words from the text and ask pupils to write them correctly. You will need to prepare these in advance and check carefully. Award points for correct answers on each board.
2. Display some jumbled phrases from the text, e.g. *foot au je dimanche joue le*. Pupils rewrite the phrase correctly in their exercise books or on the board. They could work in teams, producing one answer per team on paper.
3. Display an incorrect word or phrase in French and ask pupils to spot the mistake and correct it.

This can also be done as 'spot the missing word' or 'spot the word that is in the wrong place'.

4. Ask pupils to spell certain words from memory. Differentiate by first reading out a few words in French and then giving a few in English for them also to write out in French.
5. *Mini-dictée:* Read four or five short sentences in French for pupils to write out. Again, this could be a group exercise.
6. Give pupils phrases in English to write out in French.

Comprehension follow-up

1. Ask questions in English about the text.
2. Ask questions in French about the text.
3. True or false?
4. Who ... ?

Vocabulary treasure hunt

1. Find the word for ...
2. Find (three) opinions.

Grammar treasure hunt

1. Find (three) adjectives.
2. Find (two) feminine adjectives.
3. Find a verb in the *nous* form.
4. Find a plural noun.
5. Find a negative.

A variation on pairwork

Musical pass the mobile phone: One pupil controls the music, facing away from the class. While the music is playing, a toy or old mobile phone is passed from pupil to pupil. As soon as the music stops, the music operator (who is ideally also equipped with a phone) says the first statement of a dialogue. The other pupil who has ended up with the phone replies. They can, if they like, disguise their voice. The music operator tries to guess who is speaking. The game then continues.

Symbols used in these teaching notes

➕ extension material/suggestion for extending an activity

Ⓡ reinforcement material/suggestion for reinforcing language

PLTS example of an activity which supports personal learning and thinking skills development

💭 thinking skills activity (workbooks only)

🖱 ICT activity

Module 1: C'est perso (Pupil Book pp. 6–25)

Unit & Learning objectives	PoS & Framework objectives	Key language	Grammar and other language features
1 Mon autoportrait (pp. 8–9) Talking about likes and dislikes Using regular –er verbs (je, tu, il/elle)	**2.1c** knowledge of language **2.2a** listen for gist **2.2d** pronunciation and intonation **2.2e** ask and answer questions **3c** apply grammar **4d** make links with English **1.4/Y7** Speaking – (a) social and classroom language **2.4/Y7** Writing – (a) sentences and texts as models **3.2/Y7** Culture – (a) young people: interests/opinions **3.2/Y7** Culture – (b) challenging stereotypes **4.6/Y7** Language – (b) negatives	J'aime … Tu aimes … ? Il/Elle aime … la musique, les animaux, les mangas, etc. Je n'aime pas … l'injustice, le hard rock, les araignées, etc. C'est … génial, cool, nul, etc.	**G** the definite article (le, la, l', les) **G** –er verbs (singular) – j'aime/je n'aime pas for likes and dislikes – questions using intonation – connectives: et, aussi, mais
2 Mon kit de survie (pp. 10–11) Talking about your survival kit Using avoir (je, tu, il/elle)	**2.1b** memorising **2.1d** previous knowledge **2.1e** use reference materials **2.2a** listen for gist **4a** use language in the classroom, etc. **4b** communicate in pairs, etc. **4.6/Y7** Language – (a) questions **4.6/Y7** Language – (b) negatives	J'ai … Tu as … Il/Elle a … un appareil photo, une gourde, des chips, etc. Je n'ai pas de … cahier, etc. C'est … essentiel, important	**G** avoir (present singular) **G** qu'est-ce que … ? – understanding dictionary definitions
3 Comment je me vois (pp. 12–13) Describing yourself Understanding adjective agreement (singular)	**2.1a** identify patterns **2.1d** previous knowledge **2.2c** respond appropriately **2.2h** redraft to improve writing **4b** communicate in pairs, etc. **4e** use a range of resources **4.2/Y7** Language – high-frequency words **4.5/Y7** Language – (a) present tense verbs	Je suis/Je ne suis pas … Tu es … Il/Elle est … branché(e), curieux/curieuse, drôle, etc. Tu es d'accord? Je suis d'accord. Je ne suis pas d'accord.	**G** adjective agreement (singular) **G** être (present singular) – intensifiers: très, assez
4 Et les autres? (pp. 14–15) Talking about other people Understanding adjective agreement (plural)	**2.1c** knowledge of language **2.2a** listen for gist **2.2c** respond appropriately **3a** spoken and written language **3c** apply grammar **4f** language for interest/enjoyment **1.1/Y7** Listening – gist and detail **2.4/Y7** Writing – (b) building text **5.3** Strategies – English/other languages **5.6** Strategies – reading aloud	C'est un garçon/une fille. Il a …/Elle a … les yeux bleus/gris, etc. les cheveux longs/courts et bruns/roux, etc. Il/Elle est … grand(e), petit(e), de taille moyenne Il/Elle s'appelle …	**G** adjective agreement (plural) **G** possessive adjectives (mon/ma/mes, ton/ta/tes)

C'est perso 1

Unit & Learning objectives	PoS & Framework objectives	Key language	Grammar and other language features
5 Il est hypercool! (pp. 16–17) Describing a musician Using the present tense (*je, tu, il/elle*)	**2.1b** memorising **2.2d** pronunciation and intonation **2.2h** redraft to improve writing **2.2j** adapt previously learned language **3c** apply grammar **4e** use a range of resources **2.5/Y7** Writing – different text types **4.1/Y7** Language – letters and sounds **5.2** Strategies – memorising **5.8** Strategies – evaluating and improving	Review of vocabulary from Units 3 & 4: *Il/Elle s'appelle…* *Il/Elle aime…* *Il/Elle est…* *Il/Elle a…*	**G** the present tense (singular: *aimer, s'appeler, être, avoir*) – pronunciation of *eau*
Bilan et Révisions (pp. 18–19) Pupils' checklist and practice exercises			
En plus: C'est moi! (pp. 20–21) Introducing yourself in detail	**2.2b** skim and scan **2.2c** respond appropriately **2.2g** write clearly and coherently **2.2i** reuse language they have met **3d** use a range of vocab/structures **4a** use language in the classroom, etc. **5.5** Strategies – reference materials	Review of language from the module	– developing writing skills – developing presentation skills
Studio Grammaire (pp. 22–23) Detailed grammar summary and practice exercises			**G** the present tense (regular *-er* verbs, singular) **G** irregular verbs (*avoir, être* – present, singular) **G** adjectives (agreement) **G** possessive adjectives
À toi (pp. 118–119) Self-access reading and writing at two levels			

1 Mon autoportrait (Pupil Book pp. 8–9)

Learning objectives
- Talking about likes and dislikes
- Using regular –er verbs (je, tu, il/elle)

Framework objectives
1.4/Y7 Speaking – (a) social and classroom language: ex. 3
2.4/Y7 Writing – (a) sentences and texts as models: ex. 7
3.2/Y7 Culture – (a) young people: interests/opinions: ex. 1
3.2/Y7 Culture – (b) challenging stereotypes: Module 1 introduction (pp. 6–7)
4.6/Y7 Language – (b) negatives: ex. 4

Grammar
- the definite article (le, la, l', les)
- –er verbs (singular)

Key language
J'aime ...
Je n'aime pas ...
Tu aimes ... ?
Il/Elle aime ...
Oui, j'aime ça.
Non, je n'aime pas ça.
les animaux
les araignées
les chats
les chiens
le cinéma
les consoles de jeux
la danse
le foot
le hard rock
l'injustice
les insectes
les jeux vidéo
les mangas
les maths
la musique
la Nintendo DS
les pizzas
le racisme
le rap
les reptiles
le roller
le rugby
les spaghettis
le sport
la tecktonik
le tennis
la violence
les voyages
les weekends
C'est ...
génial/cool/bien/ennuyeux/nul

PLTS
C Creative thinkers

Cross-curricular
English: the definite article

Resources
CD 1, tracks 2–3
Accès Studio pages 4–5, 6–7, 12–13 & 14–15
Cahier d'exercices A & B, page 2
Accès Studio ActiveTeach:
p.004 Flashcards
ActiveTeach:
p.008 Video 1
p.008 Video worksheet 1
p.009 Grammar
p.009 Grammar practice
p.009 Thinking skills

Accès Studio Unit 1 (pp. 4–5) can be used before this unit to review greetings.

Accès Studio Unit 2 (pp. 6–7) can be used with this unit to review numbers and ages.

Accès Studio Unit 5 (pp. 12–13) can be used with this unit to review the definite article, in the context of classroom items.

Accès Studio Unit 6 (pp. 14–15) can be used with this unit for further practice of *j'aime/je n'aime pas* and to review vocabulary for sports and hobbies.

In conjunction with the module introduction (pages 6–7)
Have a discussion with the class on what France means to them. As well as the better known and more traditional elements, cover the aspects of modern France that will appeal to them – fashion houses such as Dior and Yves St Laurent, French football teams and other sports stars, etc.

Starter 1
Aim
To review greetings and giving your name

Introduce yourself: *Bonjour. Je m'appelle ...* Pupils introduce themselves to you, speaking as a class. Then ask pupils to introduce themselves to the person sitting next to them. Review *Au revoir* in the same way.

Next play a game. Tell pupils that each row in the class is a team – make sure numbers are equal. The aim is to be the first team to complete introductions. The person at the back starts. Each person in turn says *Bonjour*, gives his/her name and says *Au revoir* to the person in front. The person at the front of the row runs to the back person to complete the introductions.

Alternative Starter 1:
Use *Accès Studio* ActiveTeach p. 004 Flashcards to review and practise the language for greetings.

1 Mon autoportrait   C'est perso

1 Écoute. Qui est-ce? (1–6) (AT 1.2)
Listening. Pupils listen to six conversations and look at the texts. They identify who is speaking each time.

Audioscript CD 1 track 2

1 J'aime: les weekends, le cinéma.
   Je n'aime pas: le rap, la violence.
2 J'aime: les consoles de jeux, le sport, les pizzas.
   Je n'aime pas: le racisme, le hard rock.
3 J'aime: les animaux, les voyages.
   Je n'aime pas: le foot, la danse, l'injustice.
4 J'aime: les chats, les spaghettis.
   Je n'aime pas: le rugby, les reptiles.
5 J'aime: les mangas, la tecktonik.
   Je n'aime pas: le tennis, les chiens, la Nintendo DS.
6 J'aime: la musique, le roller.
   Je n'aime pas: les insectes, les jeux vidéo, les maths.

Answers
1 Olivia 2 Alex 3 Samira 4 Marielle
5 Samuel 6 Hugo

2 Copie et remplis le tableau avec les mots de l'exercice 1. (AT 3.2)
PLTS C

Reading. Pupils copy and complete the grid using the words in exercise 1. This exercise helps pupils practise using cognates as a reading strategy.

> **Studio Grammaire: the definite article**
> Use the *Studio Grammaire* box to review the definite article. There is more information and further practice on Pupil Book p. 84.

3 En tandem. Pose cinq questions à ton/ta camarade. (AT 2.2)
Speaking. In pairs: pupils take it in turn to ask and answer five questions about likes/dislikes. A framework is supplied for support.

R Pupils write five things they like and five things they dislike, using *j'aime* and *je n'aime pas*.

> Use the pronunciation box to review and practise using intonation to form questions. See also Pupil Book p. 44.

Starter 2
Aim
To review talking about likes/dislikes with *j'aime/je n'aime pas*

Write up the following. Give pupils two minutes to write three sentences with each opening.

J'aime …   Je n'aime pas …

Hear some answers. Choose a few good examples and ask some pupils, *Tu aimes (les mangas)?* They answer using *Oui, j'aime ça.* or *Non, je n'aime pas ça.*

4 Qu'est-ce qu'ils mentionnent? Écoute et écris leurs opinions. (1–5) (AT 1.3)
Listening. Pupils listen to five conversations and note what the people mention and their opinions.

Audioscript CD 1 track 3

1 – Tu aimes le sport?
   – Oui, j'aime ça. C'est cool.
2 – Tu aimes la tecktonik?
   – Non, je n'aime pas ça. C'est ennuyeux.
3 – Et toi? Tu aimes le roller?
   – Oui, j'aime ça. C'est bien.
4 – Tu aimes le cinéma?
   – Oui, j'aime ça. C'est génial.
5 – Tu aimes le rugby?
   – Non, je n'aime pas ça. C'est nul.

Answers
1 sport, b
2 tecktonik, d
3 roller, c
4 cinéma, a
5 rugby, e

> **Studio Grammaire: –er verbs (present singular)**
> Use the *Studio Grammaire* box to review the present tense singular of –er verbs, using *aimer* as the example. There is more information and further practice on Pupil Book p. 22.

5 En tandem. Pose des questions à ton/ta camarade. (AT 2.3)
Speaking. In pairs: pupils take it in turn to ask and answer questions about likes/dislikes, this time giving their opinion of each activity. A framework is supplied for support.

1 C'est perso 1 Mon autoportrait

6 Lis et réponds aux questions. (AT 3.3)
Reading. Pupils read the four short texts and then identify who is being described in each of the questions which follow.

Answers
1 Mo **2** Lucas **3** Chloé **4** Morgane **5** Chloé

+ Pupils rework the texts for Chloé and Lucas using the third person. This can be done orally or in writing.

7 Choisis cinq personnes célèbres. Décris leurs préférences. (AT 4.3)
Writing. Pupils choose five famous people and write about their likes and dislikes. An example is given. Draw pupils' attention to the tip box on using connectives.

Plenary
Give pupils three minutes working in pairs to complete ActiveTeach p. 009 Thinking skills, Worksheet 1.1 Inventing categories, which involves categorising vocabulary. Ask the class for answers.

Alternative Plenary:
Use ActiveTeach p. 009 Grammar practice to review regular –er verbs.

Workbook A, page 2

Answers
1 1 c 2 f 3 a 4 e 5 b 6 g 7 d
2 1 J'aime la musique. ✔
   2 J'aime le cinéma. ✔
   3 Je n'aime pas la violence. ✘
   4 Je n'aime pas les reptiles. ✘
   5 J'aime les chats et les chiens. ✔
3 (See answers to exercise 2.)

Workbook B, page 2

Answers
1 1 J'aime la musique, c'est cool. ✔
   2 J'aime le rugby, c'est génial. ✔
   3 Je n'aime pas l'injustice, c'est nul. ✘
   4 J'aime les chats et aussi les chiens. ✔✔
   5 J'aime les insectes mais je n'aime pas les reptiles. ✔✘
2 1 J'aime la musique. (C'est cool.)
   2 Je n'aime pas les reptiles. (C'est nul.)
   3 J'aime le foot et aussi les jeux vidéo.
   4 J'aime les animaux mais je n'aime pas les maths.

1 Mon autoportrait C'est perso 1

Worksheet 1.1 Inventing categories

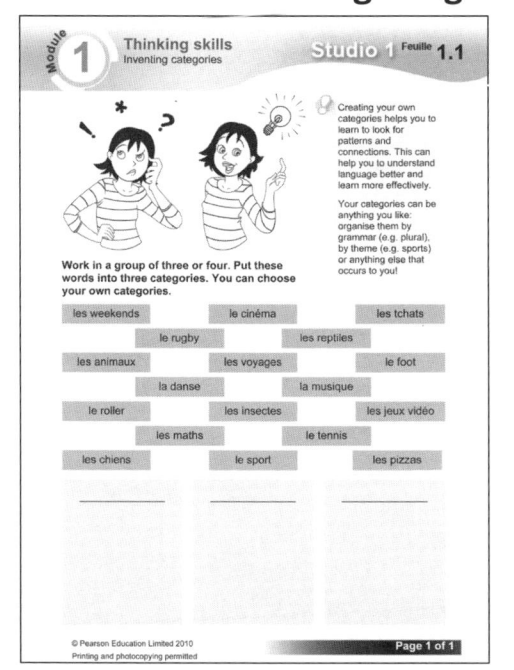

Answers
(Answers will vary. Groups might include masculine, feminine, plural, interests, likes, dislikes, etc.)

Video

The video component provides opportunities for speaking activities in a plausible and stimulating context. The StudioFR team – Marielle, Samira, Hugo and Alex – operate from their base in the medieval cellars of Châlons-en-Champagne, which have been lent to them by the Town Hall. They are making video reports about the town to send to StudioGB, their counterpart in the UK. Each video is around three minutes long.

Episode 1: Salut!

Marielle, the presenter, introduces the team from their studio in the medieval cellars of Châlons-en-Champagne. Video worksheet 1 can be used in conjunction with this episode.

Answers to video worksheet (ActiveTeach)

1 A [PLTS T]
  B They are recording a video show for English-speaking learners of French.
  C An old building in the town where they live
  D [In this order:] Hugo Marielle Samira Alex
2 A Because she spoke too fast.
  B She says speaking slowly is boring.
  C He agrees with Samira.
  D Because he thinks Marielle already knows how to spell it! Then he remembers it's for the film.
  E 14
  F It's bad/rubbish! It's true! Cut! too fast
3 A 12
  B 13
  C First to say he doesn't want to introduce himself, then to say he doesn't like hard rock music.
  D To show he likes cameras.
  E He says he doesn't like talking but Hugo says he loves talking about cameras.
  F the team How are you?
     talkative See you soon!
  G 22 October (two weeks before 5 November)
  H (Pupils' own answers)

C'est perso 1

2 Mon kit de survie (Pupil Book pp. 10–11)

Learning objectives
- Talking about your survival kit
- Using *avoir* (*je, tu, il/elle*)

Framework objectives
4.6/Y7 Language – (a) questions: ex. 1
4.6/Y7 Language – (b) negatives: ex. 4

Grammar
- *avoir* (present singular)
- *qu'est-ce que ...?*

Key language
J'ai ...
Tu as ...
Il/Elle a ...
un appareil photo
une barre de céréales
un bâton de colle
un cahier
des chips
des clés
une clé USB
une gourde
des kleenex
des lunettes de soleil
un magazine
un miroir
un MP3
un portable
un portemonnaie
un paquet de mouchoirs
des surligneurs fluo
une trousse
Je n'ai pas de ...
C'est ...
essentiel/important

PLTS
- Independent enquirers

Resources
CD 1, tracks 4–5
Accès Studio pages 10–11 & 18–19
Cahier d'exercices A & B, page 3
ActiveTeach:
p.010 Video 2
p.010 Video worksheet 2
p.010 Flashcards
p.010 Thinking skills
p.010 Learning skills
p.011 Class activity

Accès Studio Unit 4 (pp. 10–11) can be used with this unit for further practice of the indefinite article and to review vocabulary for school bag items.

Accès Studio Unit 8 (pp. 18–19) can be used with this unit for further dictionary work.

Starter 1
Aim
To introduce language for school bag/survival kit items; To use reading strategies

Write up the following, jumbling the order of the second column. Give pupils two minutes working in pairs to match the French and English versions.

un appareil photo	a camera
une barre de céréales	a cereal bar
des lunettes de soleil	sunglasses
une gourde	a water bottle
un portemonnaie	a purse
un portable	a mobile phone
des chips	some crisps
un paquet de mouchoirs	a packet of tissues

Ask pupils to swap answers with another pair. Check answers as a class. Ask the class how they worked out the meanings of the French items. Point out the usefulness of reading strategies such as recognising cognates, using grammar and using logic.

Alternative Starter 1:
Use ActiveTeach p. 010 Flashcards to review and practise further language for school bag items.

Studio Grammaire: *avoir* (present singular)
Use the *Studio Grammaire* box to review the present singular forms of *avoir*. There is more information and further practice on Pupil Book p. 22.

1 C'est quel sac? Écoute et écris les bonnes lettres. (1–4) (AT 1.2)
Listening. Pupils listen and look at the pictures of items in different people's bags. They write the letter of the bag being described each time.

Audioscript CD 1 track 4

1 – Thomas, qu'est-ce que tu as dans ton kit de survie?
 – Alors ... J'ai une clé USB, un appareil photo, un portable et un MP3.
2 – Chloé, qu'est-ce que tu as dans ton kit de survie?
 – Alors, moi, j'ai un portemonnaie, des chips, une gourde et une barre de céréales.
 – Tu n'as pas de cahier?
 – Euh ... Non, je n'ai pas de cahier.
3 – Charlotte, qu'est-ce que tu as dans ton kit de survie?
 – Voyons ... J'ai des kleenex, des clés, un bâton de colle et aussi une trousse avec des surligneurs fluo.
4 – Et toi, Gaëlle? Qu'est-ce que tu as dans ton kit de survie?
 – Alors, moi, j'ai un paquet de mouchoirs, un miroir, un magazine et puis des lunettes de soleil.

2 Mon kit de survie   C'est perso 1

> **Answers**
> **1** b **2** a **3** c **4** d

> **Studio Grammaire: *qu'est-ce que...?***
> Use the *Studio Grammaire* box to review the use of *qu'est-ce que* in questions. There is more information and further practice on Pupil Book p. 44.

2 Copie et remplis le tableau avec les noms de l'exercice 1. Fais attention au genre des noms! (AT 3.1)

PLTS I

Reading. Pupils copy and complete the grid using the nouns from exercise 1.

Before pupils start, read together through the tip box on using a dictionary. Point out how to find or check the gender of nouns. Then ask pupils to use their dictionaries to find the gender and meaning of the following words: (*un*) *peigne*, (*une*) *brosse à dents*, (*un*) *carnet*.

Throughout *Studio 1* Pupil Book there is support on dictionary use; this is highlighted and developed in the Teacher's Guide. The Pupil Book also has a useful summary on page 130.

> **Answers**
> **masculine singular**
> *un* portemonnaie – *a purse*
> un appareil photo – a camera
> un portable – a mobile phone
> un MP3 – an MP3 player
> un bâton de colle – a gluestick
> un paquet de mouchoirs – a packet of tissues
> un miroir – a mirror
> un magazine – a magazine
> **feminine singular**
> *une* gourde – *a water bottle*
> une barre de céréales – a cereal bar
> une clé USB – a memory stick
> une trousse – a pencil case
> **plural**
> *des* chips – *some crisps*
> des kleenex – some tissues
> des clés – some keys
> des surligneurs fluo – some fluorescent highlighters
> des lunettes de soleil – some sunglasses

Starter 2
Aim
To review survival kit language

Give pupils three minutes working in pairs to complete ActiveTeach p. 010 Thinking skills, Worksheet 1.2 Odd one out! Accept all plausibly argued answers.

3 En tandem. Pose des questions à ton/ta camarade. (AT 2.2)
Speaking. Pupils take it in turn to ask and answer questions about what they have in their bags. A framework is supplied for support.

4 Écoute et mets les objets dans l'ordre d'importance pour Renaud. (1–6) (AT 1.3)
Listening. Pupils listen and put the objects pictured in order of importance for Renaud, matching each item to the correct opinion (from **a–f**). Some vocabulary is glossed for support.

> **Audioscript**   **CD 1 track 5**
> **1** *Alors ... Dans mon kit de survie, j'ai un portable. Pour moi, c'est important.*
> **2** *J'ai un crayon. Pour moi, c'est essentiel.*
> **3** *Ensuite, j'ai une règle. C'est très important.*
> **4** *J'ai un stylo. C'est très, très important, ça.*
> **5** *J'ai un MP3. Mais pour moi, ce n'est pas très important.*
> **6** *Et dans mon kit de survie, j'ai aussi une calculatrice. Pour moi, ce n'est pas du tout important. Je suis fort en calcul!*

> **Answers**
> **4** d **1** a **3** c **6** b **2** e **5** f

5 En tandem. Mets les objets dans ton sac dans l'ordre d'importance pour toi. Compare avec ton/ta camarade. (AT 2.3)
Speaking. In pairs: pupils list the items in their bag in their personal order of importance. They then compare lists with a partner. A sample answer is given.

6 Fais une liste en anglais du kit de survie de Zahra. (AT 3.2)
Reading. Pupils read the text and write a list in English of what is in Zahra's survival kit. *des feutres* is glossed for support.

> **Answers**
> pencil case, pencils, coloured pencils, felt pens, rubber, gluestick, mobile phone, water bottle, sandwich

1 C'est perso   2 Mon kit de survie

7 Choisis un contexte. Utilise un dictionnaire et prépare ton kit de survie. (AT 4.3)

Writing. Pupils choose a context in which they might need a survival kit, from the pictures shown. Using a dictionary, they write a sentence about what they would put in their kit. A sample answer is given.

Pupils list by gender three of the new words they looked up and learn them at home. They then test each other in pairs on this vocabulary.

Plenary
Give pupils three minutes working in pairs to complete ActiveTeach p. 010 Learning skills, Worksheet 1.3 Using a dictionary (i). Ask the class for answers.

Alternative Plenary:
Use ActiveTeach p. 011 Class activity to play matching pairs with survival kit items.

Workbook A, page 3

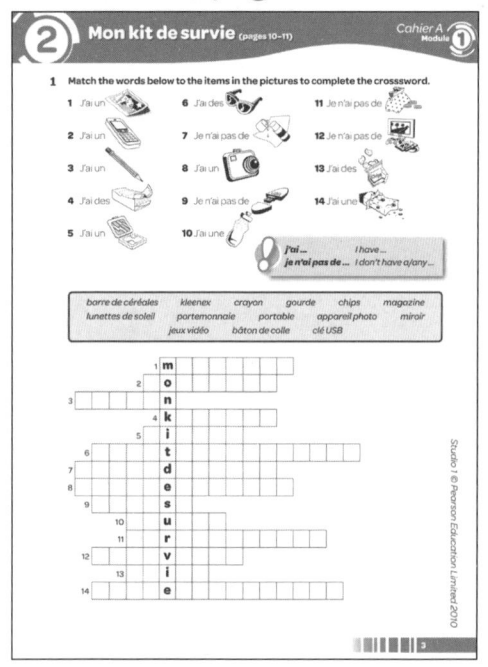

Answers
1 1 magazine 2 portable 3 crayon 4 kleenex
   5 miroir 6 lunettes de soleil 7 bâton de colle
   8 appareil photo 9 clé USB 10 gourde
   11 portemonnaie 12 jeux vidéo 13 chips
   14 barre de céréales

Workbook B, page 3

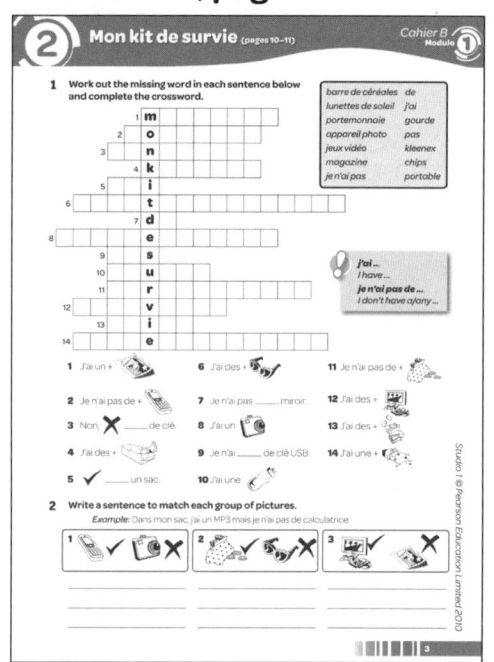

Answers
1 1 magazine 2 portable 3 je n'ai pas 4 kleenex
   5 J'ai 6 lunettes de soleil 7 de
   8 appareil photo 9 pas 10 gourde
   11 portemonnaie 12 jeux vidéo
   13 chips 14 barre de céréales
2 1 Dans mon sac, j'ai un portable, mais je n'ai pas d'appareil photo.
   2 Dans mon sac, j'ai un portemonnaie, mais je n'ai pas de lunettes de soleil.
   3 Dans mon sac, j'ai des jeux vidéo, mais je n'ai pas de magazine.

2 Mon kit de survie C'est perso 1

Worksheet 1.2 Odd one out!

Worksheet 1.3 Using a dictionary (i)

Answers
(If there is a valid reason, other answers may be acceptable.)
1 une barre de céréales – feminine
2 un magazine – begins with 'm'
3 des chips – they are edible
   or des kleenex – begins with 'k' or doesn't have an 's' on the end
4 un stylo – masculine and begins with 's'
5 un sandwich – edible, begins with 's' and is masculine
6 un crayon – masculine
7 des surligneurs fluo – plural
8 aimer – a verb
9 des lunettes de soleil – plural
10 ennuyeux – an adjective

Answers
A (Answers will vary.)
B 1 a 2 b 3 b 4 c 5 a 6 b
C 1 b 2 d 3 e 4 a 5 c
D (Answers will vary.)

Video
Episode 2: Mon kit
The team show StudioGB what they need to have in their bags to survive their daily routine. Video worksheet 2 can be used in conjunction with this episode.

Answers to video worksheet (ActiveTeach)
1 A They are presenting the things they have which help them do their jobs in the team.
  B [F3.1] (Pupils' own answers)
  C (In this order:) Marielle Samira Alex Hugo
2 A (Any six from:) matériel, journaliste, recherches, informations, scoop, essentiel, accès, Internet, technique
  B ordinateur (computer), portable (mobile phone)
3 A She has the keys to the studio!
  B Gadgets and technology
4 A It's not the latest model but it's OK.
  B It can process videos and photos.
  C first quite good It's great!
5 A It's the very latest model.
  B mirror, sunglasses, camera!
  C [PLTS T/E] She's embarrassed to admit that she carries a pen in order to sign autographs!
  D Are you sure? That's strange!

23

3 Comment je me vois (Pupil Book pp. 12–13)

C'est perso 1

Learning objectives
- Describing yourself
- Understanding adjective agreement (singular)

Framework objectives
4.2/Y7 Language – high-frequency words: ex. 2
4.5/Y7 Language – (a) present tense verbs: ex. 3

Grammar
- adjective agreement (singular)
- *être* (present singular)

Key language
Je suis/Je ne suis pas…
Tu es…
Il/Elle est…
branché(e)
charmant(e)
curieux/curieuse
drôle
généreux/généreuse
gentil(le)
intelligent(e)
modeste
poli(e)
Tu es d'accord?
Je suis d'accord.
Je ne suis pas d'accord.

PLTS
R Reflective learners

Cross-curricular
ICT: e-mailing

Resources
CD 1, tracks 6–7
Accès Studio pages 16–17 & 26–27
Cahier d'exercices A & B, page 4
ActiveTeach:
p.012 Grammar skills
p.013 Grammar
p.013 Grammar practice

Accès Studio Unit 7 (pp. 16–17) can be used with this unit for further practice of adjective agreement and position (and to review colour vocabulary).

Accès Studio Unit 12 (pp. 26–27) can be used for further practice of *être*.

Starter 1
Aim
To review *avoir* and introduce/review the present singular of *être*; To use reading strategies

Write up the following. Give pupils three minutes to complete the table, using the sentences to work out the verb forms.

J'ai des clés.   Elle a un portable.
Tu es charmant.   Je suis intelligente.
Tu as un bâton de colle. Il est modeste.

	avoir	être
I		
you		
he/she	a	

Check answers and ask pupils to translate the sentences into English.

1 Écoute. Qui est-ce? (1–9) (AT 1.1)
Listening. Pupils listen to nine people describing themselves and identify the speaker each time.

Audioscript   CD 1 track 6

1 Je suis charmant.
2 Je suis branché.
3 Je suis curieuse.
4 Je suis intelligente.
5 Je suis polie.
6 Je suis drôle.
7 Je suis gentil.
8 Je suis généreuse.
9 Je suis modeste.

Answers
1 Yanis 2 Frank 3 Ophélie 4 Malika 5 Samira
6 Nicolas 7 Valentin 8 Luna 9 Nassim

Studio Grammaire: adjective agreement (singular)
Use the *Studio Grammaire* box to review the changes to adjectives in the feminine form. There is more information and further practice on Pupil Book p. 23.

Pupils follow the adjective patterns to work out the feminine forms of the following adjectives: *petit* (small), *paresseux* (lazy), *impoli* (rude), *heureux* (happy), *grand* (big), *facile* (easy).

3 Comment je me vois   C'est perso   1

2   Écoute et écris les bonnes lettres pour Abdel (a, b ou c). (1–3) (AT 1.3)

Listening. Pupils listen to Abdel completing a quiz with a friend and write the letters of Abdel's responses. Draw pupils' attention to the tip box on using intensifiers to make their own speech and writing more interesting and personal.

Audioscript   CD 1 track 7

− Alors, Abdel, comment es-tu? Numéro 1: Tu es modeste?
  Voici les réponses:
  a Je suis très modeste.
  b Je suis assez modeste.
  c Je ne suis pas modeste.
− c Je ne suis pas modeste.
− D'accord. Numéro 2: Alors, tu es drôle?
  Voici les réponses:
  a Je suis très drôle.
  b Je suis assez drôle.
  c Je ne suis pas drôle.
− a Je suis très drôle.
− Numéro 3: Abdel, tu es intelligent?
  a Je suis très intelligent.
  b Je suis assez intelligent.
  c Je ne suis pas intelligent.
− b Je suis assez intelligent. Eh oui ...

Answers
1 c   2 a   3 b

Starter 2
Aim
To recognise adjective agreement

Pupils listen as you read out a series of adjectives. They indicate the gender of each as follows: masculine – stand up; feminine – hands on head; could be either from the spoken form – both arms in the air.

Read out the adjectives one at a time: *branché, gentille, drôle, charmant, généreuse, modeste, poli, curieux, intelligente.*

Finish by prompting with the masculine form of each adjective and asking pupils to say and spell the feminine form.

Studio Grammaire: *être* (present singular)

Use the *Studio Grammaire* box to review the present singular forms of *être*. There is more information and further practice on Pupil Book p. 22.

3   En tandem. Fais le quiz. Demande si ton/ta camarade est d'accord. (AT 2.3)

Speaking. In pairs: pupils do the quiz on their own, then ask their partner if they agree with the answers they have given. A language box and a sample exchange are supplied.

4   Lis le texte et termine les phrases en anglais. (AT 3.4)

Reading. Pupils read the text and complete the sentences summarising it in English.

Answers
1 curious   2 intelligent   3 important
4 music and mangas   5 spaghetti

5   Lis le texte. Vrai (V) ou faux (F)? (AT 3.3)

Reading. Pupils read the text and decide whether the statements about it are true (V) or false (F).

Answers
1 V   2 F   3 V   4 F   5 F   6 V

6   Décris-toi et un copain/une copine. (AT 4.3)

PLTS R

Writing. Pupils write a description of themselves and a friend. A framework is supplied. When they have finished, ask them to read their text over and make corrections as necessary.

If you have connections with a partner school, pupils could e-mail their texts to their French peers to introduce themselves.

Plenary

Go round the class. The first pupil makes a statement describing himself/herself (e.g. *Je suis branché(e).*) The next pupil responds to this (*Je suis d'accord./Je ne suis pas d'accord.*), then makes a statement about himself/herself for the next pupil to reply to, and so on round the class.

Alternative Plenary:
Use ActiveTeach p. 013 Grammar practice to review *avoir* and *être*.

1 C'est perso — 3 Comment je me vois

Workbook A, page 4

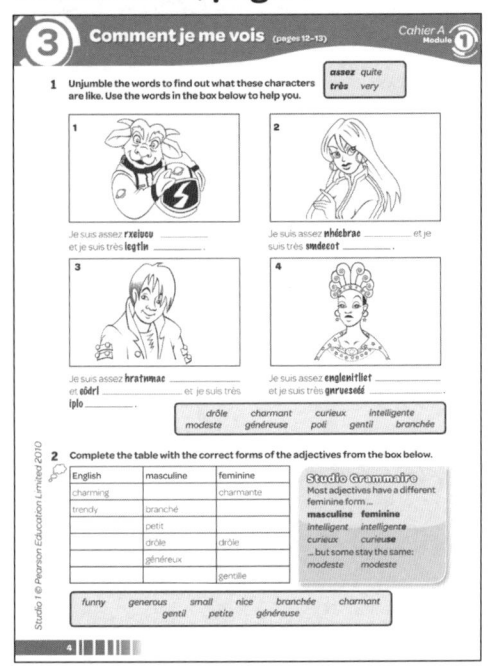

Answers

1
1. Je suis assez curieux et je suis très gentil.
2. Je suis assez branchée et je suis très modeste.
3. Je suis assez charmant et drôle et je suis très poli.
4. Je suis assez intelligente et je suis très généreuse.

2

English	masculine	feminine
charming	charmant	charmante
trendy	branché	branchée
small	petit	petite
funny	drôle	drôle
generous	généreux	généreuse
nice	gentil	gentille

Workbook B, page 4

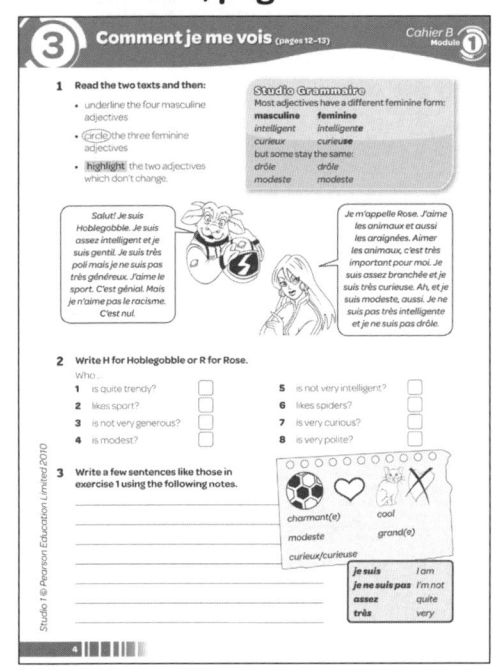

Answers

1 (underlined:) intelligent, gentil, poli, généreux
(circled:) branchée, curieuse, intelligente
(highlighted:) modeste, drôle

2 1 R 2 H 3 H 4 R 5 R 6 R 7 R 8 H

3 (Example answer:)
Je m'appelle X. J'aime le foot(ball). Aimer le foot(ball), c'est très important pour moi. Je suis assez charmant et je suis très modeste. Je ne suis pas très curieux et je ne suis pas cool. Je suis grand.

Worksheet 1.4 Accents

Module 1 Grammar — Accents — Studio 1 Feuille 1.4

Accents help with the pronunciation of a word. It is important to remember accents when you are writing in French.

A What are these accents called? Match them up correctly.

1 ç 2 é 3 ô 4 ù

- acute accent (accent aigu)
- grave accent (accent grave)
- circumflex accent (accent circonflexe)
- cedilla (cédille)

B True or false? Write T or F.

You may not know the answers, but think carefully and don't just guess. Looking at the Mini-dictionnaire section of Studio will help.

1 Acute accents only occur on the letter 'e'.
2 A grave accent is used so that you can tell the difference between words which sound the same, e.g. a/à, ou/où.
3 The circumflex accent is often used where an 's' followed in the past.
4 Cedillas can occur on any letter.
5 A cedilla softens a 'k' sound into an 's' sound.
6 You will never find a cedilla before an 'i' or an 'e'.
7 If you miss out an accent, this is considered a spelling mistake in French.
8 Grave accents can occur on the letters 'a', 'e' or 'u'.
9 You can find a circumflex accent on consonants.

C Put the missing accents into these sentences. There is one accent missing per sentence.

1 J'aime les jeux video.
2 J'aime les gateaux et aussi la capoeira.
3 Qu'est-ce que tu as dans ton sac a dos?
4 Tu aimes le foot? Non, je n'aime pas ca.
5 Mon ami Nathan est assez drole.
6 Dans mon kit de survie, j'ai un portable. Pour moi, c'est tres important.
7 Etre intelligent, c'est important pour moi.
8 C'est un garcon. Il a les yeux bleus.

© Pearson Education Limited 2010
Printing and photocopying permitted
Page 1 of 1

Answers

A 1 cedilla 2 acute accent 3 circumflex accent 4 grave accent

B 1 T 2 T 3 T 4 F (Cedillas can only occur on the letter 'c'.) 5 T 6 T 7 T 8 T 9 F (Circumflex accents can only be found on vowels.)

C
1 J'aime les jeux vidéo.
2 J'aime les gâteaux et aussi la capoeira.
3 Qu'est-ce que tu as dans ton sac à dos?
4 Tu aimes le foot? Non, je n'aime pas ça.
5 Mon ami Nathan est assez drôle.
6 Dans mon kit de survie, j'ai un portable. Pour moi, c'est très important.
7 Être intelligent, c'est important pour moi.
8 C'est un garçon. Il a les yeux bleus.

4 Et les autres? (Pupil Book pp. 14–15)

C'est perso 1

Learning objectives
- Talking about other people
- Understanding adjective agreement (plural)

Framework objectives
1.1/Y7 Listening – gist and detail: ex. 4
2.4/Y7 Writing – (b) building text: ex. 6
5.3 Strategies – English/other languages: ex. 1 PLTS suggestion
5.6 Strategies – reading aloud: ex. 3

Grammar
- adjective agreement (plural)
- possessive adjectives (*mon/ma/mes, ton/ta/tes*)

Key language
C'est un garçon/une fille.
Il a …/Elle a …
les yeux bleus/gris/marron/verts
les cheveux longs/courts/mi-longs/frisés/raides/blonds/bruns/noirs/roux
Il/Elle est …
grand(e)
petit(e)
de taille moyenne
Il/Elle s'appelle …

PLTS
S Self-managers

Resources
CD 1, tracks 8–9
Accès Studio pages 16–17 & 20–21
Cahier d'exercices A & B, page 5
Accès Studio ActiveTeach:
p.016 Flashcards
ActiveTeach:
p.014 Grammar
p.014 Grammar practice
p.015 Grammar
p.015 Grammar practice

Accès Studio Unit 7 (pp. 16–17) can be used with this unit to review or introduce colour vocabulary and adjective agreement and position.

Accès Studio Unit 9 (pp. 20–21) can be used to review or introduce vocabulary for family members and the possessive adjectives *mon, ma, mes*.

Starter 1
Aim
To review language for describing hair and eyes

Write up the following. Ask pupils to find someone in the class who fits each description. If necessary, ask pupils to review the colours included in each one before finding members of the class who match them. You could also use the opportunity to clarify the meanings of *il* and *elle*.

1. *Il a les cheveux blonds. Il a les yeux marron.*
2. *Elle a les cheveux noirs. Elle a les yeux bleus.*
3. *Il a les cheveux roux. Il a les yeux verts.*
4. *Elle a les cheveux bruns. Elle a les yeux gris.*

To check answers, ask pupils to translate the sentences into English.

Alternative Starter 1:
Use *Accès Studio* ActiveTeach p. 016 Flashcards to review and practise colours.

1 Écoute. Qui est-ce? (1–5) (AT 1.3)
Listening. Pupils listen to five descriptions and look at the pictures of people. They identify the person being described each time.

Audioscript — CD 1 track 8

1. *C'est une fille. Elle est petite. Elle a les cheveux mi-longs, noirs et raides. Elle a les yeux marron.*
2. *C'est un garçon. Il est de taille moyenne. Il a les cheveux noirs et courts. Il a les yeux verts.*
3. *C'est une fille. Elle a les cheveux longs, roux et frisés. Elle a les yeux marron.*
4. *C'est un garçon. Il est petit. Il a les yeux marron. Il a les cheveux courts et bruns.*
5. *C'est un garçon. Il est grand. Il a les cheveux courts et blonds. Il a les yeux bleus.*

Answers
1 Setsuko 2 Ludo 3 Marina 4 Youssef
5 Baptiste

R In pairs: pupils take it in turn to describe a person in the class and to identify him/her.

PLTS S
Read through the key language box on page 14 together. Check comprehension. Ask pupils to compare the French structures with their English equivalents. What differences are there? Prompt as necessary to elicit the fact that 'hair' is plural in French. Ask pupils how they can note the vocabulary in a way that will help them remember this difference.

4 Et les autres? C'est perso 1

> **Studio Grammaire: adjective agreement (plural)**
> Use the *Studio Grammaire* box to review adjective agreement (plural): *les cheveux noirs*, etc. There is more information and further practice on Pupil Book p. 23.

2 En tandem. Pose des questions à ton/ta camarade. Qui est-ce? (AT 2.3)

Speaking. In pairs: one pupil chooses one of the people pictured; the other asks questions in order to identify the person. A sample exchange is given.

➕ Pupils choose two of the characters pictured in exercise 2 and write a sentence describing each one (hair and eyes).

3 Écoute et chante. (AT 1.4)

Listening. Pupils listen to the song and sing along. *les sorties* and *sur lui* are glossed for support.

Audioscript CD 1 track 9

Timothy, Timothy, il est ton ami,
Timothy, Timothy, ton ami pour la vie!

Mon ami Timothy habite à Tahiti.
Il aime la géographie et le rugby.

Timothy, Timothy, il est ton ami,
Timothy, Timothy, ton ami pour la vie!

Mon ami Timothy adore les spaghettis.
Il est très modeste et il est assez poli.

Timothy, Timothy, il est ton ami,
Timothy, Timothy, ton ami pour la vie!

Mon ami Timothy a un kit de survie.
Il a toujours du chewing-gum sur lui.

Timothy, Timothy, il est ton ami,
Timothy, Timothy, ton ami pour la vie!

Mon ami Timothy a les cheveux longs.
Il est assez petit et a les yeux marron.

Timothy, Timothy, il est ton ami,
Timothy, Timothy, ton ami pour la vie!

Mon ami Timothy aime les sorties.
Il aime son chien Kosto et les reptiles aussi.

Starter 2

Aim
To review possessive adjectives

Write up the following, omitting the underline (used here to indicate the correct answer). Pupils select the correct form for each noun.

1. *mon / mes chips*
2. *mon / ma amie*
3. *ma / mes clé USB*
4. *ton / ta portable*
5. *ton / tes clés*
6. *ta / tes gourde*

Check answers. Ask pupils to summarise when the different forms are used.

Alternative Starter 2:
Use ActiveTeach p. 015 Grammar practice to review possessive adjectives.

4 Lis la chanson et corrige les erreurs dans les phrases. (AT 3.4)

Reading. Pupils read the text of the song in exercise 3. They then read six sentences about the song and correct the errors in them.

Answers
1. Timothy lives in **Tahiti**.
2. He loves **spaghetti**.
3. He is quite **polite**.
4. He has **long** hair.
5. He is **(quite) short**.
6. He **likes** outings.

> **Studio Grammaire: possessive adjectives**
> Use the *Studio Grammaire* box to review possessive adjectives (*mon/ma/mes* and *ton/ta/tes*). There is further practice on Pupil Book p. 23.

5 Lis le blog et copie et remplis le tableau. (AT 3.3)

Reading. Pupils copy out the table. They read Arthur's blog and complete the table with the details of his family in English.

Answers
Antonin; brother; quite tall; short, brown; green; curious, very generous
Léa; sister; medium height; long, blond, curly; blue; intelligent, not trendy
Cédric; dad; very tall; grey, short; blue; funny, quite nice, but not modest

29

1 C'est perso   4 Et les autres?

6 Choisis un membre de ta famille et écris sa description. (AT 4.4)
Writing. Pupils choose a member of their family and write a description of him/her. Two writing frames (male/female) are supplied for support, along with a list of family members (including *mon, ma* or *mes*).

Plenary
Write up the names of a few famous people (or use pictures of them – you could ask pupils to bring these in). Give pupils two minutes working in teams to prepare a short description of each person (height, hair, eyes, personality), which they then deliver from memory, each person in the team saying a sentence.

Alternative Plenary:
Use ActiveTeach p. 014 Grammar practice to review adjectives.

Workbook A, page 5

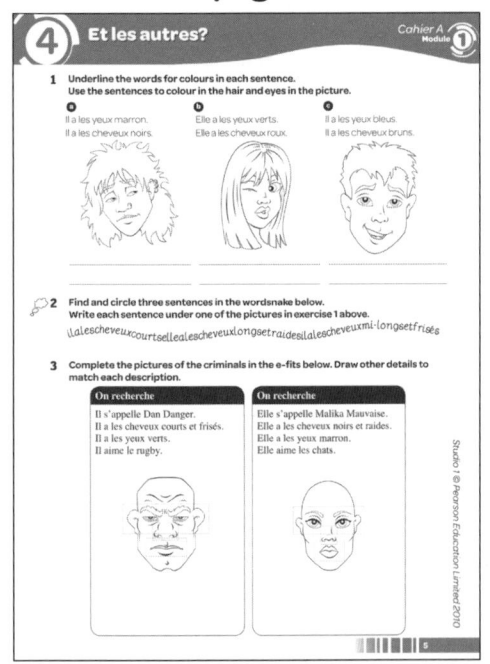

Answers
1 (Underlined:) marron, noirs, verts, roux, bleus, bruns
  (Coloured as follows:)
  a brown eyes and black hair
  b green eyes and red hair
  c blue eyes and brown hair
2 a il a les cheveux mi-longs et frisés
  b elle a les cheveux longs et raides
  c il a les cheveux courts et raides
3 (Drawings as follows:)
  Dan Danger: short, curly hair; green eyes; likes rugby
  Malika Mauvaise: black, straight hair; brown eyes; likes cats

Workbook B, page 5

Answers
1 1 a 2 b 3 a 4 b 5 c 6 c 7 d
   8 d 9 c 10 d
2 Il a les cheveux longs et frisés.
   Il est assez grand.
   Il a les yeux marron.
   Il est branché/modeste et il est aussi très modeste/branché. / Il est très branché/modeste et il est aussi modeste/branché.
   Il aime la musique, mais il n'aime pas le racisme. / Il n'aime pas le racisme, mais il aime la musique.

5 Il est hypercool! (Pupil Book pp. 16–17)

C'est perso 1

Learning objectives
- Describing a musician
- Using the present tense (*je, tu, il/elle*)

Framework objectives
2.5/Y7 Writing – different text types: ex. 7
4.1/Y7 Language – letters and sounds: ex. 2
5.2 Strategies – memorising: *Stratégie 1* (p. 25)
5.8 Strategies – evaluating and improving: ex. 8

Grammar
- the present tense (singular: *aimer, s'appeler, être, avoir*)

Key language
Review of vocabulary from Units 3 & 4:
Il/Elle s'appelle …
Il/Elle aime …
Il/Elle est …
Il/Elle a …

PLTS
T Team workers

Cross-curricular
ICT: word processing

Resources
CD 1, tracks 10–11
Cahier d'exercices A & B, page 6
ActiveTeach:
p.014 Flashcards
p.017 Class activity
p.017 Thinking skills

Starter 1
Aim
To review language for describing people; To review the first person singular of key verbs

Write up the following, leaving a gap for each word in parentheses. Give pupils three minutes to complete the text. You can supply the missing words in random order for support, if necessary.

Je [m'appelle] Jason. J'ai [les cheveux] bruns et les yeux [marron]. J'[aime] les pizzas, mais je [n']aime [pas] les spaghettis. Je [suis] branché et aussi [très] intelligent.

Check answers, asking pupils how they worked out each missing word.

Alternative Starter 1:
Use ActiveTeach p. 014 Flashcards to review adjectives for describing appearance.

1 Écoute et mets les phrases dans le bon ordre. (AT 1.2)
Listening. Pupils listen to a description of two musicians and put the sentences (a–h) in the order they hear them. *beau/belle* is glossed for support.

Audioscript CD 1 track 10

– *Il a les cheveux blonds!*
 Il est cool et beau!
 Il aime le R&B!
 Il s'appelle Cool Boy!
– *Elle a les cheveux roses!*
 Elle est très belle!
 Elle aime le rock 'n' roll!
 Elle s'appelle Pink Chick!

Answers
b, d, c, a, h, f, e, g

Use the pronunciation box to review and practise the French *eau* sound.

2 Écoute et répète aussi vite que possible. (AT 1.2)
Listening. Pupils listen to the tongue twister and repeat it as quickly as possible.

Audioscript CD 1 track 11

un beau gâteau dans un beau château
un beau gâteau dans un beau château

Studio Grammaire: present tense (singular)
Use the *Studio Grammaire* box to review the key verbs (*aimer, s'appeler, être, avoir*) in the present tense singular forms. There is more information and further practice on Pupil Book p. 22.

3 Décris les deux chanteurs. Utilise les informations du tableau. (AT 2.3)
Speaking. Pupils describe the two singers in the third person, using the details supplied. A framework is supplied.

Answers
Il s'appelle Soul Man. Il aime le soul. Il est cool et beau. Il a les cheveux noirs.
Elle s'appelle Hip Gal. Elle aime le hip-hop. Elle est belle. Elle a les cheveux blonds.

31

1 C'est perso   5 Il est hypercool!

4 Invente un chanteur/une chanteuse et décris-le/la. Dessine-le/la. (AT 2.3)
Speaking. Pupils make up and draw a singer of their own. They then describe him/her to a partner.

Starter 2
Aim
To review grammar from the module; To use reading strategies

Write up the following, jumbling the order of the second column. Give pupils three minutes to match up the sentence halves.

Elle est	belle.
Il joue	de la guitare.
Elle aime	le punk-rock.
Il est	très cool.
Elle a	les cheveux noirs.
Il n'a	pas beaucoup de talent.

Check answers, asking pupils to explain their choices and to translate each completed sentence into English.

5 Lis le texte et remplis les blancs avec les verbes de la case. (AT 3.4)
Reading. Pupils read and complete the gap-fill text, using the words supplied. *sa voix* is glossed for support.

Answers
1 J'adore   2 Elle chante   3 elle est   4 Elle a
5 Elle aime   6 Tu es

6 Lis la page web. C'est Adrien, Karim ou Félix? Écris les bons noms. (AT 3.4)
Reading. Pupils read the web page about the group BB Brunes. They then identify who is being described in each of the sentences: Adrien, Karim or Félix.

Answers
1 Adrien   2 Karim   3 Félix   4 Adrien
5 Karim   6 Karim   7 Adrien   8 Félix

7 Écris une page web pour un musicien (réel ou imaginaire). (AT 4.4)
Writing. Pupils write a web page for a musician (real or imaginary). A list of features to include in their writing is supplied. This work could be done on a computer.

8 Vérifie le texte de ton/ta camarade. (AT 3.4)

PLTS T

Reading. Pupils swap their texts from exercise 7 with a partner and check and correct each other's work. A list of language to focus on is supplied: spelling, verb endings and adjective endings. Pupils then do a second draft of their own text.

Read together through the *Stratégie* on Pupil Book p. 25, covering the *Look, say, cover, write, check* technique for mastering spelling. Set pupils the challenge of choosing and learning ten words using this approach, either in the classroom or at home.

Plenary
Review and practise key present tense verbs in the singular. Prompt with a subject pronoun and an infinitive. Pupils give you the correct form (e.g. *elle, avoir – elle a*). Move on to using English prompts to increase the challenge.

Alternative Plenary:
Use ActiveTeach p. 017 Class activity to practise sentence formation using language from the module.

Workbook A, page 6

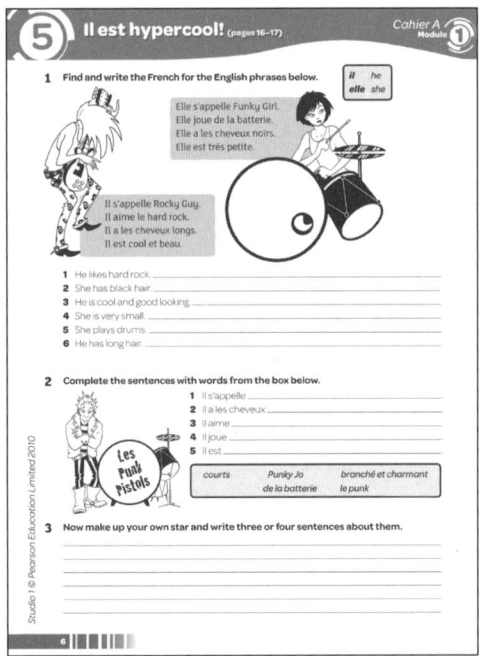

5 Il est hypercool! C'est perso

Answers

1.
   1. Il aime le hard rock.
   2. Elle a les cheveux noirs.
   3. Il est cool et beau.
   4. Elle est très petite.
   5. Elle joue de la batterie.
   6. Il a les cheveux longs.
2. Il s'appelle Punky Jo.
   Il a les cheveux courts.
   Il aime le punk.
   Il joue de la batterie.
   Il est branché et charmant.

Workbook B, page 6

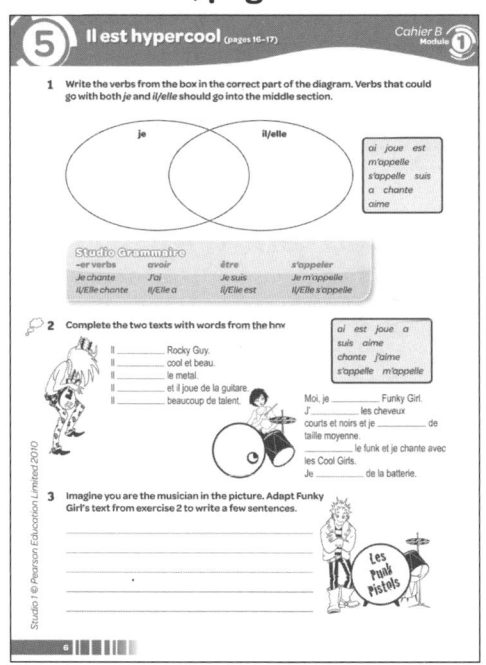

Answers

1. je: ai, m'appelle, suis
   il/elle: est, s'appelle, a
   both: joue, chante, aime
2. Il **s'appelle** Rocky Guy. Il **est** cool et beau. Il **aime** le metal. Il **chante** et il joue de la guitare. Il **a** beaucoup de talent.
   Moi, je **m'appelle** Funky Girl. **J'ai** les cheveux courts et noirs et je **suis** de taille moyenne. **J'aime** le funk et je chante avec les Cool Girls. Je **joue** de la batterie.
3. (Example answer:)
   Moi, je m'appelle Paul Punk. J'ai les cheveux courts et blonds et je suis de taille moyenne. J'aime le punk et je chante avec les Punk Pistols. Je joue de la batterie.

Worksheet 1.5 Making comments

Answers

C'est génial.	It's great.
C'est super.	It's super.
C'est intéressant.	It's interesting.
C'est bien.	It's good.
C'est important.	It's important.
C'est facile.	It's easy.
C'est difficile.	It's difficult.
À mon avis, c'est …	In my opinion, it's …
Je pense que c'est …	I think it's …
Tu es d'accord?	Do you agree?
Je suis d'accord.	I agree.
Je ne suis pas d'accord.	I don't agree.
Il faut mettre un accent.	You have to put an accent on.
Il y a un problème de prononciation.	There's a problem with pronunciation.
Il y a un problème grammatical.	There's a grammatical problem.
Il y a un problème d'orthographe.	There's a problem with spelling.
Je ne comprends pas.	I don't understand.
Tu peux m'expliquer?	Can you explain to me?

Positive phrases: C'est génial. C'est super. C'est intéressant. C'est bien. C'est important. C'est facile. Je suis d'accord.

Negative phrases: C'est difficile. Je ne suis pas d'accord. Il y a un problème de prononciation. Il y a un problème grammatical. Il y a un problème d'orthographe. Je ne comprends pas.

Other phrases: À mon avis, c'est … Je pense que c'est … Tu es d'accord? Il faut mettre un accent. Tu peux m'expliquer.

Bilan et Révisions (Pupil Book pp. 18–19)

C'est perso 1

Bilan
Pupils use this checklist to review language covered in the module, working on it in pairs in class or on their own at home. Encourage them to follow up any areas of weakness they identify. There are Target Setting Sheets included in the Assessment Pack, and an opportunity for pupils to record their own levels and targets on the *J'avance* page in the Workbook, p. 9. You can also use the *Bilan* checklist as an end-of-module plenary option.

Révisions
These revision exercises can be used for assessment purposes or for pupils to practise before tackling the assessment tasks in the Resource & Assessment File.

Resources
CD 1, track 12
Cahier d'exercices A & B, pages 7 & 8

1 Qui est-ce? Écoute et écris les bons noms. (1–4) (AT 1.2)
Listening. Pupils listen to four people describing themselves and identify each speaker from the pictures.

Audioscript — CD 1 track 12
1 *Moi, j'ai les cheveux courts et marron et j'ai les yeux verts.*
2 *J'ai les cheveux blonds, mi-longs et j'ai les yeux bleus.*
3 *Moi, j'ai les cheveux courts et noirs et j'ai les yeux marron.*
4 *J'ai les cheveux longs, frisés et noirs et j'ai les yeux marron.*

Answers
1 Frank 2 Clémence 3 Abdel 4 Marina

2 Décris les kits de survie. (AT 2.2)
Speaking. Pupils describe what is in the survival kits pictured. A sample opening is given.

Answers
a *Dans mon kit de survie, j'ai un portemonnaie, des chips, un portable, un MP3 et des lunettes de soleil.*
b *Dans mon kit de survie, j'ai une clé USB, un appareil photo, une gourde et une trousse avec des surligneurs fluo.*
c *Dans mon kit de survie, j'ai des kleenex/un paquet de mouchoirs, des clés, un bâton de colle et une barre de céréales.*

3 Lis le texte et termine les phrases en anglais. (AT 3.3)
Reading. Pupils read the text and complete the sentences that summarise it in English.

Answers
1 Lou-Anne's **sister** is called Amélie.
2 Amélie is quite **funny** and very **intelligent**.
3 She has short **black** hair.
4 Her brother plays **in a group**.
5 He has a lot of talent but he's **quite modest**.

4 Fais ton autoportrait. (AT 4.3)
Writing. Pupils write a description of themselves, including their likes and dislikes. A writing frame is supplied.

Workbook A, page 7

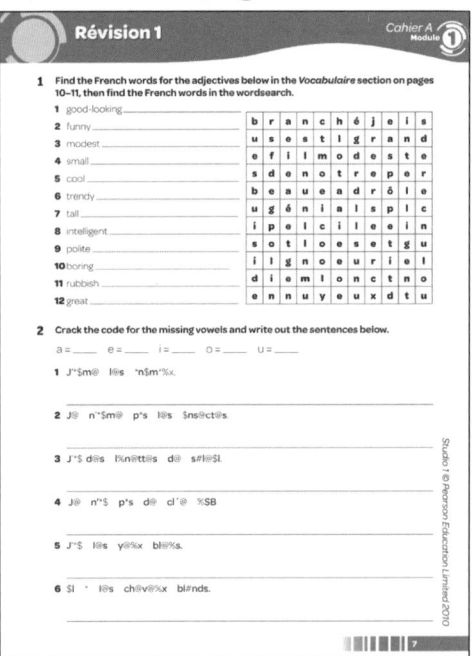

Bilan et Révisions C'est perso 1

Answers
1

b	r	a	n	c	h	é	j	e	i	s
u	s	e	l	t	l	g	r	a	n	d
e	f	i	l	m	o	d	e	s	t	e
s	d	e	n	o	t	r	e	p	e	r
b	e	a	u	e	a	d	r	ô	l	e
u	g	é	n	i	a	l	s	p	l	c
i	p	e	l	c	i	l	e	e	i	n
s	o	t	l	o	e	s	e	t	g	u
i	l	g	n	o	e	u	r	i	e	l
d	i	e	m	l	o	n	c	t	l	n
e	n	n	u	y	e	u	x	d	t	u

1 **1** beau **2** drôle **3** modeste **4** petit **5** cool
6 branché **7** grand **8** intelligent **9** poli
10 ennuyeux **11** nul **12** génial

2 a = *   e = @   i = $ o = #   u = %
  1 J'aime les animaux.
  2 Je n'aime pas les insectes.
  3 J'ai des lunettes de soleil.
  4 Je n'ai pas de clé USB.
  5 J'ai les yeux bleus.
  6 Il a les cheveux blonds.

Workbook A, page 8

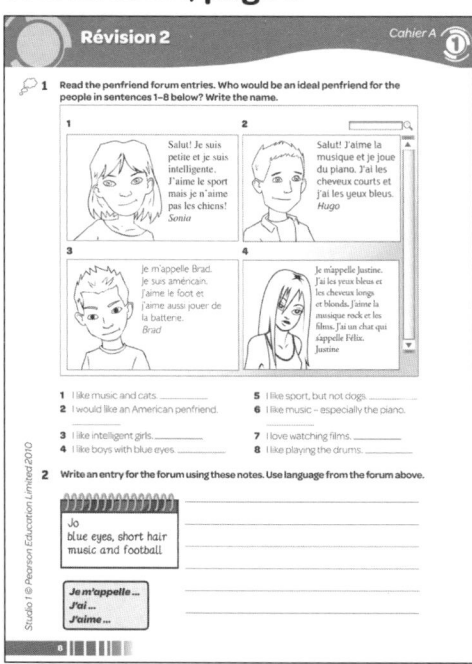

Answers
1 **1** Justine **2** Brad **3** Sonia **4** Hugo **5** Sonia
  6 Hugo **7** Justine **8** Brad
2 Je m'appelle Jo.
  J'ai les yeux bleus et les cheveux courts.
  J'aime la musique et le football.

Workbook B, page 7

Answers
1 **a** Je m'appelle Océane.
  b J'aime la musique et les mangas.
  c Je n'aime pas le racisme.
  d J'ai une barre de céréales et une clé USB.
  e C'est Leona Lewis. Elle est chanteuse.
2 **1** d **2** b **3** e **4** a **5** c

Workbook B, page 8

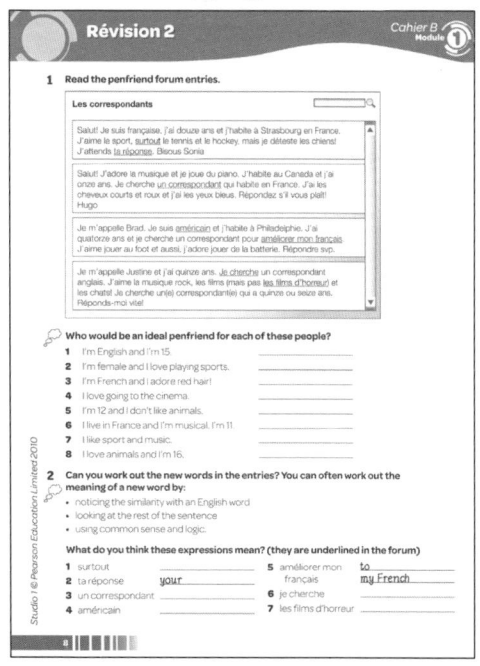

Answers
1 **1** Justine **2** Sonia **3** Hugo **4** Justine
  5 Sonia **6** Hugo **7** Brad **8** Justine
2 **1** especially **2** your reply **3** a penfriend
  4 American **5** to improve my French
  6 I'm looking for **7** horror films

C'est perso 1 — En plus: C'est moi! (Pupil Book pp. 20–21)

Learning objective
- Introducing yourself in detail

Framework objective
5.5 Strategies – reference materials: ex. 6

Key language
Review of language from the module

PLTS
E Effective participators

Resources
CD 1, track 13
ActiveTeach:
p.012 Flashcards
p.012 Grammar
p.020 Assignment 1
p.020 Assignment 1: prep

Starter
Aim
To develop reading skills: reading for gist

Give pupils one minute to skim-read the text in exercise 1 and write in English the topic of each paragraph.

Check answers, asking pupils how they identified the topic each time. Point out that when reading for gist they should look for key words and focus on the opening sentences of paragraphs, which often summarise what the paragraph is about.

Alternative Starter:
Use ActiveTeach p. 012 Flashcards to review adjectives that describe character.

1 Écoute et lis le texte. (AT 1.4, AT 3.4)
Listening. Pupils listen to Harris talking about himself and follow the text at the same time. Some vocabulary is glossed for support.

Read together through the tip box on text features (connectives, intensifiers, opinions, range of verbs, adjectives). Encourage pupils to work these features into their own speech and writing whenever they can.

Audioscript — CD 1 track 13

C'est moi! Je m'appelle Harris. Je suis québécois et je parle français. J'habite à Saint-Sauveur. C'est un petit village dans les Laurentides, au nord de Montréal. Les Laurentides sont des montagnes.

J'aime le camping et le rafting. Le rafting, c'est cool. Et le hockey sur glace, j'aime ça. J'aime aussi les couleurs de l'automne, la nature et la forêt. J'aime le ski alpin et le surf des neiges. C'est génial, mais je n'aime pas les compétitions. La motoneige, je n'aime pas ça ... C'est ennuyeux! Tu aimes le ski alpin?

Dans mon kit de survie, j'ai toujours mon portable et mon MP3 car j'aime la photographie et la musique. Mon portable est très, très important pour moi. En hiver, j'ai aussi mes gants et mon bonnet.

Je suis assez intelligent et très drôle, mais je ne suis pas très généreux. Je suis de taille moyenne. J'ai les cheveux mi-longs, raides et marron et j'ai les yeux gris.

Mon père a un traîneau à chiens. C'est super! Les chiens s'appellent Bernard et Babette. Ils ont les yeux bleus. Ils sont très drôles et aussi très intelligents. Je joue tous les jours avec les chiens.

Mon chanteur préféré s'appelle Corneille. Il est génial. Il a les cheveux frisés et noirs. Il a les yeux marron. Il chante et il joue de la guitare. Il est charmant et beau et il a beaucoup de talent.

R Pupils identify in the text in exercise 1 all instances of the features listed in the tip box.

2 Relis le texte. Mets les images dans le bon ordre (a–f). (AT 3.4)
Reading. Pupils read the text in exercise 1 again and put the pictures into the order they are mentioned.

Answers
c, d, f, e, b, a

3 Choisis un titre pour accompagner les images de l'exercice 2. (AT 3.4)
Reading. Pupils choose a caption for each picture in exercise 2.

Answers
1 e 2 f 3 d 4 a 5 b 6 c

4 Trouve l'équivalent des phrases dans le texte de l'exercice 1. (AT 3.4)
Reading. Pupils find in the exercise 1 text the French for the English sentences given.

Answers
1 Je suis québécois et je parle français.
2 J'aime aussi les couleurs de l'automne, la nature et la forêt.
3 Mais je n'aime pas les compétitions.
4 Mon portable est très, très important pour moi.
5 Je suis très drôle, mais je ne suis pas très généreux.
6 Il chante et il joue de la guitare.

5 Présente-toi! (AT 4.1–4)
Writing. Pupils write a detailed presentation of themselves following the framework supplied.

6 À trois. Fais des présentations. (AT 2.1–4)
PLTS E

Speaking. Read together through the tip box on preparing for the presentation. In groups of three: the first pupil gives his/her presentation from exercise 5; the second comments on the language and pronunciation of the presentation; the third identifies a favourite sentence in the presentation. Each pupil takes a turn at each role.

Plenary
Put the class into teams. Prompt each team in turn with one of the English headings in the box in exercise 5. Each team works together to form a correct sentence in response, then one person tells you the sentence. Award two points for a completely correct answer, and one point for an answer with a small mistake.

Note: This *Studio* Teacher's Guide suggests lots of team games. To save time, you may want to set up permanent teams at the start of term. You could keep a running total of points scored and award a prize to the winning team at the end of each term.

Worksheet 1.6 Ma star préférée et moi!

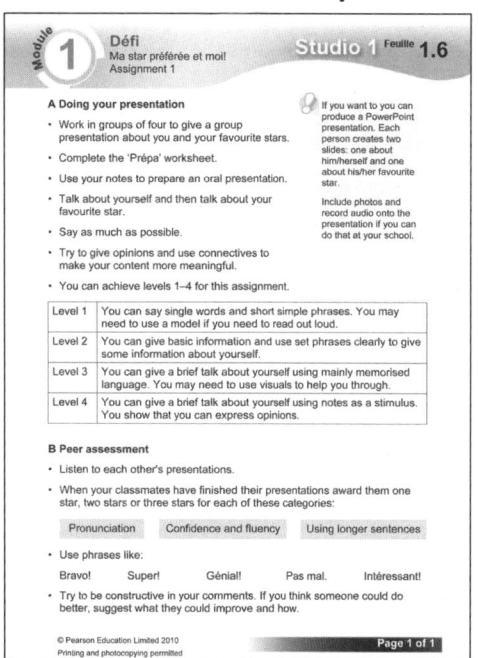

Worksheet 1.7 Ma star préférée et moi! Prépa

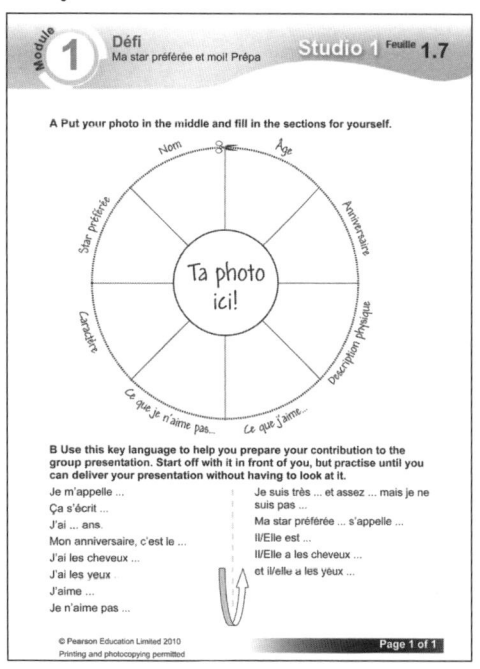

Studio Grammaire (Pupil Book pp. 22–23)

C'est perso 1

The *Studio Grammaire* section provides a more detailed summary of the key grammar covered in the module, along with further exercises to practise these points. The activities on ActiveTeach pages 22 and 23 are repeated from elsewhere in the module.

Grammar topics
- verbs – the present tense (regular, singular)
- irregular verbs (*avoir*, *être* – present, singular)
- adjectives (agreement)
- possessive adjectives (*mon/ma/mes, ton/ta/tes*)

Verbs – the present tense
Regular verbs

1 Write out the verb *danser* (to dance) in the present tense and translate it into English.

Pupils complete the verbs by supplying the endings and then translate them into English.

Answers
je dans**e**	I dance/I am dancing
tu dans**es**	you dance/you are dancing
il/elle dans**e**	he/she dances/he/she is dancing

2 Write out the verbs using the correct form of the present tense.

Pupils complete gap-fill sentences by supplying the correct form of the verb given.

Answers
1 Je **joue** de la guitare.
2 Je **chante** tous les jours.
3 Tu **aimes** les consoles de jeux?
4 Tu **parles** français?
5 Il **habite** à Saint-Sauveur.
6 Elle **aime** les animaux.

Irregular verbs

3 Fill in the gaps in these sentences, then translate them into English.

Pupils complete gap-fill sentences by supplying the whole verb. They then translate the sentences into English.

Answers
1 Dans mon kit de survie, j'**ai** un portable.
   In my survival kit I've got a mobile phone.
2 Tu **as** un animal? Have you got an animal/a pet?
3 Il **a** un frère. He has (got) a/one brother.
4 Elle **a** une sœur. She has (got) a/one sister.
5 Il **a** beaucoup de talent. He has (got) lots of talent.
6 Elle **a** une guitare. She has (got) a guitar.

4 Unjumble the forms of *être*, then match them to the English.

Pupils work out the anagrams, then match the French and English verbs.

Answers
1 il **est** – he is
2 je **suis** – I am
3 tu **es** – you are
4 elle **est** – she is

Adjectives

5 Choose the correct adjectives to describe the faces.

Pupils complete the three texts by choosing from the two adjective options each time.

Answers
1 Il a le visage **vert**. Il a les yeux **rouges** et les cheveux **courts, jaunes** et **frisés**.
2 Elle a le visage **jaune**. Elle a les yeux **bleus**. Elle a les cheveux **verts**.
3 Il a le visage **bleu**. Il a les cheveux **mi-longs, noirs** et **frisés**. Il a les yeux **verts**.

6 Translate the sentences into French.

Pupils translate the English sentences into French, paying particular attention to the agreement of adjectives.

Answers
1 Il est généreux.
2 Elle est gentille.
3 Elle est curieuse.
4 Il est branché, mais il n'est pas intelligent.
5 Il est ennuyeux.

Possessive adjectives

7 Copy out the profile and fill it in.

Pupils copy out and complete the personal profile with their own details.

8 Change the profile so that your friend can fill it in.

Pupils rewrite the profile in exercise 7, replacing the *mon, ma, mes* possessive adjectives with *ton, ta, tes*.

Answers
Ton nom
Ta date de naissance
Ton numéro de téléphone
Ton e-mail
Ta couleur préférée
Ton animal préféré
Ton film préféré
Ta star préférée
Ton groupe préféré
Tes passions

C'est perso 1 À toi (Pupil Book pages 118–119)

Self-access reading and writing

A Reinforcement

1 Complète les phrases. (AT 3.2)
Reading. Pupils match the sentence halves, writing out the complete sentences.

Answers
1 *Je m'appelle Alice.*
2 *J'ai 14 ans.*
3 *J'aime les spaghettis.*
4 *Je n'aime pas la musique classique.*
5 *Je suis assez gentille.*

2 Qui est-ce? Associe les images et les descriptions. (AT 3.2)
Reading. Pupils match the pictures and the descriptions.

Answers
1 d 2 b 3 c 4 a

3 Décris les personnes. (AT 4.2)
Writing. Pupils write a description of the two people pictured.

Answers
a C'est une fille. Elle a les cheveux mi-longs, blonds et frisés. Elle a les yeux bleus. Elle est petite.
b C'est un garçon. Il a les cheveux courts et bruns. Il a les yeux marron. Il est grand.

B Extension

1 Complète le dialogue. (AT 4.2)
Writing. Pupils complete the dialogue, using the picture prompts to fill the gaps.

Answers
● Tu **aimes** le camping?
■ Non, je n'aime pas ça. C'est **ennuyeux**. Tu es d'accord?
● Non, je ne suis pas d'accord. C'est **génial/bien/cool**.

2 Écris des dialogues. Utilise le dialogue de l'exercice 1 comme modèle. (AT 4.4)
Writing. Pupils write out their own dialogues, using the picture prompts supplied and the dialogue in exercise 1 as a model.

Answers
● Tu **aimes** le tennis?
■ Oui, j'aime ça. C'est **génial/bien/cool**. Tu es d'accord?
● Non, je ne suis pas d'accord. C'est **nul/ennuyeux**.

● Tu **aimes** le roller?
■ Non, je n'aime pas ça. C'est **nul/ennuyeux**. Tu es d'accord?
● Non, je ne suis pas d'accord. C'est **génial/bien/cool**.

● Tu **aimes** la danse?
■ Oui, j'aime ça. C'est **génial/bien/cool**. Tu es d'accord?
● Oui, je suis d'accord. C'est **génial/bien/cool**.

3 Choisis la phrase correcte. (AT 3.3)
Reading. Pupils read the text then complete the sentences by selecting the correct options.

Answers
1 *assez polie* 2 *très patiente* 3 *la danse*
4 *le hip-hop* 5 *bleus* 6 *guitare*

4 Décris-toi. Choisis six adjectifs. Classe les adjectifs dans l'ordre d'importance pour toi. Écris six phrases. (AT 4.4)
Writing. Pupils choose six adjectives describing their character and rate them in order of personal importance. A range of adjectives and an example are given.

Module 2: Mon collège (Pupil Book pp. 26–47)

Unit & Learning objectives	PoS & Framework objectives	Key language	Grammar and other language features
1 Mes matières (pp. 28–29) Talking about school subjects Asking questions	**2.1d** previous knowledge **2.2a** listen for gist **2.2c** respond appropriately **2.2e** ask and answer questions **3d** use a range of vocab/structures **4e** use a range of resources **1.1/Y7** Listening – gist and detail **4.3/Y7** Language – gender and plurals **4.6/Y7** Language – (a) questions **5.1** Strategies – patterns	*le français, la géographie, les arts plastiques,* etc. *Tu aimes … ?/Est-ce que tu aimes … ?* *J'aime …* *J'aime beaucoup …* *J'aime assez …* *J'adore …* *Je n'aime pas …* *Je déteste …* *C'est ma matière préférée.*	**G** forming questions (intonation/with *Est-ce que … ?*) – the definite article with likes/dislikes – connectives to create longer sentences – accents
2 C'est génial! (pp. 30–31) Giving opinions and reasons Agreeing and disagreeing	**2.1d** previous knowledge **2.2g** write clearly and coherently **2.2h** redraft to improve writing **2.2i** reuse language they have met **3a** spoken and written language **4a** use language in the classroom, etc. **1.3/Y7** Listening – (a) interpreting intonation and tone **1.3/Y7** Speaking – (b) using intonation and tone **4.4/Y7** Language – sentence formation	*C'est …* *intéressant, ennuyeux,* etc. *On a beaucoup de devoirs.* *Le/La prof est sympa/ trop sévère.* *Moi aussi.* *T'es fou/folle.* *parce que*	– listening skills: using tone of voice – connectives and intensifiers
3 J'ai cours! (pp. 32–33) Describing your timetable Using the 12-hour clock	**2.2a** listen for gist **2.2f** initiate/sustain conversations **2.2i** reuse language they have met **3f** compare experiences **4a** use language in the classroom, etc. **4d** make links with English **3.1/Y7** Culture – aspects of everyday life **5.4** Strategies – working out meaning	*Quelle heure est-il?* *Il est …* *neuf heures, neuf heures et quart,* etc. *l'emploi du temps* *lundi, mardi, mercredi, jeudi, vendredi* *À (neuf heures), j'ai (sciences).* *tous les jours* *le matin, l'après-midi* *le (mercredi) après-midi* *la récréation/récré* *le déjeuner*	– the definite article with likes and dislikes; no definite article when referring to school subjects without an opinion – time: giving the current time and saying when something happens – listening skills: using context
4 Au collège en France (pp. 34–35) Describing your school day Using *on* to say 'we'	**2.1b** memorising **2.2d** pronunciation and intonation **3c** apply grammar **3d** use a range of vocab/structures **4b** communicate in pairs, etc. **4e** use a range of resources **1.5/Y7** Speaking – (a) presenting **3.2/Y7** Culture – (a) young people: interests/opinions **4.1/Y7** Language – letters and sounds	*On a cours (le lundi, …).* *On commence/finit les cours à …* *On a (quatre) cours le matin/l'après-midi.* *On étudie (neuf) matières.* *À la récré, on bavarde et on rigole.* *On mange à la cantine.*	**G** *on* form (*–er* verbs, *avoir* and *être*) – speaking skills: adapting model language

2 Mon collège

Unit & Learning objectives	PoS & Framework objectives	Key language	Grammar and other language features
5 Miam-miam! (pp. 36–37) Talking about food Using the partitive article (*du/de la/de l'/des*)	**2.2j** adapt previously learned language **3a** spoken and written language **3c** apply grammar **4a** use language in the classroom, etc. **4d** make links with English **4f** language for interest/enjoyment **1.4/Y7** Speaking – (a) social and classroom language **4.3/Y7** Language – gender and plurals	*Je mange … du fromage, de la pizza, des crudités,* etc. *avec … des frites,* etc. *Bon appétit!*	**G** the partitive article (*du, de la, de l', des*) **G** *Qu'est-ce que … ?* and *Est-ce que … ?* – writing skills: adapting model language – plural nouns (*–s*)
Bilan et Révisions (pp. 38–39) Pupils' checklist and practice exercises			
En plus 1: Mon collège au paradis (pp. 40–41) Schools in other French-speaking countries	**2.1c** knowledge of language **2.1d** previous knowledge **2.2b** skim and scan **2.2c** respond appropriately **3e** different countries/cultures **4d** make links with English **5.3** Strategies – English/other languages **5.7** Strategies – planning and preparing	Review of language from the module	– reading skills: reading for gist; near-cognates; using context – preparing for a videoconference
En plus 2: Joyeux Noël! (pp. 42–43) Talking about winter celebrations	**2.1e** use reference materials **2.2i** reuse language they have met **2.2k** deal with unfamiliar language **3d** use a range of vocab/structures **3f** compare experiences **4e** use a range of resources	*les bonnes choses à manger, les cadeaux, la messe de minuit,* etc. *la veille/le jour de Noël Joyeux Noël!*	– speaking skills: adapting model language; using a dictionary
Studio Grammaire (pp. 44–45) Detailed grammar summary and practice exercises			**G** asking questions (intonation, *est-ce que … ? qu'est-ce que … ?*) **G** using *on* **G** the partitive article
À toi (pp. 120–121) Self-access reading and writing at two levels			

1 Mes matières (Pupil Book pp. 28–29)

Mon collège 2

Learning objectives
- Talking about school subjects
- Asking questions

Framework objectives
1.1/Y7 Listening – gist and detail: ex. 4
4.3/Y7 Language – gender and plurals: ex. 3
4.6/Y7 Language – (a) questions: ex. 3
5.1 Strategies – patterns: ex. 6

Grammar
- forming questions (intonation/ with *Est-ce que … ?*)

Key language
le français, le théâtre
la géographie/la géo, la musique, la technologie
l'anglais (m), l'EPS (f), l'histoire (f), l'informatique (f)
les arts plastiques (m), les maths (f), les sciences (f)
Tu aimes/Est-ce que tu aimes … ?
J'aime …
J'aime beaucoup …
J'aime assez …
J'adore …
Je n'aime pas …
Je déteste …
C'est ma matière préférée.

PLTS
I Independent enquirers

Cross-curricular
ICT: present survey results

Resources
CD 1, tracks 14–16
Accès Studio pages 12–13 & 14–15
Cahier d'exercices A & B, page 12
ActiveTeach:
p.028 Flashcards
p.029 Class activity
p.029 Learning skills

Accès Studio Unit 5 (pp. 12–13) can be used as an introduction to this module on school.
Accès Studio Unit 6 (pp. 14–15) can be used with this unit for further practice of *j'aime/je n'aime pas*.

Starter 1
Aim
To review language for expressing likes and dislikes; To use reading strategies

Write up the following, jumbling the order of the phrases. Give pupils two minutes to match the symbols to the correct phrases.

- 😊😊 *j'adore/j'aime beaucoup*
- 😊 *j'aime*
- 😐 *j'aime assez*
- 🙁 *je n'aime pas*
- 🙁🙁 *je déteste*

Check answers, asking pupils to explain how they worked them out. Ask them to translate *assez* and *beaucoup*.

1 Écoute les questions. C'est quelle matière? (1–12) (AT 1.1)
Listening. Pupils listen to 12 questions and note the letter of the correct picture for the school subject mentioned in each.

Audioscript   CD 1 track 14
1 Tu aimes le français?
2 Tu aimes la géographie?
3 Est-ce que tu aimes la technologie?
4 Tu aimes les sciences?
5 Tu aimes l'anglais?
6 Est-ce que tu aimes les maths?
7 Est-ce que tu aimes l'EPS?
8 Tu aimes les arts plastiques?
9 Est-ce que tu aimes l'histoire?
10 Tu aimes la musique?
11 Tu aimes l'informatique?
12 Est-ce que tu aimes le théâtre?

Answers
1 b 2 c 3 e 4 l 5 f 6 k 7 g 8 j 9 h
10 d 11 i 12 a

R Pupils working in pairs take it in turn to quickly sketch a subject for their partner to name.

Studio Grammaire: asking questions
Use the *Studio Grammaire* box to review asking questions using rising intonation and using *Est-ce que … ?* There is more information and further practice on Pupil Book p. 44.

2 Écoute. Note les matières et les opinions. (1–6) (AT 1.2)
Listening. Pupils listen to six conversations. For each they note the subject discussed (from pictures a–l in exercise 1) and the opinion given (using the symbols in the key language box).

43

2 Mon collège   1 Mes matières

Audioscript CD 1 track 15

1 *Tu aimes les maths?*
   Oui, j'aime les maths.
2 *Est-ce que tu aimes la musique?*
   Oui, j'adore la musique!
3 *Tu aimes l'EPS?*
   Non, je n'aime pas l'EPS.
4 *Est-ce que tu aimes les sciences?*
   Ah, non! Je déteste les sciences!
5 *Tu aimes la géographie?*
   Alors … J'aime assez la géographie.
6 *Est-ce que tu aimes le théâtre?*
   Ah, oui, j'aime beaucoup le théâtre. C'est ma matière préférée!

Answers
1 k ☺   2 d ☺☺   3 g ☹   4 l ☹☹
5 c 😐   6 a ☺☺

3 En tandem. Pose des questions à ton/ta camarade. (AT 2.2–3)

Speaking. In pairs: pupils ask and answer questions on their opinion of school subjects. A sample exchange is given. Draw their attention to the tip box on using the definite article with likes/dislikes.

Starter 2
Aim
To review language for likes/dislikes and school subjects

Draw the following symbols on the board. Give pupils three minutes to write five sentences, each using one of the symbols and a school subject of their choice.

Check answers, asking some pupils to read out sentences and others to translate what they hear, to check comprehension.

☺☺ ☺☺ ☺ 😐 ☹ ☹☹ ☹☹

Alternative Starter:
Use ActiveTeach p. 029 Class activity to review school subjects and opinions.

4 Écoute. Tu entends *assez* ou *aussi* dans chaque phrase? Note le bon mot. (1–5) (AT 1.2)

Listening. Pupils listen to five sentences and note whether they hear *assez* or *aussi* each time. Before playing the recording, draw their attention to the pronunciation box on *assez/aussi*.

Audioscript CD 1 track 16

1 *J'aime assez les sciences.*
2 *J'aime aussi les maths.*
3 *J'adore l'EPS. J'aime aussi le français.*
4 *J'aime assez l'histoire, mais je préfère la géo.*
5 *J'aime assez la technologie et j'aime aussi les arts plastiques.*

Answers
1 assez   2 aussi   3 aussi   4 assez   5 assez, aussi

5 Lis les textes. Regarde les symboles et écris le bon prénom. (AT 3.3)

Reading. Pupils read what six people say about their subject preferences, then identify which person is represented by each set of subject/opinion symbols. You may want to warn pupils that some subjects are mentioned in more than one text, so they need to look closely at the opinions in order to differentiate.

Answers
a Clarisse   b Manu   c Leïla   d Élisa   e Yanis
f Clarisse   g Leïla   h Florian

6 Écris ton opinion sur tes matières. (AT 4.3–4)

Writing. Pupils write sentences giving their own opinion of all the subjects mentioned in exercise 1. An example is given. Draw pupils' attention to the tip box on connectives and encourage them to use these in their writing. Also draw their attention to the tip box on remembering to use the correct accents in their writing.

7 Fais un sondage sur six matières. (AT 2.3–4)

PLTS

Speaking. Pupils choose six subjects and do a survey to find out other pupils' opinions of them. An example grid to note answers and a sample exchange are given.

Pupils could use a computer to create a graph showing the results of their survey and to write some sentences on their findings.

1 Mes matières Mon collège 2

Plenary
Create a chain round the class. The first pupil asks *Est-ce que tu aimes* + a school subject? The second pupil responds with an opinion. The third asks another question. Continue like this round the class.

Workbook A, page 12

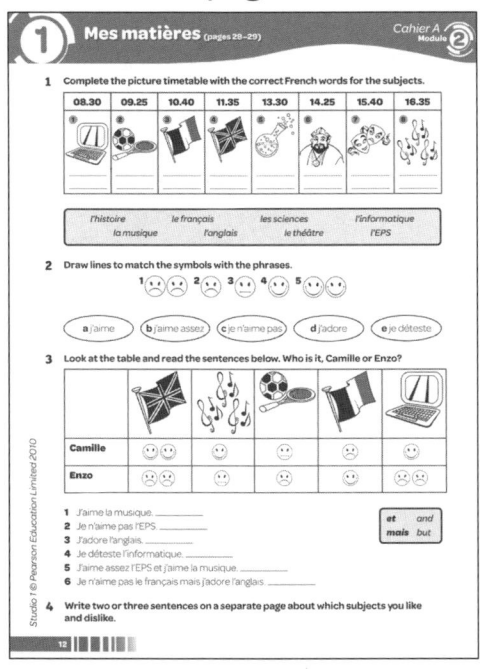

Answers
1 1 l'informatique 2 l'EPS 3 le français
   4 l'anglais 5 les sciences 6 l'histoire
   7 le théâtre 8 la musique
2 1 e 2 c 3 b 4 a 5 d
3 1 Camille 2 Enzo 3 Camille 4 Enzo
   5 Camille 6 Camille

Workbook B, page 12

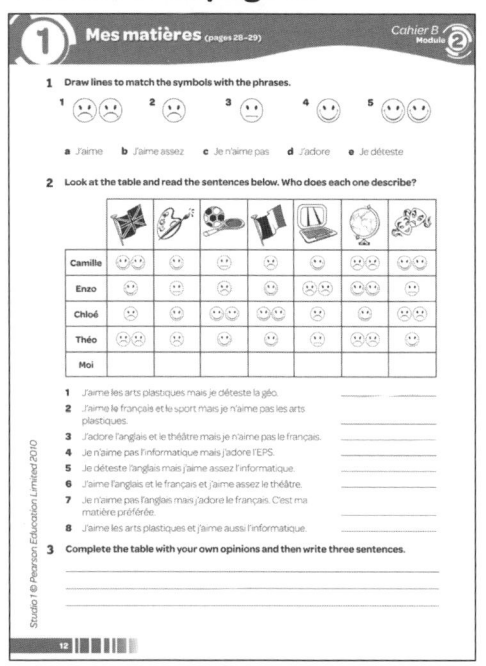

Answers
1 1 e 2 c 3 b 4 a 5 d
2 1 Camille 2 Théo 3 Camille 4 Chloé
   5 Théo 6 Enzo 7 Chloé 8 Camille

Worksheet 2.1 Learning new words

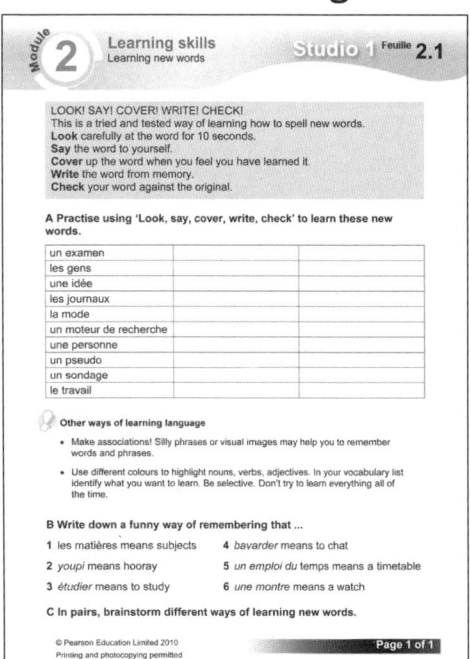

Answers
(Answers will vary.)

2 C'est génial! (Pupil Book pp. 30–31)

Learning objectives
- Giving opinions and reasons
- Agreeing and disagreeing

Framework objectives
1.3/Y7 Listening – (a) interpreting intonation and tone: ex. 1
1.3/Y7 Speaking – (b) using intonation and tone: ex. 3
4.4/Y7 Language – sentence formation: ex. 8

Key language
C'est…
difficile
génial
nul
marrant
ennuyeux
intéressant
facile
On a beaucoup de devoirs.
Le/La prof est sympa.
Le/La prof est trop sévère.
Moi aussi.
T'es fou/folle.
parce que

PLTS
T Team workers

Cross-curricular
ICT: word processing

Resources
CD 1, tracks 17–18
Cahier d'exercices A & B, page 13
ActiveTeach:
p.030 Flashcards

Starter 1
Aim
To review and introduce adjectives for giving an opinion

Write up the following, jumbling the order of the second column. Give pupils working in pairs three minutes to match the French and English versions.

génial	great
nul	rubbish
ennuyeux	boring
difficile	difficult
facile	easy
intéressant	interesting
sévère	strict
marrant	fun
sympa	nice

Check answers, asking pupils to explain how they worked them out.

1 Écoute les opinions. Écris P (positif) ou N (négatif). (1–8) (AT 1.3)
Listening. Do this task with Pupil Books closed: the aim is to develop the skill of listening for tone of voice to help work out unknown language (draw pupils' attention to the tip box on this). Pupils listen to eight people talking about school subjects and note P if the person's opinion is positive or N if it is negative. *t'es fou/folle* is glossed for support.

Audioscript CD 1 track 17
1 Les maths? Ah, non! C'est nul!
2 C'est intéressant, l'informatique. J'adore ça!
3 J'aime le théâtre. C'est marrant.
4 Tu aimes la géographie? T'es fou! C'est ennuyeux!
5 C'est facile, les arts plastiques. Et le prof est sympa.
6 Beurk! L'histoire! On a beaucoup de devoirs. Je déteste ça.
7 Tu aimes les sciences? T'es fou! C'est difficile. Et la prof est trop sévère.
8 L'anglais, c'est ma matière préférée. C'est génial!

Answers
1 N **2** P **3** P **4** N **5** P **6** N **7** N **8** P

2 Lis les opinions. Paul est toujours positif. Nadia est toujours négative. Qui dit quoi? (AT 3.1)
Reading. Pupils read the opinions and decide who says each one: Paul, who is always positive, or Nadia, who is always negative.

Answers
Paul: *3*, 5, 6, 7, 8, 9
Nadia: *1*, 2, 4, 6, 10

3 En tandem. Une personne est Paul. L'autre personne est Nadia. Invente une dispute! (AT 2.3–4)
Speaking. In pairs: pupils discuss school subjects, taking it in turn to play the part of Paul (being positive) and Nadia (being negative). A sample exchange is given.

46

2 C'est génial! Mon collège 2

Starter 2
Aim
To review adjectives for giving an opinion on school subjects

Write up the following. Give pupils three minutes to write a sentence for each subject, using *c'est* + an adjective. Model an example: *L'anglais, c'est intéressant.* If necessary, write up some adjectives for support.

*le théâtre   les maths   le français
les sciences   l'histoire*

Check answers, asking pupils to translate their sentences into English.

Alternative Starter 2:
Use ActiveTeach p. 030 Flashcards to review and practise the adjectives used to give opinions on school subjects.

4 Écoute. Copie et complète le tableau. (1–5) (AT 1.4)
Listening. Pupils copy out the table. They listen to five conversations in which people give their opinion on school subjects, together with a reason for their opinion. They complete the table with the details. *Pourquoi?* and *parce que* are glossed for support.

Audioscript   CD 1 track 18

1 – Tu aimes les arts plastiques?
   – Oui, j'aime les arts plastiques.
   – Pourquoi?
   – Parce que c'est marrant.
2 – Est-ce que tu aimes les maths?
   – Non! Je déteste les maths!
   – Pourquoi?
   – Parce que c'est difficile!
3 – Est-ce que tu aimes l'EPS?
   – Euh, oui, j'aime l'EPS.
   – T'es folle! Tu aimes l'EPS? Pourquoi?
   – Ben, parce que c'est facile.
4 – Tu aimes le français?
   – Non, je n'aime pas le français.
   – Tu n'aimes pas le français? T'es fou! Pourquoi?
   – Parce qu'on a beaucoup de devoirs!
5 – Est-ce que tu aimes la musique?
   – Ah, oui! J'adore la musique!
   – Pourquoi tu aimes la musique, alors?
   – Parce que la prof est sympa.
   – Ah, oui. Elle est sympa.

Answers

	Matière	Opinion	Raison
1	les arts plastiques	☺	marrant
2	les maths	☹☹	difficile
3	l'EPS	☺	facile
4	le français	☹	beaucoup de devoirs
5	la musique	☺☺	la prof est sympa

5 Lis le tchat et réponds aux questions en anglais. (AT 3.4)
Reading. Pupils read the chat and answer the questions on it in English.

Answers
1 Emma   2 Yasmine   3 Samuel   4 Frédéric
5 Samuel   6 Emma   7 Yasmine
8 (pupil's own opinion)

6 Écris ton opinion sur six matières. (AT 4.3)
Writing. Pupils write six sentences giving their opinion on six different subjects. An example is given.

7 Relis les textes et trouve ces descriptions en français. (AT 3.4)
Reading. Pupils re-read the texts in exercise 5 and find the French for the six English phrases listed.

Answers
1 très marrant   2 assez ennuyeux   3 trop sévère
4 trop difficile   5 très sympa   6 un peu difficile

Pupils working in pairs take it in turn to prompt with a subject and to respond with an opinion, using an intensifier + an adjective.

8 Réponds à Frédéric, Emma, Samuel ou Yasmine. (AT 4.4)

PLTS T

Writing. Pupils choose one of the four people in exercise 5 and write a reply to him/her, giving their own opinions and the reasons for them. This could be done on a computer. A sample opening is given. Draw pupils' attention to the tip box on including connectives and intensifiers to extend their sentences. When they have finished, pupils swap with a partner to check each other's work: they identify errors but don't correct them. Pupils then write a second draft.

2 Mon collège   2 C'est génial!

Plenary
Make a series of statements about school subjects, including intensifiers, e.g. *La géographie, c'est très intéressant.* Pupils need to contradict you, e.g. *Mais non! La géographie, c'est assez ennuyeux.* Continue, with pupils taking over the role of making the initial statement.

Workbook A, page 13

Workbook B, page 13

Answers
1 Salut Tom!
Mon nouveau collège, c'est **génial**! On a beaucoup de devoirs mais c'est assez **facile**.
L'EPS, c'est ma matière **préférée**. Le foot, c'est très **marrant** et j'adore jouer au rugby. J'aime aussi **la musique** parce que **le prof** est sympa. Je **n'aime pas** les arts plastiques. C'est un peu **difficile** pour moi et **je déteste** la géo, **c'est nul** et la prof est **trop sévère**.
Hugo
2 1 teacher too strict
   2 great
   3 favourite subject
   4 likes it – teacher nice
   5 doesn't like – a bit difficult
   6 loves playing it
   7 gets lots – quite easy
   8 football – it's fun
3 (Example answer:)
Salut!
Mon nouveau collège, c'est **nul**! On a beaucoup de devoirs.
L'informatique, c'est ma matière **préférée**. J'aime **l'informatique** parce que **c'est génial**. Je **déteste** l'EPS. C'est très **difficile** pour moi. J'aime les arts plastiques, c'est assez facile.

Answers
1 1 Les sciences, c'est nul.
   2 Les maths, c'est intéressant.
   3 Les arts plastiques, c'est facile.
   4 La technologie, c'est marrant.
   5 La géo, c'est difficile.
   6 Le français, c'est génial.
   7 L'anglais, c'est difficile
2 1 Jade **2** Tom **3** Tom **4** Lucas **5** Jade
   6 Lucas **7** Jade **8** Lucas

3 J'ai cours! (Pupil Book pp. 32–33)

Mon collège 2

Learning objectives
- Describing your timetable
- Using the 12-hour clock

Framework objectives
3.1/Y7 Culture – aspects of everyday life: ex. 4
5.4 Strategies – working out meaning: ex. 7

Key language
Quelle heure est-il?
Il est ...
neuf heures
neuf heures cinq/dix/vingt/vingt-cinq
neuf heures et quart/et demie
dix heures moins vingt-cinq/vingt/dix/cinq
dix heures moins le quart
midi
minuit
midi/minuit et demi
l'emploi du temps
lundi, mardi, mercredi, jeudi, vendredi
À (neuf heures), j'ai (sciences).
tous les jours
le matin
l'après-midi
la récréation/la récré
le déjeuner

PLTS
C Creative thinkers

Resources
CD 1, tracks 19–21
Accès Studio pages 6–7 & 8–9
Cahier d'exercices A & B, page 14
Accès Studio ActiveTeach:
p.007 Class activity
ActiveTeach:
p.032 Flashcards
p.033 Thinking skills

Accès Studio Units 2 & 3 (pp. 6–9) can be used to introduce or review numbers 1–31.
Accès Studio Unit 3 (pp. 8–9) can be used for further practice of days of the week.

Starter 1
Aim
To review numbers 1–20

Ask pupils to stand up. Play round the class, with each pupil taking a turn to speak. If a pupil can't think of the next number or makes a mistake, he/she is out.

First do a round of the numbers 1–20 in French. Repeat this, but when a number is divisible by 4, the pupil says *Fou!* instead of the number. Repeat again, this time replacing numbers divisible by 3 as well – these are replaced with *Folle!* For a number divisible by both 3 and 4, the pupil must say *Fou et folle!*

Alternative Starter 1:
Use *Accès Studio* ActiveTeach p. 007 Class activity to review and practise numbers 1–20.

1 Écoute et lis. (1–7) (AT 1.2, AT 3.2)
Listening. Pupils listen to seven statements saying what time it is and what school subject the speaker has, following the text in their books.

Audioscript CD 1 track 19

1 Il est neuf heures. J'ai maths.
2 Il est neuf heures et quart. J'ai français.
3 Il est neuf heures et demie. J'ai technologie.
4 Il est dix heures moins le quart. J'ai EPS.
5 Il est neuf heures dix. J'ai sciences.
6 Il est dix heures moins vingt. J'ai anglais.
7 Il est midi. J'ai histoire-géo.

2 Écoute. C'est quelle montre? (1–8) (AT 1.3)
Listening. Pupils listen to eight conversations and identify the time given in each, noting the letter of the correct clock.

Audioscript CD 1 track 20

1 – Quelle heure est-il?
  – Il est trois heures dix.
  – Trois heures dix? J'ai anglais!
2 – Quelle heure est-il?
  – Il est deux heures et quart.
  – Deux heures et quart? Alors, j'ai musique.
3 – Quelle heure est-il?
  – Il est dix heures et demie.
  – Dix heures et demie? Oh non! J'ai sciences.
4 – Quelle heure est-il?
  – Euh ... Il est onze heures.
  – Il est onze heures? Chouette! J'ai arts plastiques.
5 – Quelle heure est-il?
  – Il est quatre heures moins le quart.
  – Quoi? Quatre heures moins le quart? J'ai français! Au revoir!
6 – Quelle heure est-il?
  – Il est midi.
  – Il est midi? Alors, j'ai informatique. C'est ma matière préférée!
7 – Quelle heure est-il?
  – Voyons ... Il est une heure moins vingt.
  – Une heure moins vingt ... Beurk! J'ai mathématiques.

49

2 Mon collège   3 J'ai cours!

8 – Quelle heure est-il?
   – Il est neuf heures vingt-cinq.
   – Neuf heures vingt-cinq? Youpi! J'ai théâtre! J'adore ça!

Answers
1 d 2 h 3 b 4 g 5 e 6 f 7 a 8 c

3 En tandem. Fais trois dialogues. (AT 2.3–4)

Speaking. In pairs: pupils put together three dialogues, using the framework and picture prompts supplied. Before they start, read together through the key language box on time. Also draw their attention to the tip box on using the definite article with likes and dislikes (unlike in English) and omitting the definite article when referring to school subjects when no opinion is being expressed.

Starter 2
Aim
To review the language for time

Write up the following. Give pupils three minutes in pairs to write a sentence for each time. Model the first as an example: *Il est deux heures et demie.*

2.30   4.45   3.00   12.30   8.15   6.55   10.35

Check answers: *deux heures et demie, cinq heures moins le quart, trois heures, midi/minuit et demi, huit heures et quart, sept heures moins cinq, onze heures moins vingt-cinq.*

Alternative Starter 2:
Use ActiveTeach p. 032 Flashcards to review and practise the language for time.

4 Regarde l'emploi du temps de Thomas. Écris en anglais six choses qui sont différentes de ton emploi du temps. (AT 3.4)

Reading. Pupils read Thomas's timetable and write in English six differences between his timetable and their own.

Answers
(Possible answers:)
earlier start time, later finish time, no school on Wednesday afternoons, two breaks, study periods, homework help period, some subjects not studied (e.g. drama), some different subjects (e.g. German), only one class/form period a week, most lessons 55 minutes long, use of the 24-hour clock

5 Copie et complète les phrases pour Thomas. (AT 4.2)

Writing. Using the information in the timetable, pupils copy and complete the sentences. You could supply the missing times in random order for support if necessary. *tous les jours* is glossed for support. Draw pupils' attention to the tip box on times, highlighting the difference between giving the current time and saying when something happens (*à …*).

Answers
1 Le lundi à **huit heures et demie**, j'ai maths.
2 Le mardi à **neuf heures vingt-cinq**, j'ai anglais.
3 Tous les jours à **dix heures vingt**, j'ai la récréation.
4 Le mercredi à **onze heures et demie**, j'ai histoire-géo.
5 Tous les jours à **midi et demi**, j'ai le déjeuner.
6 Le jeudi à **une heure et demie**, j'ai français.
7 Le vendredi à **quatre heures moins vingt**, j'ai sciences.

Pupils draw up their own timetable in French and write seven sentences about it like the ones in exercise 5.

6 En tandem. Jeu de mémoire. Pose six questions sur ton emploi du temps à ton/ta camarade. (AT 2.3)

Speaking. In pairs: pupils play a memory game. The first pupil closes his/her book. The other, looking at the timetable, prompts with a time; the first pupil gives a sentence with the time and the subject. After six prompts, they swap roles. A sample exchange is given.

7 Écoute. Thomas a un problème. Qu'est-ce qui se passe? (AT 1.4–5)
PLTS C

Listening. Pupils listen to the conversation between Thomas and his teacher and work out what Thomas's problem is. Some vocabulary is glossed for support. Before you play the recording, read through the tip box on listening skills together.

Audioscript CD 1 track 21

– Madame, madame! S'il vous plaît!
– Oui, Thomas?
– Pardon, madame. J'ai perdu mon emploi du temps. À huit heures et demie, j'ai permanence?
– Oui. À huit heures et demie, tu as permanence.
– Et à neuf heures vingt-cinq … ?
– Euh, voyons … À neuf heures vingt-cinq, tu as … anglais.
– Et après la récréation, j'ai technologie?
– Non. Après la récréation, tu as français. Et à onze heures et demie, tu as allemand.

3 J'ai cours! Mon collège

– Ah, oui! J'ai allemand. J'aime le français parce que c'est facile, mais l'allemand, c'est un peu difficile. Bon, merci, madame.
– De rien.
– Au revoir, madame
– Au revoir, Thomas.

Answer
Thomas has lost his timetable and is checking with his teacher which classes he has that morning.

Plenary
Play a team game to review times. Prepare a sheet of paper for each team with the following prompts on it. Leave a space by each prompt for the time in words to be written in. (Use just six prompts for a shorter game.)

| 1.00 | 2.05 | 3.10 | 4.15 | 5.20 | 6.25 |
| 7.30 | 8.35 | 9.40 | 10.45 | 11.50 | 12.55 |

Put the class into teams and put each team's sheet of paper with a pen at the front of the class in a place where the team can easily get to it. Set a time limit. Each team member in turn comes to the front of the class and writes one of the times. The team with the most correct times at the end of the allotted time is the winner.

Workbook A, page 14

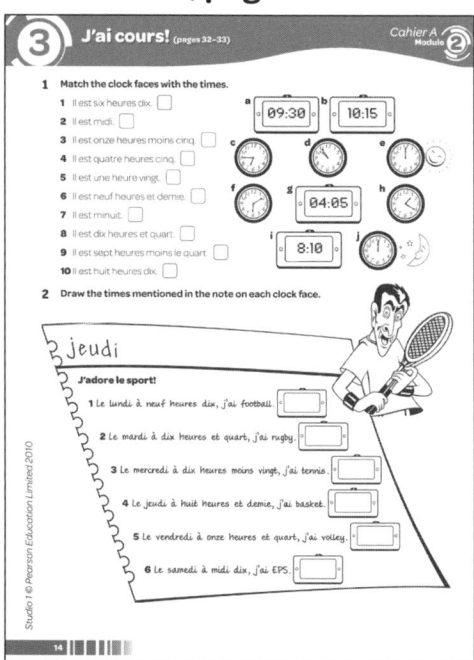

Answers
1 1 f 2 e 3 d 4 g 5 h 6 a 7 j 8 b
   9 c 10 i
2 1 9:10 2 10:15 3 9:40 4 8:30 5 11:15 6 12:10

Workbook B, page 14

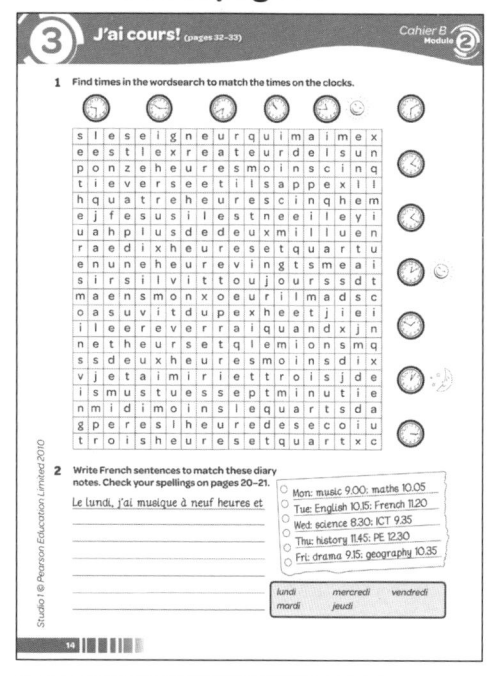

Answers
1 9.30: neuf heures et demie
10.15: dix heures et quart
6.40: sept heures moins vingt
10.55: onze heures moins cinq
11.45: midi moins le quart
6.10: six heures dix
4.05: quatre heures cinq
1.20: une heure vingt
12.10: midi dix
1.50: deux heures moins dix
12.05: minuit cinq
3.15: trois heures et quart

2 Le lundi, j'ai musique à neuf heures et maths à dix heures cinq.
Le mardi, j'ai anglais à dix heures et quart et français à onze heures vingt.
Le mercredi, j'ai sciences à huit heures et demie et informatique à dix heures moins vingt-cinq.
Le jeudi, j'ai histoire à midi moins le quart et EPS à midi et demi.
Le vendredi, j'ai théâtre à neuf heures et quart et géo à onze heures moins vingt-cinq.

2 Mon collège 3 J'ai cours!

Worksheet 2.2 Nonsense!

Module 2 — Thinking skills — Nonsense! — Studio 1 Feuille 2.2

A Find the logical mistakes in these texts. There is one mistake per text. Rewrite a logical version for yourself.

1 Moi, je déteste les maths! C'est cool! Le français, c'est difficile, mais c'est marrant. Le dessin, c'est assez ennuyeux.

2 Tu aimes l'histoire? Pourquoi? T'es fou! Mon prof est très sympa et on a beaucoup de devoirs. L'histoire, c'est trop difficile pour moi!

3 Moi, j'aime le théâtre. Mon prof de théâtre est très sympa. Mais ma matière préférée, c'est la géo, parce que j'adore le sport. Mon sport préféré, c'est le tennis.

4 On commence les cours à huit heures et demie. Aujourd'hui, c'est vendredi. À huit heures et demie j'ai anglais. C'est ma matière préférée, parce que c'est ennuyeux. Après la récréation j'ai EPS. C'est génial parce que j'adore le sport. On a le déjeuner à midi vingt. On mange à la cantine.

B Make up six nonsense sentences of your own. Ask your partner to find the logical mistakes.

Answers

A 1 Moi, **j'aime** les maths! C'est **cool**! OR Moi, **je déteste** les maths! C'est **nul**! Le français, c'est difficile, mais c'est marrant. Le dessin, c'est assez ennuyeux.

2 Tu aimes l'histoire? Pourquoi? T'es fou! Mon prof **n'est pas** très sympa et on a beaucoup de devoirs. L'histoire, c'est trop difficile pour moi!

3 Moi, j'aime le théâtre. Mon prof de théâtre est très sympa. Mais ma matière préférée, c'est **l'EPS**, parce que j'adore le sport. Mon sport préféré, c'est le tennis.

4 On commence les cours à huit heures et demie. Aujourd'hui, c'est vendredi. À huit heures et demie, j'ai anglais. C'est ma matière préférée, parce que c'est **intéressant**. Après la récréation, j'ai EPS. C'est génial parce que j'adore le sport. On a le déjeuner à midi vingt. On mange à la cantine.

B (Answers will vary.)

4 Au collège en France (Pupil Book pp. 34–35)

Mon collège 2

Learning objectives
- Describing your school day
- Using *on* to say 'we'

Framework objectives
1.5/Y7 Speaking – (a) presenting: ex. 4
3.2/Y7 Culture – (a) young people: interests/opinions: ex. 5
4.1/Y7 Language – letters and sounds: ex. 3

Grammar
- *on* form (*–er* verbs, *avoir* and *être*)

Key language
On a cours (le lundi, …).
On commence les cours à …
On a (quatre) cours le matin/ l'après-midi.
On étudie (neuf) matières.
À la récré, on bavarde et on rigole.
On mange à la cantine.
On finit les cours à …

PLTS
R Reflective learners

Cross-curricular
ICT: word processing/creating a blog

Resources
CD 1, tracks 22–23
Cahier d'exercices A & B, page 15
ActiveTeach:
p.034 Video 3
p.034 Video worksheet 3
p.035 Learning skills

Starter 1

Aim
To review singular verb forms of regular *–er* verbs + *avoir* and *être*

Write up the following table. Give pupils three minutes to copy and complete it.

	aimer	bavarder	détester	avoir	être
		to chat			to be
je		bavarde			
tu			détestes		es
il/elle	aime			a	

Check answers. Ask pupils what the ending is for the *il/elle* form of regular *–er* verbs and the *il/elle* form of *avoir* and *être*.

1 Écoute et lis. (1–8) (AT 1.4, AT 3.4)
Listening. Pupils listen to Manon talking about her school, and follow the text at the same time.

Audioscript — CD 1 track 22

1 Bonjour. Je m'appelle Manon. J'ai onze ans et je suis en sixième. Voici mon collège.
2 On a cours le lundi, le mardi, le mercredi matin, le jeudi et le vendredi. On n'a pas cours le mercredi après-midi. Youpi!
3 On commence les cours à huit heures et demie.
4 On a quatre cours le matin et trois ou quatre cours l'après-midi.
5 On étudie neuf matières.
6 À la récré, on bavarde et on rigole.
7 À midi et demi, c'est le déjeuner. On mange à la cantine. Miam-miam! C'est bon!
8 On finit les cours à cinq heures. On est fatigués!

2 Que dit Manon? Complète les phrases en anglais. (AT 3.4)
Reading. Pupils read the text in exercise 1 again, then complete the sentences that summarise it in English.

Answers
1 My name is **Manon**. This is my **school**.
2 We don't have lessons on **Wednesday** afternoon.
3 We start lessons at **8.30/half past eight**.
4 We have **four** lessons in the morning and **three or four** in the afternoon.
5 We study **nine** subjects.
6 At **break(time)**, we chat and have a laugh.
7 At lunchtime, we eat in **the canteen**.
8 We finish lessons at **5.00/five o'clock**. We're tired!

Studio Grammaire: *on*
Use the *Studio Grammaire* box to cover *on*. There is more information and further practice on Pupil Book pp. 44–45. Suggest to pupils that they use table layouts to note and learn verb forms and demonstrate ways of highlighting verb endings to help memorise them.

3 Écoute et répète. (AT 1.1)
Listening. Read together through the pronunciation box on how to say *on*. Then play the recording for pupils to repeat.

Audioscript — CD 1 track 23

on, mon, onze, bon, bonjour

2 Mon collège 4 Au collège en France

Starter 2
Aim
To review the *on* form

Write up the following, jumbling the order of the second column. Give pupils three minutes to match the sentence halves.

1	On a	a	*cours le mercredi.*
2	On n'a	b	*pas cours le samedi.*
3	On commence à	c	*neuf heures.*
4	On étudie	d	*neuf matières.*
5	On rigole	e	*à la récré.*
6	On finit	f	*à trois heures.*
7	On est	g	*fatigués.*

4 Imagine que tu parles avec Manon. Dis-lui six choses sur ton collège. (AT 2.3–4)
Speaking. Pupils imagine they're talking to Manon. Using Manon's text as a model, they tell her six things about their own school. Sample sentence openings are given.

5 Lis le texte et mets les images dans le bon ordre. (AT 3.4)
Reading. Read together through the cultural note on special lessons in French schools. Pupils then read Ludo's text and put the pictures in the correct order. *je dois travailler* is glossed for support.

Answers
d, b, a, c, e

Pupils translate the text in exercise 5 aloud, one sentence each round the class.

6 Relis le texte et corrige les phrases. (AT 3.4)
Reading. Pupils read the text in exercise 5 again and correct the sentences about it.

Answers
1 Ludo **aime** les cours à son nouveau collège.
2 Il **déteste** son emploi du temps.
3 Au collège, on commence les cours à **huit** heures.
4 Le mardi, on étudie **des cours théoriques de musique.**
5 Le **jeudi**, on a chorale.
6 Ludo **aime (bien)** ça parce que c'est **marrant**.
7 Ludo joue **du saxophone**.
8 La famille de Ludo **n'aime pas** ça.

7 Écris un blog sur ton collège. (AT 4.4)
PLTS R

Writing. Pupils write a blog about their own school. A sample opening is given. This could be done as a word-processing exercise; alternatively you could work with the ICT department to help pupils to set up their own blog. Get pupils to read and correct a partner's work. Pupils then look at their own work and identify two things they should review in order to improve their French.

Pupils could make their blogs accessible to your partner school, if you have one, or exchange e-mails with French pupils using the information they have put together.

Plenary
Ask pupils to tell you what *on* means and to give you the *on* forms of the verbs *aimer, avoir* and *être*. Then prompt in English using verbs from Manon's text in exercise 1 (e.g. 'we study') for pupils to respond with the French (e.g. *on étudie*). Cover regular *–er* verbs first, then *on finit, on a, on est*. You could increase the level of challenge by including some negative forms.

Workbook A, page 15

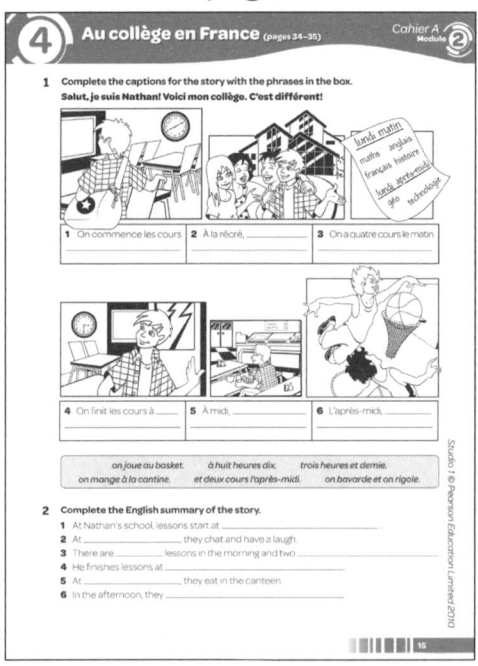

4 Au collège en France Mon collège

Answers

1 1 On commence les cours à huit heures dix.
  2 À la récré, on bavarde et on rigole.
  3 On a quatre cours le matin et deux cours l'après-midi.
  4 On finit les cours à trois heures et demie.
  5 À midi, on mange à la cantine.
  6 L'après-midi, on joue au basket.
2 1 8.10/ten past eight **2** break
  3 four; in the afternoon **4** 3.30/half past three
  5 12.00/twelve o'clock/midday **6** play basketball

Workbook B, page 15

Answers

1 1 b **2** f **3** e **4** c **5** d **6** a
2 1 different **2** basketball **3** 8.10/ten past eight
  4 in the morning **5** in the afternoon
  6 3.30/half past three **7** plays basketball

Worksheet 2.3 Working out the meaning of new words

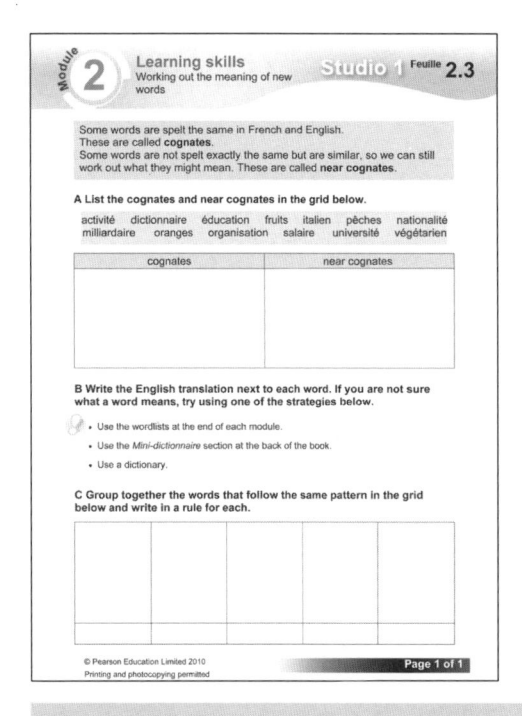

Answers
A and B

Cognates	Near cognates	English
	activité	activity
	dictionnaire	dictionary
éducation		education
fruits		fruits
	italien	Italian
	pêches	peaches
	nationalité	nationality
	milliardaire	multi-millionaire
oranges		oranges
organisation		organisation
	salaire	salary
	université	university
	végétarien	vegetarian

C italien, végétarien: Adjectives ending in –ien
oranges, pommes, fruits, pêches: Fruits in the plural
nationalité, activité, université: Nouns ending in é, translated by –y
éducation, organisation: Nouns ending in –tion
salaire, milliardaire: Nouns ending in –aire

2 Mon collège 4 Au collège en France

Video

Episode 3: Au collège
Alex is taking us around his school, *le collège Saint Étienne*. Video worksheet 3 can be used in conjunction with this episode.

Answers to video worksheet (ActiveTeach)

1 A [F3.1] (The most obvious things are:)
   It starts very early (it is still dark).
   They don't wear uniform.
   Pupils greet each other with a kiss.
   The same subject can occur twice in a day. (Here, it is English.)
   (There will be more suggestions; please discuss them as they occur.)
   B It's a hidden camera.
   C English, maths, (break), French, PE, (lunch), history/geography, English again.
   D It is PE (EPS). Probably difficult for the team to film.

2 A It's 8 o'clock on Friday.
   B She says 'salut'
   C 'une bonne copine'

3 A What he actually says is: 'We have a laugh, we chat and we see friends from other classes.' (On rigole, on bavarde et on voit des copains des autres classes.)
   B It means 'You filmed without me?' confirming the impression that she's quite taken with her role as the presenter.
   C – maths
       – technology
       – PE (EPS)
   D Because he is using a 'secret camera'.
   E sympa   sévère   intéressant   préféré
   F récré

4 A Because he is about to enter the staff room with his hidden camera.
   B prof (short for *professeur*) and géo (short for *géographie*)

5 [PLTS T/E] (Answers will vary.)

2 5 Miam-miam! (Pupil Book pp. 36–37)

Learning objectives
- Talking about food
- Using the partitive article (*du/de la/de l'/des*)

Framework objectives
1.4/Y7 Speaking – (a) social and classroom language: ex. 5
4.3/Y7 Language – gender and plurals: ex. 3

Grammar
- the partitive article (*du, de la, de l', des*)
- *Qu'est-ce que...?* and *Est-ce que...?*

Key language
Je mange...
du fromage
du poisson
du poulet
du steak haché
du yaourt
de la pizza
de la glace à la fraise
de la mousse au chocolat
de la tarte au citron
des crudités
avec...
de la purée de pommes de terre
des frites
des haricots verts
Bon appétit!

PLTS
S Self-managers

Resources
CD 1, tracks 24–26
Accès Studio pages 6–7 & 24–25
Cahier d'exercices A & B, page 16
ActiveTeach:
p.036 Video 4
p.036 Video worksheet 4
p.036 Flashcards
p.036 Grammar
p.036 Grammar practice
p.036 Grammar skills
p.037 Class activity
p.037 Grammar
p.037 Grammar practice
p.037 Grammar skills

Accès Studio Unit 2 (pp. 6–7) can be used with this unit to review or introduce numbers 1–21.

Accès Studio Unit 11 (pp. 24–25) can be used with this unit to review or introduce food and drink vocabulary.

Starter 1
Aim
To review parts of speech (noun/subject, adjective, verb)

Give pupils three minutes working in pairs to complete ActiveTeach p. 036 Worksheet 2.4 Parts of speech, exercises A and B. Ask the class for their answers.

1 Écoute. Qu'est-ce qu'ils mangent à la cantine? Écris les *deux* bonnes lettres pour chaque personne. (1–5) (AT 1.4)
Listening. Read together through the cultural note on lunch in French schools. Pupils then listen to five conversations about what pupils eat in the canteen at school. They note the letters of the two correct pictures for each person.

Audioscript CD 1 track 24

1 – Bonjour. Qu'est-ce que tu manges?
– Je mange du poulet avec des frites.
– Et comme dessert?
– Comme dessert, je mange de la mousse au chocolat.
– Merci. Bon appétit!

2 – Salut! Qu'est-ce que tu manges?
– Je mange du poisson avec de la purée de pommes de terre.
– Et qu'est-ce que tu manges comme dessert?
– De la tarte au citron. Miam-miam! J'adore ça!
– Alors, bon appétit!

3 – Pardon. Qu'est-ce que tu manges aujourd'hui?
– Je mange du steak haché avec des haricots verts.
– C'est bon?
– Oui, c'est délicieux!
– Est-ce que tu manges aussi un dessert?
– Oui, je mange du yaourt nature.

4 – Salut! Qu'est-ce que tu manges?
– Euh... je mange des crudités...
– Oui...
– ... et après, de la pizza.
– Est-ce que tu manges un dessert?
– Non. Je ne mange pas de dessert.

5 – Bonjour. Qu'est-ce que tu manges?
– Je mange du fromage – du Camembert et un peu de Brie.
– Et qu'est-ce que tu manges comme dessert?
– Comme dessert, je mange de la glace à la fraise. J'adore la glace!
– Alors, bon appétit!
– Merci.

Answers
1 c,h **2** b,i **3** d,e **4** j,f **5** a,g

2 Mon Collège 5 Miam-miam!

2 En tandem. Jeu de mémoire. (AT 2.3)
Speaking. In pairs: pupils play a memory game. The first pupil closes his/her book. The other prompts with the letter of one of the pictures in exercise 1. The first pupil says the name of the food. After four prompts, they swap roles. *je ne sais pas* is glossed for support.

> **Studio Grammaire: the partitive article**
> Use the *Studio Grammaire* box to cover the partitive article (*du, de la, de l', des*). There is more information and further practice on Pupil Book p. 45.

3 Écris une phrase pour chaque personne de l'exercice 1. (AT 4.3)
Writing. Pupils write a sentence for each of the people in exercise 1. An example is given.

> **Answers**
> 1 Je mange du poulet avec des frites et de la mousse au chocolat.
> 2 Je mange du poisson avec de la purée de pommes de terre et de la tarte au citron.
> 3 Je mange du steak haché avec des haricots verts et du yaourt.
> 4 Je mange des crudités et de la pizza.
> 5 Je mange du fromage et de la glace à la fraise.

4 Écoute et répète. (AT 1.1)
Listening. Read through the pronunciation box on cognates together. Then play the recording for pupils to repeat.

Audioscript — CD 1 track 25

chocolat, dessert, mousse, pizza, steak, tarte

> **Starter 2**
> **Aim**
> To review the definite article and partitive article
>
> Give pupils three minutes working in pairs to complete ActiveTeach p. 036 Worksheet 2.4 Parts of speech, exercises C and D. Ask the class for their answers.
>
> **Alternative Starter 2:**
> Use ActiveTeach p. 036 Grammar activity to review the partitive article.

5 En tandem. Fais un dialogue. Puis change les détails. (AT 2.4)
Speaking. In pairs: pupils practise the dialogue, using the picture prompts supplied. They then make up their own dialogues by substituting other foods. They take it in turn to ask and answer the questions.

> **Studio Grammaire: *qu'est-ce que/est-ce que***
> Use the *Studio Grammaire* box to explain the difference between *qu'est-ce que* and *est-ce que*. There is more information and further practice on Pupil Book p. 44.

6 Écris ton menu de cantine idéal. (AT 4.3–4)
Writing. Pupils write their own ideal school canteen menu. Draw their attention to the tip box on adapting language given as a model.

7 Lis, écoute et chante! (AT 1.4–5, AT 3.4–5)
Listening. Pupils listen to the song, following the text at the same time. Play the song again and encourage pupils to sing along. Some vocabulary is glossed for support.

Audioscript — CD 1 track 26

À la cantine aujourd'hui,
Les enfants ont mangé...
Trois steaks hachés,
Deux yaourts nature
Et une portion de pizza Reine!

À la cantine aujourd'hui,
Les enfants ont mangé...
Quatre gros poissons,
Trois steaks hachés,
Deux yaourts nature
Et une portion de pizza Reine!

À la cantine aujourd'hui,
Les enfants ont mangé...
Cinq poulets-frites,
Quatre gros poissons,
Trois steaks hachés,
Deux yaourts nature
Et une portion de pizza Reine!

À la cantine aujourd'hui,
Les enfants ont mangé...
Six tartes au citron,
Cinq poulets-frites,
Quatre gros poissons,
Trois steaks hachés,
Deux yaourts nature
Et une portion de pizza Reine!

5 Miam-miam! Mon collège 2

8 Écris d'autres couplets pour la chanson. (AT 4.3–4)
Writing. Pupils write other verses for the song. An example is given. Draw their attention to the tip box on making nouns plural by adding –s.

9 Chante tes couplets. (AT 2.4–5)
Speaking. Pupils sing the verses they have written in exercise 8. You could make a recording of everyone's efforts.

PLTS S

Read together through the *Stratégie* on Pupil Book p. 47, which covers cognates and near-cognates. Pupils carry out the task given there (identifying English cognates among the vocabulary listed on pp. 46 and 47).

Plenary
Play a game in teams to review the partitive article. Teams nominate one person to write for them. Prompt with French words for food and drink (e.g. *un yaourt*). Following team discussion, the allotted person writes down the word with the appropriate partitive (e.g. *du yaourt*). Keep the pace quite quick, so that teams have to work together. To increase the challenge, you could use food/drink words from Unit 11 of *Accès Studio* (pp. 24–25), as well as the vocabulary from this unit.

Alternative Plenary:
Use ActiveTeach p. 037 Class activity to review general vocabulary from the module.

Workbook A, page 16

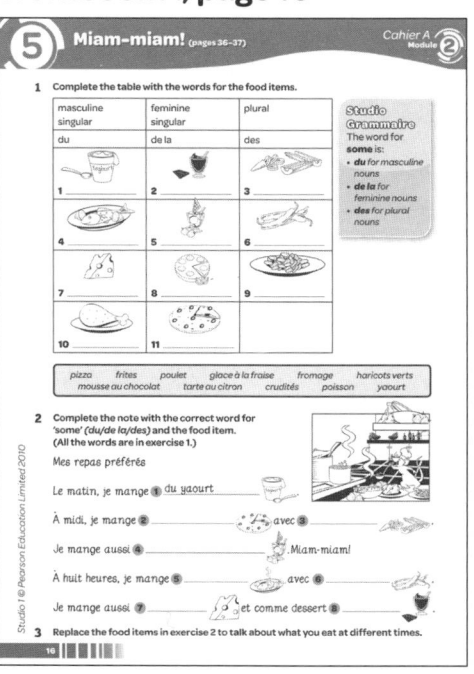

Answers
1. **1** yaourt **2** mousse au chocolat **3** crudités **4** poisson **5** glace à la fraise **6** haricots verts **7** fromage **8** tarte au citron **9** frites **10** poulet **11** pizza
2. **1** du yaourt **2** de la pizza **3** des crudités **4** de la glace (à la fraise) **5** du poisson **6** des haricots verts **7** du fromage **8** de la mousse au chocolat

Workbook B, page 16

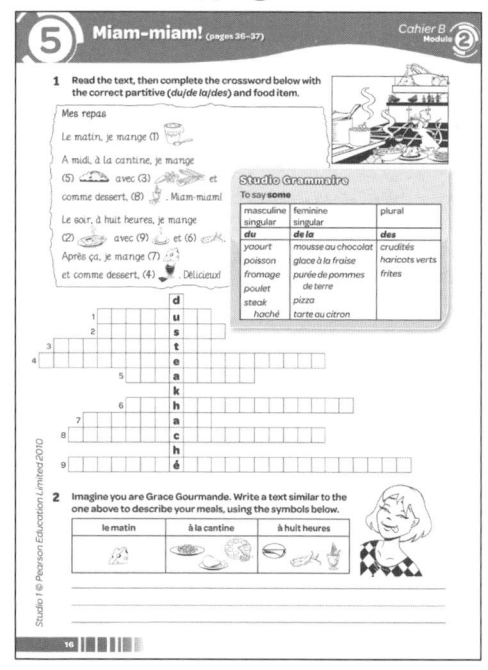

Answers
1. **1** du yaourt **2** du poisson **3** des crudités **4** de la mousse au chocolat **5** de la pizza **6** des haricots verts **7** du fromage **8** de la glace à la fraise **9** de la purée de pommes de terre
2. Le matin, je mange du fromage. À la cantine, je mange du poulet avec des frites comme dessert, une tarte au citron.
Le soir, à huit heures, je mange du steak haché avec des haricots verts et comme dessert, de la glace.

59

2 Mon collège 5 Miam-miam!

Worksheet 2.4 Parts of speech

A In these sentences, underline the subject, circle the verb, and put a square around the adjective in the sentence, if there is one.
1 J'adore la technologie et les sciences.
2 Je déteste l'EPS, c'est nul.
3 Tu aimes la musique?
4 La prof est sympa.
5 On finit les cours à quatre heures.
6 Je mange tous les jours une pizza.

B Circle the adjectives. If the word is not an adjective, write what part of speech it is, e.g. noun/verb.

ennuyeux génial nul marrant facile histoire sympa appétit difficile midi vendredi assez intéressant est

C Read the explanation and fill in the gaps, then put the nouns in the right column.

The is the definite article. There are ____ definite articles in French: *le*, __ and *les*. *le* becomes *l'* before a _____ or silent ____.
The indefinite article is *a* or *some* in the plural. *un* comes before _____ nouns, *une* comes before _____ nouns and *des* before _____ nouns.

	masculine	feminine	plural
definite article			
indefinite article			

le français un cours des haricots verts
la cantine les devoirs une prof

The partitive article (*du* (masculine singular), *de la* (feminine singular), *de l'* (in front of vowels or silent h) or *des* (plural)) means *some*.

D Circle the correct partitive article for each sentence.
1 Je mange *de la/du* tarte au citron.
2 Tu manges *des/du* frites?
3 Il mange *du/de la* poulet.
4 Elle mange *du/de la* yaourt.
5 Est-ce que tu manges *des/de la* crudités?

Worksheet 2.5 Questions

- You can ask a question using rising intonation, making your voice go up at the end.
  Tu aimes le français?
- You can use 'Est-ce que …?'
  Est-ce que tu aimes la musique?
- Or you can use specific question words:
  Qu'est-ce que …? What?
  Comment? How?
  Qui? Who?
  Quel/le …? What/Which?

A Unjumble these questions.
1 t'appelles-tu Comment? _____
2 as-tu Quel âge? _____
3 habites-tu Où? _____
4 tu l'informatique Est-ce que aimes? _____
5 Tu le dessin aimes? _____
6 manges tu Qu'est-ce que? _____
7 heure est-il Quelle? _____
8 manges Est-ce que de la viande tu? _____

B Match the questions above with the answers below.
a J'habite à Nantes.
b J'ai douze ans.
c Non, je déteste l'informatique.
d Non, je suis végétarien.
e Je mange du poisson et de la purée de pommes de terre.
f Il est quatre heures.
g Je m'appelle Tony.
h J'adore le dessin, c'est ma matière préférée.

C Translate these questions into French.
1 Do you like maths? _____
2 What time is it? _____
3 What do you eat? _____
4 Who is your favourite teacher? _____
5 How old are you? _____

Answers

A

	subject	verb	adjective
1	J'	adore	
2	Je	déteste	nul
3	Tu	aimes	
4	La prof	est	sympa
5	On	finit	
6	Je	mange	

B Adjectives: ennuyeux, génial, nul, marrant, facile, sympa, difficile, intéressant
histoire – noun   vendredi – noun
appétit – noun   assez – intensifier
midi – noun   est – verb

C *The* is the definite article. There are **three** definite articles in French: *le*, *la* and *les*. *le* and *la* become *l'* before a **vowel** or silent **'h'**.
The indefinite article is *a* or *some* in the plural. *un* comes before **masculine singular** nouns, *une* comes before **feminine singular** nouns and *des* before **plural** nouns.

	masculine	feminine	plural
definite article	le français	la cantine	les devoirs
indefinite article	un cours	une prof	des haricots verts

D
1 Je mange **de la** tarte au citron.
2 Tu manges **des** frites?
3 Il mange **du** poulet.
4 Elle mange **du** yaourt.
5 Est-ce que tu manges **des** crudités?

Answers

A
1 Comment t'appelles-tu?
2 Quel âge as-tu?
3 Où habites-tu?
4 Est-ce que tu aimes l'informatique?
5 Tu aimes le dessin?
6 Qu'est-ce que tu manges?
7 Quelle heure est-il?
8 Est-ce que tu manges de la viande?

B
1 g Je m'appelle Tony.
2 b J'ai douze ans.
3 a J'habite à Nantes.
4 c Non, je déteste l'informatique.
5 h J'adore le dessin, c'est ma matière préférée.
6 e Je mange du poisson et de la purée de pommes de terre.
7 f Il est quatre heures.
8 d Non, je suis végétarien.

C
1 Tu aimes les maths?/Est-ce que tu aimes les maths?
2 Quelle heure est-il?
3 Qu'est-ce que tu manges?
4 Qui est ton prof(esseur) préféré?
5 Quel âge as-tu?

5 Miam-miam! Mon collège 2

Video

Episode 4: À la cantine

StudioFR takes us around the canteen, where they interview the chef who explains what's on the menu. Video worksheet 4 can be used in conjunction with this episode.

Answers to video worksheet (ActiveTeach)
1. A [F3.1] (Answers will vary.)
   B (Answers will vary.)
   C Salad (cucumber, carrots), cold meats (charcuterie), fish, minced steak, croquette potatoes, green beans, pizza, pineapple, grapes, apples, fruit salad, raspberry tarts, apple purée, meringues
   D The chef says they are 'meringues maison'. (*maison* = house/home)
   E Yes, she speaks at a much more sensible speed.
2. A Friday
   B Coucou
   C Pizza is only on Wednesdays.
   D He asks eagerly if there is any pizza.
   E [PLTS **C**] chef/rendezvous
3. A Meringues are available, and they are his favourite dessert.
   B 500
   C What are you going to eat today?
   D He's too busy drooling over the desserts.
   E She tells him to point the camera at HER.
   F 'Bon appétit' – Enjoy your meal.
   G He has missed the fruit salad.
4. (Answers will vary.)

Bilan et Révisions (Pupil Book pp. 38–39)

Bilan
Pupils use this checklist to review language covered in the module, working on it in pairs in class or on their own at home. Encourage them to follow up any areas of weakness they identify. There are Target Setting Sheets included in the Assessment Pack, and an opportunity for pupils to record their own levels and targets on the *J'avance* page in the Workbook, p. 19. You can also use the *Bilan* checklist as an end-of-module plenary option.

Révisions
These revision exercises can be used for assessment purposes or for pupils to practise before tackling the assessment tasks in the Resource & Assessment File.

Resources
CD1, track 27
Cahier d'exercices A & B, pages 17 & 18

1 Écoute. Copie et complète le tableau. (1–6) (AT 1.3)
Listening. Pupils copy out the table. They listen to six conversations and complete the table – for each conversation, they note the letter of the subject mentioned and draw the appropriate face symbol for the opinion of the speaker.

Audioscript — CD 1 track 27

1. – Tu aimes la géographie?
   – Non. Je n'aime pas la géographie.
2. – Tu aimes les maths?
   – Ah, oui. J'adore les maths!
3. – Est-ce que tu aimes l'EPS?
   – Non! Je déteste l'EPS!
4. – Est-ce que tu aimes les sciences?
   – Bof. J'aime assez les sciences.
5. – Tu aimes le français?
   – Oui. J'aime le français. Et toi?
   – Moi aussi, j'aime le français.
6. – Est-ce que tu aimes le théâtre?
   – J'aime beaucoup le théâtre. C'est ma matière préférée!

Answers

	matière	opinion
1	d	☹
2	a	☺☺
3	b	☹☹
4	f	😐
5	e	☺
6	c	☺☺

2 En tandem. Fais des conversations sur les matières. (AT 2.3)
Speaking. In pairs: pupils take it in turn to ask and answer on the school subjects they like and why. A sample dialogue is given.

3 Lis l'e-mail de Mélissa. Trouve les quatre bonnes phrases. (AT 3.4)
Reading. Pupils read the e-mail. They then read the sentences about it and identify the four that are correct.

Answers
2, 3, 5, 6

4 Écris un paragraphe sur ta journée scolaire. (AT 4.4)
Writing. Pupils write a paragraph about their own school day. A list of points to cover is given. Draw their attention to the tip box on using Mélissa's text as a model.

Bilan et Révisions — Mon collège 2

Workbook A, page 17

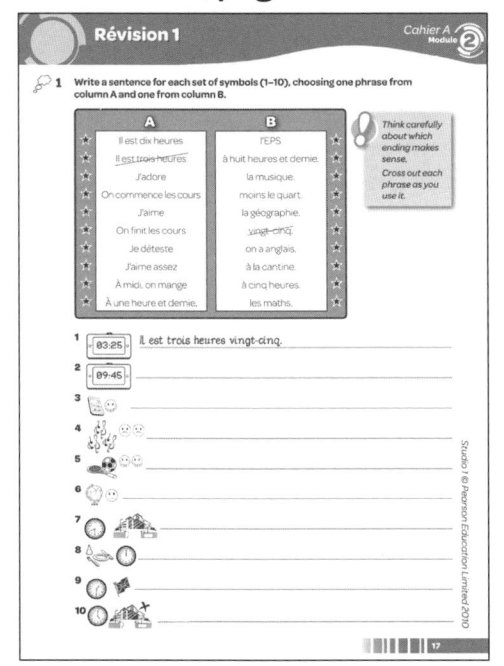

Answers
1. Il est trois heures vingt-cinq.
2. Il est dix heures moins le quart.
3. J'aime les maths.
4. Je déteste la musique.
5. J'adore l'EPS.
6. J'aime assez la géographie.
7. On commence les cours à huit heures et demie.
8. À midi, on mange à la cantine.
9. À une heure et demie, on a anglais.
10. On finit les cours à cinq heures.

Workbook A, page 18

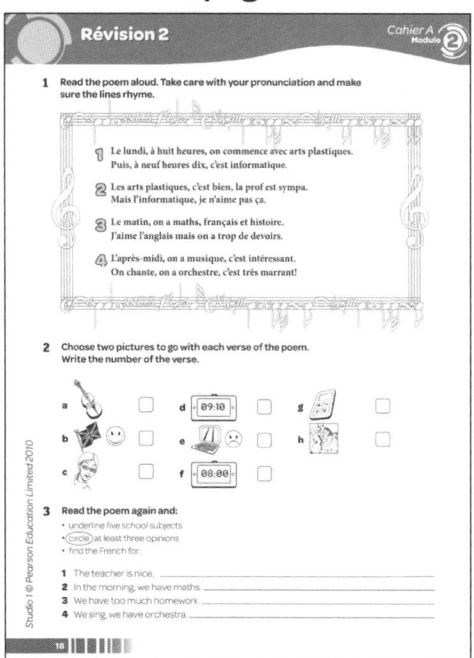

Answers
2. **a** 4 **b** 3 **c** 2 **d** 1 **e** 2 **f** 1 **g** 3 **h** 4
3. (Five underlined from:) arts plastiques, informatique, maths, français, histoire, anglais, musique
(Three circled from:) c'est bien, je n'aime pas ça, j'aime, c'est intéressant, c'est très marrant
   1. La prof est sympa.
   2. Le matin, on a maths.
   3. On a trop de devoirs.
   4. On chante, on a orchestre.

2　Mon collège　Bilan et Révisions

Workbook B, page 17

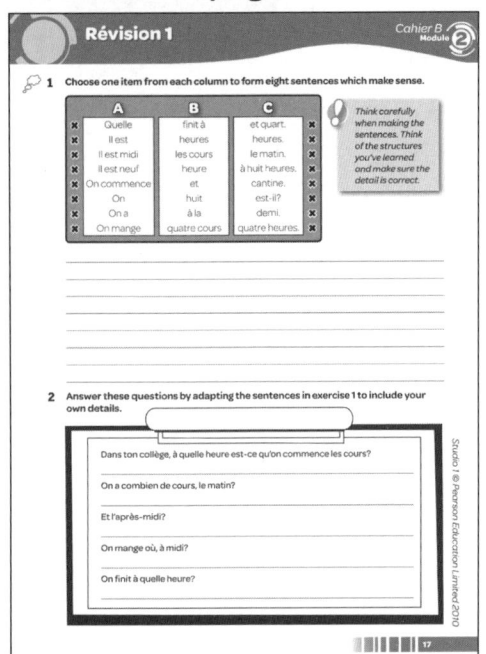

Answers
1. Quelle heure est-il?
   Il est huit heures.
   Il est midi et demi.
   Il est neuf heures et quart.
   On commence les cours à huit heures.
   On finit à quatre heures.
   On a quatre cours le matin.
   On mange à la cantine.

Workbook B, page 18

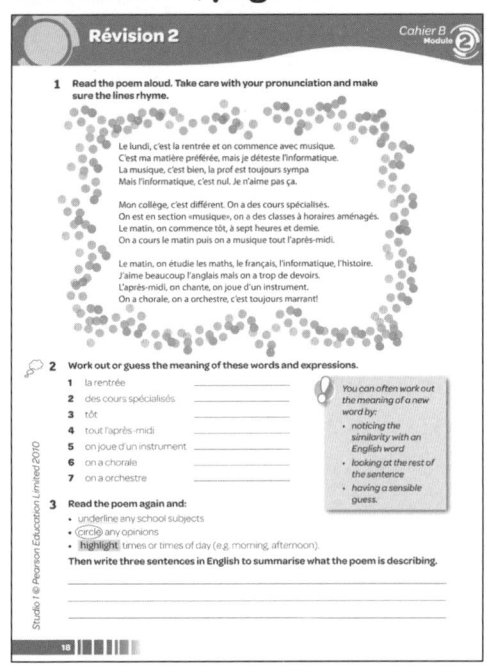

Answers
2 1 return to school   2 specialist lessons   3 early
   4 all afternoon   5 we play an instrument
   6 we have choir   7 we have orchestra
3 (Underlined:)   musique, informatique, maths,
                   français, histoire, anglais
   (Circled:)   C'est ma matière préférée, mais je
                   déteste l'informatique.
                   c'est bien, la prof est toujours sympa
                   c'est nul. Je n'aime pas ça.
                   c'est différent.
                   J'aime beaucoup
                   on a trop de devoirs.
                   c'est toujours marrant!
   (Highlighted:) le matin, à sept heures et demie,
                   l'après-midi

En plus 1: Mon collège au paradis
(Pupil Book pp. 40–41)

Learning objectives
- Schools in other French-speaking countries
- Developing reading skills

Framework objectives
5.3 Strategies – English/other languages: ex. 3
5.7 Strategies – planning and preparing: ex. 6

Key language
Review of language from the module

PLTS
C Creative thinkers

Cross-curricular
Geography: French-speaking countries

Resources
CD 1, track 28
ActiveTeach:
p.041 Assignment 2
p.041 Assignment 2: prep

Starter
Aim
To introduce some different countries where French is spoken

Write up the following, omitting the underlining (which shows the answers). Give pupils three minutes working in pairs to identify in which of these countries French is one of the main languages.

Canada / Brazil / Mexico / Algeria / Belgium / Ivory Coast / South Africa / Finland / Morocco

1 Regarde les textes, la carte et les photos. Il s'agit de quoi dans les textes? (AT 3.4)

PLTS C

Reading. Pupils look at the texts, the map and the photos and work out what the texts are about. Before they start, read together through the tip box on reading for gist.

Answers
The texts are about school life in other French-speaking countries, the island paradises of Mayotte and les Comores.

2 Écoute et lis. Quelles sont les trois choses qu'ils ne mentionnent pas? (AT 1.4, AT 3.4)

Listening. Pupils listen to the texts from exercise 1 in which two boys talk about their schools. They then read the list of topics and identify the three topics which are not mentioned by the speakers.

Audioscript — CD 1 track 28

– *Bonjour. Ça va? Je m'appelle Mohamed. J'habite à la Mayotte. C'est une île dans l'océan Indien, à l'est de l'Afrique. À la Mayotte, on parle français. Mon collège est assez bien équipé – on a un tableau noir, des livres, des crayons, etc. Mais on n'a pas de gymnase, alors on fait l'EPS sur la plage! On commence les cours à sept heures moins dix et on finit à quatre heures. On n'a pas de cantine au collège – on apporte notre déjeuner. Normalement, je mange du riz et des fruits (des bananes, des mangues et des ananas).*

– *Salut! Je m'appelle Fouad. Moi, j'habite aux Comores – des îles dans l'océan Indien où on parle français. J'aime mon collège, mais c'est difficile d'apprendre, parce qu'on n'a pas d'équipement scolaire. On n'a pas de tableau noir, pas de papier et pas beaucoup de livres... Le matin, on commence les cours à sept heures et on finit à onze heures. L'après-midi, on recommence les cours à trois heures. Il fait trop chaud pour les cours entre onze heures et trois heures! On n'a pas de cantine au collège, alors je mange à la maison.*

Answers
3, 5, 8

3 Qu'est-ce que c'est en anglais? Devine! (AT 3.4)

Reading. Pupils translate into English the ten French phrases taken from the text in exercise 1. Draw their attention to the tip box on using near-cognates to work out meaning.

2 Mon collège   En plus 1: Mon collège au paradis

Answers
1 the Indian Ocean
2 Africa
3 gym
4 well equipped
5 normally
6 rice
7 bananas
8 mangos
9 school equipment
10 fruit

4 Vérifie tes réponses à l'exercice 3 dans le Mini-dictionnaire ou dans un dictionnaire. (AT 3.4)

Reading. Pupils use the *Mini-dictionnaire* section at the back of the Pupil Book, or a French–English dictionary, to check their answers to exercise 3.

5 Lis et complète la traduction sans utiliser un dictionnaire. Devine! (AT 3.4)

Reading. Pupils complete the translation of the six sentences without using a dictionary. Draw their attention to the tip box on using context to work out meaning.

Answers
1 I live in Mayotte. It's an **island** in the Indian Ocean, to the **east** of Africa.
2 We don't have a gym, so we do PE on the **beach**.
3 We don't have a canteen at school – we **bring** our lunch.
4 It's difficult to **learn** because we don't have any school equipment.
5 It's too **hot** for lessons **between** 11 o'clock and 3 o'clock.
6 We don't have a canteen at school, so I eat at **home**.

6 En tandem. Imagine que tu fais une vidéoconférence avec Mohamed ou Fouad. Utilise les questions. (AT 2.4)

Speaking. In pairs: pupils imagine that they are having a videoconference with Mohamed or Fouad, taking it in turn to ask and answer questions. The questions and a sample opening to the exchange are supplied. Draw their attention to the tip box on preparing for the task and reviewing their work.

Plenary

Ask pupils to summarise the strategies for working out unknown words which they have learned so far. Prompt as necessary to cover using picture clues, looking for key words, using cognates, using context, using what they know, using a dictionary/wordlist. Encourage pupils to write a checklist of these and to refer to it until the strategies become automatic.

Worksheet 2.6 Mon blog

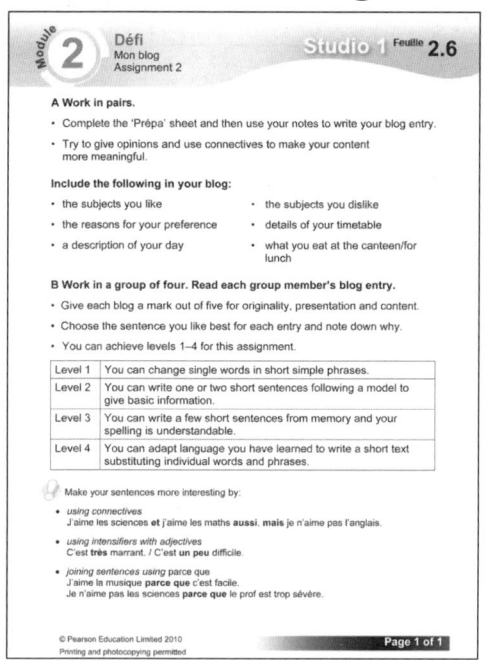

Worksheet 2.7 Mon blog. Prépa

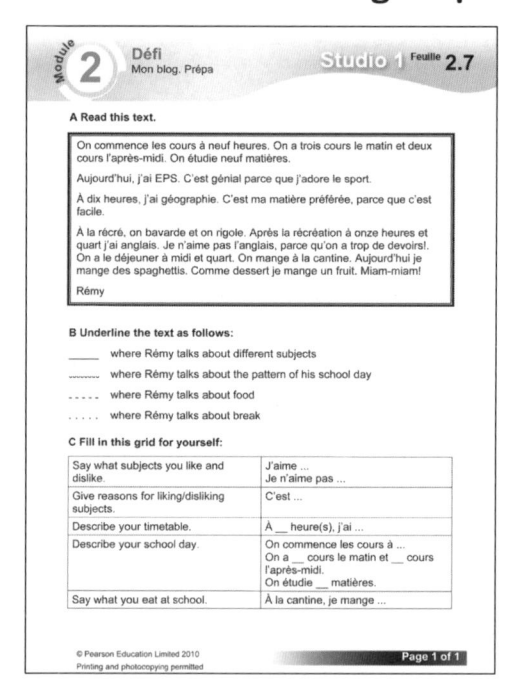

Answers

B On commence les cours à neuf heures. On a trois cours le matin et deux cours l'après-midi. On étudie neuf matières.

Aujourd'hui, j'ai EPS. C'est génial parce que j'adore le sport. À dix heures, j'ai géographie. C'est ma matière préférée, parce que c'est facile.

À la récré, on bavarde et on rigole.

Après la récréation à onze heures et quart j'ai anglais. Je n'aime pas l'anglais, parce qu'on a trop de devoirs!

On a le déjeuner à midi et quart. On mange à la cantine. Aujourd'hui je mange des spaghettis. Comme dessert je mange un fruit. Miam-miam!

Rémy

C (Answers will vary.)

En plus 2: Joyeux Noël! (Pupil Book pp. 42–43)

Mon collège 2

Learning objectives
- Talking about winter celebrations
- Developing speaking skills

Key language
les bonnes choses à manger
les cadeaux
la messe de minuit
les décorations
les chants de Noël
les vacances scolaires
un sapin de Noël
le père Noël
On mange de la dinde.
Douce nuit, sainte nuit
Je suis catholique/musulman(e).
la veille de Noël
le jour de Noël
Joyeux Noël!

PLTS
E Effective participators

Resources
CD 1, tracks 29–31
ActiveTeach:
p.043 Thinking skills

Starter
Aim
To introduce Christmas vocabulary

Give pupils three minutes to write out in French the six aspects of Christmas illustrated in exercise 1, in order of personal preference. While they are doing this, write your own order of preference. When time is up, read out your answers and ask pupils to give theirs.

1 Écoute. Qu'est-ce que chaque personne aime le plus à Noël? Écris la bonne lettre. (1–6) (AT 1.4–5)

Listening. Pupils listen to six conversations about Christmas and identify what each person likes most about it, noting the letter of the correct picture. Some vocabulary is glossed for support.

You could use this recording to illustrate the use of *tu* with children/teenagers and *vous* with adults. This is covered more fully in Module 4.

Audioscript CD 1 track 29

1
– Pardon. Tu aimes Noël?
– Ah, oui, c'est génial, Noël!
– Qu'est-ce que tu aimes le plus à Noël?
– J'aime les cadeaux! Le père Noël m'apporte toujours beaucoup de cadeaux. J'adore les cadeaux!
– Merci. Au revoir.
– Au revoir et Joyeux Noël!

2
– Bonjour! Est-ce que vous aimez Noël?
– Noël? Ah, oui, bien sûr! J'aime beaucoup Noël!
– Qu'est-ce que vous aimez le plus à Noël?
– Alors, j'aime les bonnes choses à manger. On mange de la dinde et une bûche de Noël. C'est délicieux!
– Merci. Joyeux Noël!

3
– Bonjour. Je peux te demander si tu aimes Noël?
– Ben, moi, je suis musulmane. On ne fête pas Noël.
– Oh, excuse-moi. Tu ne fêtes pas Noël…
– Non, mais j'aime beaucoup les vacances scolaires! On a deux semaines de vacances! Youpi!

4
– Et toi, tu fêtes Noël?
– Oui, chez moi on fête Noël.
– Qu'est-ce que tu aimes le plus à Noël?
– J'aime beaucoup les décorations. On a beaucoup de décorations chez nous. On a un sapin de Noël avec beaucoup de boules et des guirlandes. Je trouve ça très beau.
– Merci. Joyeux Noël!
– À vous aussi.

5
– Pardon. Bonjour. Est-ce que vous fêtez Noël?
– Ah, oui. Noël, c'est très important pour moi. Je suis catholique.
– Qu'est-ce que vous aimez le plus à Noël?
– J'aime la messe de minuit. La veille de Noël, je vais à la messe de minuit avec ma famille. On aime beaucoup ça.
– Merci. Au revoir.
– Au revoir et Joyeux Noël!

6
– Salut!
– Salut! / Bonjour! / Ça va?
– Est-ce que vous aimez Noël?
– Ah, oui! / Noël, c'est super! / J'adore Noël!
– Qu'est-ce que tu aimes le plus à Noël?
– Moi? Euh … Qu'est-ce que j'aime le plus … ?
– Les chants de Noël!
– Ah, oui! J'adore chanter les chants de Noël! Douce nuit, sainte nuit …
– Ah, non! C'est trop religieux, ça! Moi, je préfère Mon beau sapin, Roi des forêts …
– Ah, non, je déteste cette chanson! Moi, j'aime Vive le vent, vive le vent, vive le vent d'hiver, Qui s'en va sifflant, soufflant, Dans les grands sapins verts. Oh!
– Écoutez! On va chanter quelque chose ensemble. On va chanter «Petit papa Noël». D'accord?
– OK. / D'accord. / Si tu veux.
– Allez! Un, deux, trois!
– Petit papa Noël, Quand tu descendras du ciel, Avec tes jouets par milliers, N'oublie pas mon petit soulier …

En plus 2: Joyeux Noël! Mon collège 2

Answers
1 b *2* a *3* f *4* d *5* c *6* e

2 Qu'est-ce que c'est en anglais? Devine, puis vérifie dans le Mini-dictionnaire. (AT 3.2)

Reading. Using reading strategies, pupils translate into English the eight French phrases taken from the recording in exercise 1. They then check their answers in the *Mini-dictionnaire* section at the back of the Pupil Book.

Answers
a a Christmas tree
b We eat turkey
c I'm a Muslim
d Father Christmas
e I'm a Catholic
f Silent night, holy night
g Christmas Eve
h Merry Christmas!

3 Écoute à nouveau et complète les phrases avec les mots de l'exercice 2. (1–6) (AT 1.4–5)

Listening. Pupils listen to the recording for exercise 1 again and complete the gap-fill sentences, using the expressions in exercise 2.

Audioscript   CD 1 track 30

As for exercise 1

Answers
1 **Le père Noël** m'apporte toujours beaucoup de cadeaux.
2 **On mange de la dinde** et une bûche de Noël. C'est délicieux!
3 **Je suis musulmane.** On ne fête pas Noël.
4 On a **un sapin de Noël** avec beaucoup de boules et des guirlandes.
5 **La veille de Noël**, je vais à la messe de minuit avec ma famille.
6 J'adore chanter les chants de Noël! **Douce nuit, sainte nuit** ...

4 En tandem. Demande à ton/ta camarade: (AT 2.4)

Speaking. In pairs: pupils ask and answer the three questions supplied about Christmas.

5 Que sais-tu de Noël en France? Fais le quiz! Utilise un dictionnaire, si nécessaire. (AT 3.4)

Reading. Pupils do the quiz on Christmas in France. They can use a dictionary to work out what the answer options mean, but encourage them to use reading strategies first.

Answers
(For reference only – pupils listen to check their own answers in exercise 6.)
1 a *2* b *3* a *4* a *5* b *6* b *7* a *8* a

6 Écoute et vérifie. (AT 1.4)

Listening. Pupils listen and check their answers to the quiz in exercise 5.

Audioscript   CD 1 track 31

À Noël, en France, on décore la maison avec un sapin de Noël et des guirlandes.
On n'envoie pas de cartes de Noël, mais on envoie des cartes de vœux pour le Nouvel An.
Le père Noël apporte des cadeaux le 24 ou le 25 décembre. Ça dépend de ta région ou de ta famille.
On mange de la dinde la veille de Noël, c'est-à-dire le 24 décembre.
On mange aussi des huîtres et du foie gras.
Comme dessert, on mange une bûche de Noël. C'est un gâteau roulé, au chocolat. C'est délicieux!
On chante des chants de Noël, comme «Douce nuit» et «Mon beau sapin».
À Noël, on dit «Joyeux Noël» et au Nouvel An on dit «Bonne Année!»

7 Fais un mini exposé sur Noël dans ton pays. (AT 2.4–5)

PLTS E

Speaking. Pupils do a short presentation on Christmas in their own country. Draw their attention to the tip box on adapting the model text and using a dictionary.

8 Écris un poème de Noël en acrostiche. Dessine des images aussi. (AT 4.4)

Writing. Pupils write and illustrate an acrostic poem about Christmas in French. A sample opening is given.

Plenary

Put the class into teams. Give the teams three minutes to come up with as many facts about how Christmas is celebrated in France as they can. Award two points for each completely correct answer, one point for an answer with an error. The team with the most points wins.

2 Mon collège   En plus 2: Joyeux Noël!

Worksheet 2.8 Joyeux Noël!

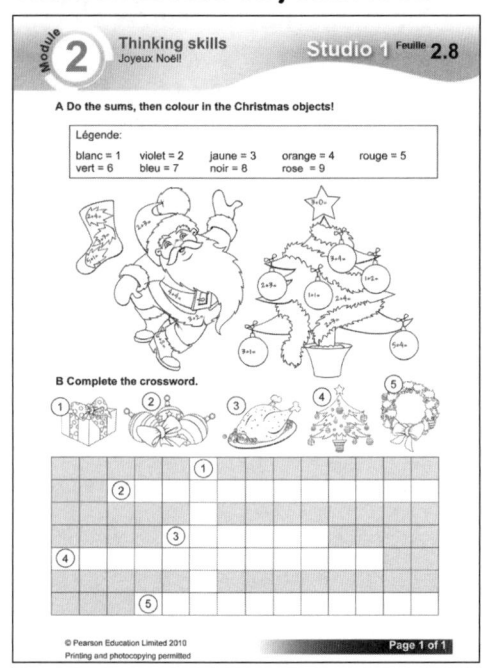

Answers

B

				①						
		② d	é	c	o	r	a	t	i	o	n	s
				a						
			③ d	i	n	d	e			
④ a	r	b	r	e	d	e	N	o	ë	l
				a						
		⑤ g	u	i	r	l	a	n	d	e	s

Studio Grammaire (Pupil Book pp. 44–45)

Mon collège 2

The *Studio Grammaire* section provides a more detailed summary of the key grammar covered in the module, along with further exercises to practise these points.

Grammar topics
- asking questions
- using *on*
- the partitive article

Asking questions

1 Say the statements as questions by making your voice go up at the end. Then write them out as questions, using *est-ce que*.

Pupils make the six statements into questions, first orally (using intonation), then in writing (using *est-ce que*).

Answers
1 *Est-ce que* tu aimes la technologie?
2 *Est-ce que* tu aimes les sciences?
3 *Est-ce qu'*il adore la géographie?
4 *Est-ce qu'*elle déteste le français?
5 *Est-ce qu'*il aime l'EPS?
6 *Est-ce qu'*elle déteste l'histoire?

2 Choose the correct option to complete each question. Then copy out the question and answer.

Pupils write out the complete questions and answers, choosing *est-ce que* or *qu'est-ce que* as appropriate.

Answers
1 *Est-ce que* tu manges de la glace? Oui, je mange de la glace.
2 *Est-ce que* tu manges du steak haché? Non, je mange du poulet.
3 *Qu'est-ce que* tu manges? Je mange du poisson avec des frites.
4 *Est-ce que* tu manges un dessert? Non, je ne mange pas de dessert.
5 *Qu'est-ce qu'*il mange aujourd'hui? Il mange du yaourt.
6 *Est-ce qu'*elle mange à la cantine? Oui, elle mange à la cantine.

Using *on*

3 Choose the correct form of the verb and copy out the text. Then translate the text into English.

Pupils write out the complete text, choosing between the two options for each verb. They then translate the text into English.

Answers
Je m'appelle Louise et mon amie s'appelle Anna. On **a** onze ans et on **est** en sixième. On **commence** les cours à huit heures et demie. On **étudie** huit matières. On **adore** les arts plastiques, mais on n'**aime** pas les maths. À la récré, on **bavarde** et on **rigole**. À midi et quart, on **mange** à la cantine. On **finit** les cours à cinq heures.

I am called Louise and my friend is called Anna. We are 11 years old and we are in Year 7. We start lessons at half past eight. We study eight subjects. We love art, but we don't like maths. At break, we chat and have a laugh. At quarter past 12, we eat in the canteen. We finish lessons at five o'clock.

4 Copy and complete the sentences with the *on* form of the verb. Then translate the sentences into English.

Pupils write out the sentences using the *on* form of the verbs. They then translate them into English.

Answers
1 On **joue** au tennis. – We play tennis.
2 On **travaille** au collège. – We work at school.
3 On **regarde** un DVD. – We watch a DVD.
4 On **écoute** la radio. – We listen to the radio.
5 On **surfe** sur Internet. – We surf the Internet.
6 On **parle** français. – We speak French.

The partitive article

5 Choose the correct option and copy out the sentences.

Pupils write out the sentences using the correct form of the partitive article.

Answers
1 Aujourd'hui, je mange **du** steak haché.
2 Tu manges **de la** mousse au chocolat?
3 Tous les jours, elle mange **des** frites.
4 À la cantine, on mange **de la** pizza.
5 Est-ce qu'il mange **des** crudités?
6 Comme dessert, je mange **de la** tarte au citron.

2 Mon collège Studio Grammaire

6 Translate the sentences into French. You can adapt the sentences in exercise 5. Remember to include the partitive article.

Pupils translate the six sentences into French, using the sentences in exercise 5 as a model, and taking care to use the correct form of the partitive article.

Answers
1 Aujourd'hui, je mange de la glace à la fraise.
2 Tu manges du poulet?
3 Tous les jours, elle mange du fromage.
4 À la cantine, on mange de la purée de pommes de terre.
5 Est-ce qu'il mange des haricots verts?
6 Comme dessert, je mange du yaourt.

Mon collège 2 — À toi (Pupil Book pages 120–121)

Self-access reading and writing

A Reinforcement

1 Lis les phrases et dessine les heures. (AT 3.2)

Reading. Pupils read the sentences giving times and draw a clock for each one.

Answers
(Clocks drawn by pupils should show the following times:)
1 9.00 **2** 3.10 **3** 7.15 **4** 1.30 **5** 9.45 **6** 3.55

2 Copie et complète les phrases. (AT 4.3)

Writing. Pupils write out the sentences, supplying the French for the picture prompts. The answers are supplied in random order.

Answers
1 À neuf heures, j'ai **géographie**.
2 À dix heures dix, j'ai **français**.
3 À onze heures et quart, j'ai **théâtre**.
4 À une heure et **demie**, j'ai **sciences**.
5 À deux heures moins le **quart**, j'ai **informatique**.
6 À trois heures moins **dix**, j'ai **arts plastiques**.

3 Lis les phrases. C'est possible ou absurde? (AT 3.3)

Reading. Pupils read the sentences and decide whether each one is possible (writing *possible*) or is nonsense (writing *absurde*).

Answers
1 *absurde* 2 *absurde* 3 *possible* 4 *absurde*
5 *possible* 6 *absurde*

4 Copie et corrige les phrases absurdes. Utilise tes propres idées. (AT 4.3)

Writing. Pupils write out corrected versions of the nonsense sentences in exercise 3, using their own ideas.

B Extension

1 Écris les phrases avec les mots dans le bon ordre. (AT 4.3)

Writing. Pupils write out the jumbled sentences in the correct order. Draw their attention to the tip box on accents and get them to check that their answers include accents where required.

Answers
1 J'aime la musique parce que c'est marrant.
2 J'aime le théâtre parce que c'est intéressant.
3 J'adore le français parce que c'est facile.
4 Je déteste la technologie parce que c'est ennuyeux.
5 J'aime beaucoup la géographie parce que c'est génial.
6 Je n'aime pas l'histoire parce que le prof est trop sévère.

2 Lis et note: vrai (V) ou faux (F)? (AT 3.4)

Reading. Pupils read Karim's text and then the six sentences about it. They decide whether each sentence is true (writing V) or false (writing F).

Answers
1 F 2 F 3 F 4 V 5 V 6 F

3 Corrige les phrases fausses de l'exercice 2. (AT 4.3)

Writing. Pupils rewrite the false sentences from exercise 2 so that they reflect what Karim says in his blog entry.

Answers
1 Le mercredi, Karim a **quatre** cours.
2 Il **aime beaucoup/adore** l'EPS. / L'EPS, **c'est sa matière préférée.**
3 À la récré, il mange **du chocolat**.
6 Il finit les cours à cinq heures **et** quart.

4 Écris un blog sur ton collège. Adapte le texte de Karim. (AT 4.4)

Writing. Pupils write a blog about their own school, adapting Karim's text in exercise 2. A list of details to include is given. They also need to include at least three connectives and intensifiers, as listed in the tip box.

Module 3: Mes passetemps (Pupil Book pp. 48–67)

Unit & Learning objectives	PoS & Framework objectives	Key language	Grammar and other language features
1 Mon ordi et mon portable (pp. 50–51) Talking about computers and mobiles Using regular *–er* verbs	**2.1d** previous knowledge **2.2a** listen for gist **2.2c** respond appropriately **2.2d** pronunciation and intonation **2.2g** write clearly and coherently **3b** sounds and writing **2.1/Y7** Reading – main points and detail **5.1** Strategies – patterns **4.5/Y7** Language – (a) present tense verbs	*Je joue. Je surfe sur Internet. Je tchatte sur MSN.* etc. *quelquefois, souvent, tous les jours*, etc.	**G** regular *–er* verbs (singular) – adverbs of frequency
2 Tu es sportif/ sportive? (pp. 52–53) Talking about which sports you play Using *jouer à*	**2.2d** pronunciation and intonation **2.2i** reuse language they have met **3c** apply grammar **3e** different countries/cultures **4b** communicate in pairs, etc. **4e** use a range of resources **1.5/Y7** Speaking – (a) presenting **2.4/Y7** Writing – (a) sentences and texts as models	*Je joue ... au basket, à la pétanque, sur la Wii*, etc. *Tu es sportif/sportive? Oui, je suis (assez/très) sportif/sportive. Non, je ne suis pas (très) sportif/sportive. Mon sportif/Ma sportive préféré(e) est ...*	**G** *jouer à* + a sport – preparing for a presentation – speaking skills: pronunciation, grammar and delivery
3 Qu'est-ce que tu fais? (pp. 54–55) Talking about activities Using the verb *faire*	**2.1b** memorising **2.2e** ask and answer questions **3c** apply grammar **4c** use more complex language **4d** make links with English **4f** language for interest/enjoyment **1.4/Y7** Speaking – (b) using prompts **2.3/Y7** Reading – text features **3.1/Y7** Culture – aspects of everyday life **5.4** Strategies – working out meaning	*Qu'est-ce que tu fais? Je fais ... du roller, de la natation, de l'équitation, des promenades*, etc. *en été, en hiver quand il fait beau quand il pleut* etc.	**G** *faire de* + a sport/ activity – reading strategies: patterns, rhymes, picture clues
4 J'aime faire ça! (pp. 56–57) Saying what you like doing Using *aimer* + the infinitive	**2.2a** listen for gist **2.2d** pronunciation and intonation **2.2f** initiate/sustain conversations **3c** apply grammar **3f** compare experiences **4a** use language in the classroom, etc. **1.5/Y7** Speaking – (b) expression/non-verbal techniques	*Qu'est-ce que tu aimes faire ... ? le soir, le weekend*, etc. *J'aime ... retrouver mes amies en ville écouter de la musique* etc.	**G** *aimer/adorer/ détester* + infinitive – distinguishing between verb forms (*j'aime jouer/ je joue*)

Mes passetemps 3

Unit & Learning objectives	PoS & Framework objectives	Key language	Grammar and other language features
5 Ils sont actifs! (pp. 58–59) Describing what other people do Using *ils* and *elles*	**2.1a** identify patterns **2.2b** skim and scan **2.2k** deal with unfamiliar language **3b** sounds and writing **3d** use a range of vocab/structures **4b** communicate in pairs, etc. **1.2/Y7** Listening – unfamiliar language **2.2/Y7** Reading – (a) unfamiliar language **4.5/Y7** Language – (a) set phrases about the past	*Il fait de la lutte. Elle s'entraîne (trois) fois par semaine. Il a gagné le match. Ils font de la musculation. Elles aiment le R&B.*	**G** *ils/elles* verb forms (regular *–er* verbs + *être, faire*)
Bilan et Révisions (pp. 60–61) Pupils' checklist and practice exercises			
En plus: J'adore les sports extrêmes! (pp. 62–63) Talking about extreme sports	**2.1d** previous knowledge **2.1e** use reference materials **2.2h** redraft to improve writing **3d** use a range of vocab/structures **4c** use more complex language **4g** language for a range of purposes	Review of language from the module *les sports extrêmes j'adore faire du snowboard C'est hypercool! impressionnant(e)*	**G** possessive adjectives (*son/sa/ses*) – reading skills: reading for gist and detail – writing skills: using model texts as a source of language; using a dictionary
Studio Grammaire (pp. 64–65) Detailed grammar summary and practice exercises			**G** verbs – the present tense (regular *–er* verbs) **G** *faire* (and *faire de* + a sport/activity) **G** *jouer à* + a sport/game **G** using verbs with nouns and infinitives **G** saying 'they' in French
À toi (pp. 122–123) Self-access reading and writing at two levels			

75

1 Mon ordi et mon portable (Pupil Book pp. 50–51)

Mes passetemps 3

Learning objectives
- Talking about computers and mobiles
- Using regular –er verbs

Framework objectives
2.1/Y7 Reading – main points and detail: ex. 7
5.1 Strategies – patterns: ex. 4
4.5/Y7 Language – (a) present tense verbs: ex. 6

Grammar
- regular –er verbs (singular)

Key language
Je joue.
Je surfe sur Internet.
Je tchatte sur MSN.
Je regarde des clips vidéo.
Je télécharge de la musique.
J'envoie des SMS.
Je parle avec mes ami(e)s/mes copains/mes copines.
J'envoie des e-mails.
quelquefois
souvent
tous les jours/soirs
tout le temps
de temps en temps
une/deux fois par semaine

PLTS
T Team workers

Resources
CD 2, tracks 2–4
Cahier d'exercices A & B, page 22
ActiveTeach:
p.050 Video 5
p.050 Video worksheet 5
p.050 Flashcards
p.051 Thinking skills

Starter 1
Aim
To introduce language for talking about computer use

Write up the following. Give pupils three minutes to number the computer activities 1–5 in order of personal priority, with 1 for the activity they do the most.

a J'envoie des e-mails.
b Je regarde des clips vidéo.
c Je tchatte sur MSN.
d Je surfe sur Internet.
e Je télécharge de la musique.

Ask pupils to translate each sentence into English and explain how they worked out new words. Pupils then swap lists with a partner and check their partner's preferences. Did any pairs have the same list? Finally, take a class vote on the most popular activity.

1 Écoute et écris la bonne lettre. (1–8) (AT 1.2)
Listening. Pupils listen to eight conversations and identify what each person uses his/her computer or mobile phone for, noting the letter of the correct picture and phrase.

Audioscript CD 2 track 2

1 – Bonjour. Qu'est-ce que tu fais avec ton ordinateur?
– Je regarde des clips vidéo. C'est génial!
2 – Et toi? Qu'est-ce que tu fais avec ton ordinateur?
– Euh ... Je tchatte sur MSN.
3 – Pardon. Qu'est-ce que tu fais avec ton ordinateur?
– Moi? Je télécharge de la musique.
4 – Salut! Qu'est-ce que tu fais avec ton ordinateur?
– Alors ... J'envoie des e-mails à mes copains.
5 – Et toi? Qu'est-ce que tu fais avec ton ordinateur?
– Je surfe sur Internet. J'adore ça!
6 – Pardon. Qu'est-ce que tu fais avec ton portable?
– Je parle! Je parle avec mes amis.
7 – Bonjour. Qu'est-ce que tu fais avec ton portable?
– J'envoie des SMS. J'envoie beaucoup de SMS!
8 – Et toi? Qu'est-ce que tu fais avec ton portable?
– Moi? Je joue. Je joue sur mon ordinateur et sur mon portable. J'adore les jeux vidéo!

Answers
1 d **2** c **3** e **4** h **5** b **6** g **7** f **8** a

Studio Grammaire: regular –er verbs (singular)
Use the *Studio Grammaire* box to review regular –er verbs (singular forms) and to cover the spelling change in *envoyer*. There is more information and further practice on Pupil Book p. 64.

1 Mon ordi et mon portable   Mes passetemps 3

2 En tandem. Fais un dialogue avec ton/ta camarade. (AT 2.3)

Speaking. In pairs: pupils take it in turn to ask and answer questions about what they use their computer and mobile phone for. A sample exchange is given.

3 Écoute les interviews. Note les *deux* activités et la fréquence. (1–4) (AT 1.3)

Listening. Read together through the key language box of expressions of frequency. Pupils then listen to four people being interviewed about their computer and mobile phone use. For each speaker, they identify two activities (using pictures a–h in exercise 1) and note the frequency in English.

Audioscript — CD 2 track 3

– Bonjour. J'ai avec moi Abdoul, Margot, Simon et Irina.
– Salut! / Bonjour!
– On parle de la technologie – les ordinateurs et les portables.

1 – Abdoul, qu'est-ce que tu fais avec ton ordinateur? Tu envoies des e-mails?
– Ah, oui. J'envoie tous les jours des e-mails.
– Tous les jours! Et tu télécharges de la musique?
– Oui. Je télécharge de la musique.
– Tu fais ça tous les jours aussi?
– Non. Une fois par semaine.
– Merci.

2 – Margot, qu'est-ce que tu fais? Est-ce que tu joues?
– Ah, oui! Je joue tous les soirs.
– Est-ce que tu surfes aussi sur Internet?
– Oui, de temps en temps, je surfe sur Internet.
– D'accord. Merci.

3 – Simon, ton portable est important? Tu envoies des SMS?
– Ah, oui, j'envoie tout le temps des SMS!
– Tout le temps? Et tu parles souvent avec tes copains ou ta famille?
– Oui, je parle souvent à mes copains. Mon portable, c'est essentiel!

4 – Et finalement, Irina. Est-ce que tu tchattes sur MSN?
– Sur MSN? Oui, deux fois par semaine.
– Deux fois par semaine. Et tu regardes des clips vidéo?
– Oui, quelquefois. Je regarde quelquefois des clips vidéo.

Answers
1 Abdoul: h every day, e once a week
2 Margot: a every evening, b from time to time
3 Simon: f all the time, g often
4 Irina: c twice a week, d sometimes

Starter 2
Aim
To review expressions of frequency; To review language for computer and mobile phone use

Write up the following. Give pupils three minutes to write four sentences, each using *je* and one of the verbs and expressions of frequency given. Remind pupils that they need to adapt the verb, which is given here in the infinitive.

jouer   tchatter sur MSN
télécharger de la musique   surfer sur Internet
quelquefois   souvent   tous les soirs
deux fois par semaine

Hear some answers. Ask pupils to translate their sentences into English. Ask the class what rule they used to adapt the infinitive so they could use it with *je*.

Alternative Starter 2:
Use ActiveTeach p. 050 Flashcards to review and practise the language for computer and mobile phone use.

Use the pronunciation box to review and practise the pronunciation of terminal –s and –t. Pupils find three words in exercise 4 where the terminal –s is pronounced. (**2** Je parle tous les soirs à me**s** amis. **3** De temp**s** en temps, tu envoies de**s** SMS.)

4 Lis les phrases à voix haute. (AT 2.2)
Speaking. Pupils read the sentences aloud, taking care to leave silent or pronounce each terminal –s as appropriate.

5 Écoute et vérifie. (1–5) (AT 1.2)
Listening. Pupils listen to the five sentences in exercise 4 to check whether their pronunciation was correct.

Audioscript — CD 2 track 4
1 Tu regardes tout le temps des clips vidéo!
2 Je parle tous les soirs à mes amis.
3 De temps en temps, tu envoies des SMS.
4 Quelquefois, je tchatte avec mes copines.
5 Tu joues à la console deux fois par semaine.

6 Tu fais souvent ça? Dis ce que tu fais avec ton ordinateur/ton portable. (AT 2.3)

PLTS T

Speaking. Pupils talk about the activities they do on their computer and mobile phone, including details of how frequently. An example is given.

3 Mes passetemps 1 Mon ordi et mon portable

7 Lis et choisis la bonne réponse. (AT 3.3)
Reading. Pupils read Lucas's text and answer the questions on it, choosing from the two options given each time. *les jeux* is glossed for support.

Answers
1 Lucas   2 Lucas et David   3 la mère de Lucas
4 le père de Lucas   5 le père de Lucas
6 la sœur de Lucas

8 Relis le texte. Complète les phrases en anglais. (AT 3.4)
Reading. Pupils re-read the text in exercise 7 and complete the sentences summarising it in English.

Answers
1 Lucas plays on his computer every **day**.
2 Lucas and David text each other **often**.
3 Lucas's mum downloads music **once or twice** a week.
4 His dad sends e-mails every **evening**.
5 **Sometimes** he plays Formula One games.
6 Lucas's sister watches video clips on YouTube **all the time**.

9 Écris un court paragraphe: «La technologie et moi». (AT 4.4)
Writing. Pupils write a short paragraph about their own use of technology, giving details of what they use their computer and mobile phone for and including information on frequency. A sample opening is given.

➕ Pupils also write about how a friend or family member uses his/her computer and mobile phone.

Plenary
Put the class into teams. Challenge them to write down as quickly as they can the *je* form of the seven verbs used in the unit to talk about computer/mobile phone use. You could increase the level of challenge by asking them to write the infinitive form too. The first team to complete the list correctly wins.

Workbook A, page 22

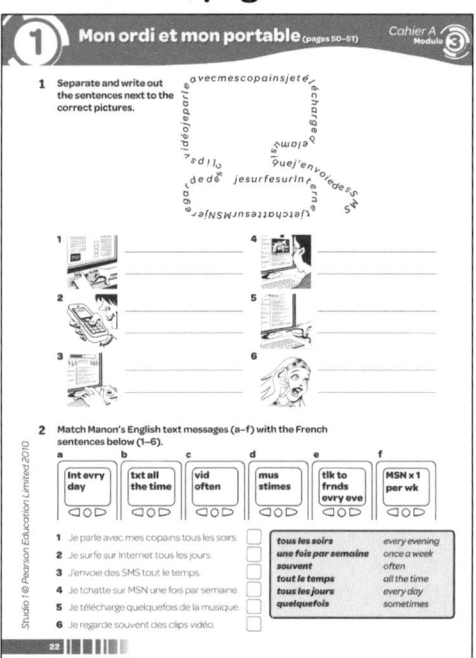

Answers
1 1 Je tchatte sur MSN.
   2 J'envoie des SMS.
   3 Je télécharge de la musique.
   4 Je regarde des clips vidéo.
   5 Je surfe sur Internet.
   6 Je parle avec mes copains.
2 1 e   2 a   3 b   4 f   5 d   6 c

Workbook B, page 22

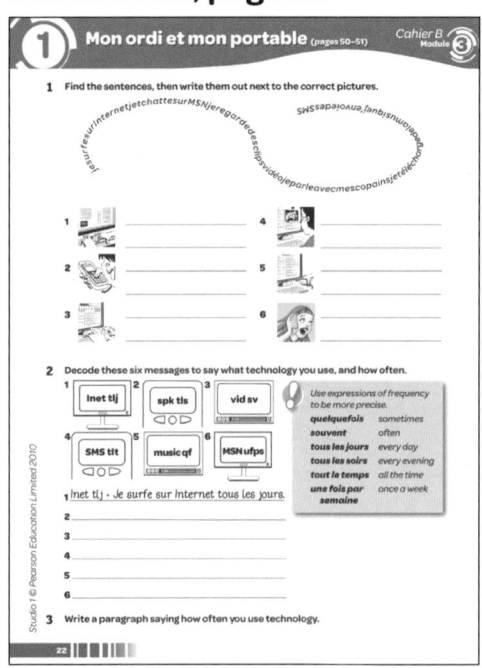

1 Mon ordi et mon portable   Mes passetemps   3

Answers
1 1 Je tchatte sur MSN.
   2 J'envoie des SMS.
   3 Je télécharge de la musique.
   4 Je regarde des clips vidéo.
   5 Je surfe sur Internet.
   6 Je parle avec mes copains.
2 1 Je surfe sur Internet tous les jours.
   2 Je parle avec mes copains tous les soirs.
   3 Je regarde souvent des clips vidéo.
   4 J'envoie des SMS tout le temps.
   5 Quelquefois, je télécharge de la musique.
   6 Je tchatte sur MSN une fois par semaine.

Worksheet 3.1 High-frequency words

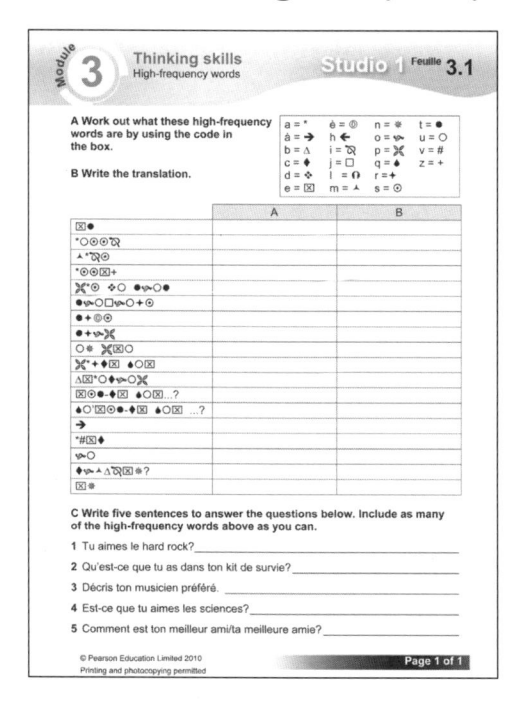

Answers

A	B
et	and
aussi	also
mais	but
assez	quite
pas du tout	not at all
toujours	always
très	very
trop	too much/too many
un peu	a bit
parce que	because
beaucoup	a lot
est-ce que … ?	? (question marker)
qu'est-ce que … ?	what?
à	at/to
avec	with
ou	or
combien?	how many/how much?
en	in

C (Answers will vary.)

Video

Episode 5: Les jeunes et la technologie
Samira, the producer, is looking for inspiration for StudioFR's next video. She's looking around at what the team is doing and has an idea. Video worksheet 5 can be used in conjunction with this episode.

Answers to video worksheet (ActiveTeach)
1 A MP3, surf, Internet, SMS, clip, vidéo
   B [PLTS T] Because she's deciding what the team's next video project should be.
   C [F1.3] (Answers will vary.)
2 A Because she's downloading music instead of working.
   B Because he thinks it should be obvious that he uses the Internet for StudioFR.
   C She is amazed that he watches videos on his phone.
   D – Ça dépend.
       – Incroyable!
       – Ça y est!
   E tous les jours – Hugo – every day
      deux fois par semaine – Marielle – twice a week
3 A sending texts, sending photos, talking with friends
   B (Choose from:) watch videos, play Internet games, chat, listen to music, download music, surf the net
   C He doesn't have a mobile phone.
   D None of them.
4 A Because he lists so many things, proving he's a technology enthusiast.
   B to download.
5 (Answers will vary.)

2 Tu es sportif/sportive?
(Pupil Book pp. 52–53)

3 *Mes passetemps*

Learning objectives
- Talking about which sports you play
- Using *jouer à*

Framework objectives
1.5/Y7 Speaking – (a) presenting: ex. 6
2.4/Y7 Writing – (a) sentences and texts as models: ex. 3

Grammar
- *jouer à* + a sport

Key language
Je joue …
au basket
au billard
au foot(ball)
au hockey
au rugby
au tennis
au tennis de table/ping-pong
au volleyball
à la pétanque
aux boules
sur la Wii
Tu es sportif/sportive?
Oui, je suis (assez/très) sportif/sportive.
Non, je ne suis pas (très) sportif/sportive.
Mon sportif/ Ma sportive préféré(e) est …

PLTS
I Independent enquirers

Cross-curricular
ICT: Internet research

Resources
CD 2, tracks 5–6
Accès Studio pages 14–15
Cahier d'exercices A & B, page 23
ActiveTeach:
p.052 Flashcards
p.052 Grammar skills

Accès Studio Unit 6 (pp. 14–15) can be used with this unit to review or introduce sports vocabulary.

Starter 1
Aim
To review regular *–er* verbs

Give pupils three minutes working in pairs to complete ActiveTeach p. 052 Grammar skills Worksheet 3.2 Regular *–er* verbs, exercises A and B. Ask the class for answers.

1 Écoute et complète le texte. (1–3) (AT 1.3)
Listening. Pupils listen to three people talking about how sporty they are and complete the gap-fill versions of the texts. The answers are supplied in random order. Before they start, read together through the cultural note on the French sports of *boules* and *pétanque*.

Audioscript CD 2 track 5

– *Je suis très sportif! Je joue au rugby, je joue au **foot** et je joue au tennis sur la Wii. De temps en temps, je joue aussi au **basket**! J'adore le sport!*
– *Je suis assez sportive. Je joue au hockey et je joue au **volleyball**. Je joue aussi au **tennis de table** sur la Wii. Le ping-pong, c'est génial!*
– *Je ne suis pas très sportif, mais je joue au **billard**. Quelquefois, je joue aux boules ou à la **pétanque** avec mes copains.*

Answers
(Also in bold in the audioscript)
1 foot **2** basket **3** volleyball **4** tennis de table
5 billard **6** pétanque

Studio Grammaire: *jouer à* + a sport
Use the *Studio Grammaire* box to cover *jouer au/à la/aux* with sports. There is more information and further practice on Pupil Book p. 65.

R Pupils working in pairs take it in turn to prompt with a sport and to give a sentence saying they play the sport, e.g. *basket – Je joue au basket*.

2 Fais un sondage. Pose la question à cinq amis et note les réponses. (AT 2.3)
Speaking. Pupils carry out a survey, asking five friends if they are sporty. Before they start, read together through the key language speech bubble (which includes symbols to use in noting responses). A sample exchange and a framework are supplied for support.

3 Écris des phrases sur cinq amis. (AT 4.3)
Writing. Pupils write up their results from exercise 2, saying how sporty their five friends are and which sports they play. Examples are given.

2 Tu es sportif/sportive? Mes passetemps 3

Starter 2
Aim
To practise using the correct form of *à*

Give pupils three minutes working in pairs to complete ActiveTeach p. 052 Grammar skills Worksheet 3.2 Regular *-er* verbs, exercise D. Ask the class for answers.

Alternative Starter 2:
Use ActiveTeach p. 052 Flashcards to review and practise the language for playing sports.

4 Écoute et lis. Écris la bonne lettre/les bonnes lettres. (1–4) (AT 1.3, AT 3.3)
Listening. Pupils listen to four people talking about their favourite sportspeople and read the text at the same time. For each speaker, they note the letter(s) of the appropriate picture(s). *il est né* is glossed for support.

Audioscript CD 2 track 6

1 *Mon sportif préféré est Frédéric Michalak. Il joue au rugby. Il joue pour Toulouse et pour la France.*
2 *Ma sportive préférée est Justine Henin. Elle joue au tennis. Elle est belge mais elle parle français.*
3 *Mon sportif préféré joue au basket. Il s'appelle Tony Parker. Il est français, mais il est né en Belgique. Il joue pour les San Antonio Spurs.*
4 *J'ai deux sportifs préférés. Mes sportifs préférés sont Karim Benzema et Florent Malouda. Benzema vient de France et Malouda vient de Guyane.*

Answers
1 d **2** a **3** e **4** b,c

5 Lis les phrases. Écris le bon nom. (AT 3.4)
Reading. Pupils read the text in exercise 4 again and identify which sportsperson is being described in each of the questions.

Answers
1 Karim Benzema **2** Tony Parker **3** Justine Henin
4 Florent Malouda **5** Frédéric Michalak
6 Tony Parker

6 Fais un mini exposé sur le sport. (AT 2.3–4)
Speaking. Pupils prepare and give a short presentation on sport, giving details of how sporty they are, which sports they play and their favourite sportsperson. An example is given. Encourage them to read through the tip box on how to tackle a presentation before they begin.

7 Fais des recherches sur Internet sur un sportif français et écris un court paragraphe. (AT 4.3–4)

PLTS

Writing. Pupils do some Internet research on a French sportsperson, using one of the suggestions supplied or their own ideas. They then write a short paragraph about him/her. Example sentence openings are supplied.

Plenary
Play a chain game round the class. Start it off: *Je suis très sportif/sportive. Je joue au tennis.* The next person repeats what you have said and adds another sport (e.g. ... *et je joue au hockey.*). Continue round the class. If someone can't remember the chain, makes a mistake or can't think of anything to add, he/she sits down and the chain starts again.

Workbook A, page 23

3 Mes passetemps   2 Tu es sportif/sportive?

Answers

1
1. Je joue au ping-pong. d
2. Je joue au hockey. g
3. Je joue au basket. f
4. Je joue sur la PlayStation. e
5. Je joue au rugby. h
6. Je joue au tennis. b
7. Je joue au volleyball. c
8. Je joue au foot. a

2
1. Il joue au football.
2. Elle joue au tennis.
3. Il joue au basket.
4. Elle joue au ping-pong.
5. Il joue au tennis.
6. Il joue au rugby.

Workbook B, page 23

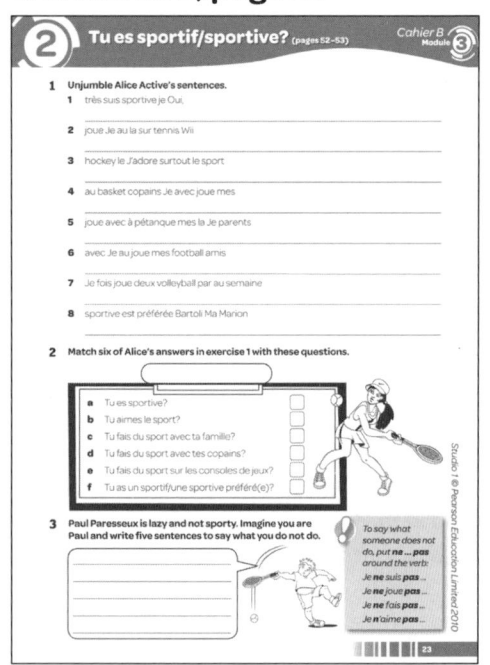

Answers

1
1. Oui, je suis très sportive.
2. Je joue au tennis sur la Wii.
3. J'adore le sport, surtout le hockey.
4. Je joue au basket avec mes copains.
5. Je joue à la pétanque avec mes parents.
6. Je joue au football avec mes amis.
7. Je joue au volleyball deux fois par semaine.
8. Ma sportive préférée est Marion Bartoli.

2 a 1 b 3 c 5 d 4/6 e 2 f 8

3 (Example answers:)
Je ne joue pas au tennis.
Je ne joue pas au football.
Je ne joue pas à la pétanque.
Je ne fais pas de sport.
Je ne suis pas sportif.

Worksheet 3.2 Regular –er verbs

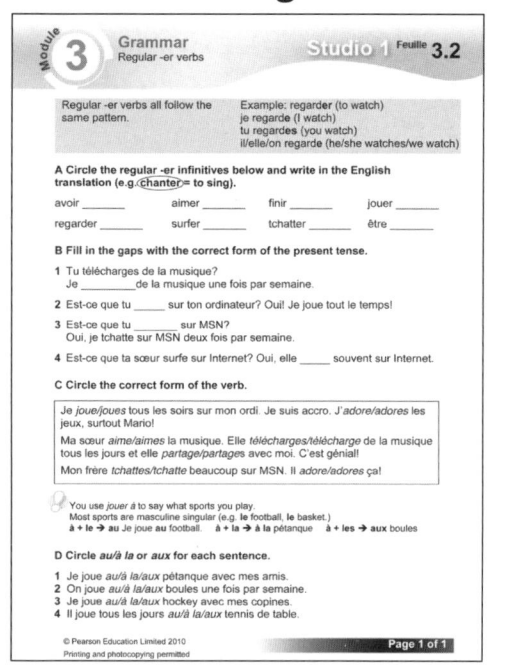

Answers

A
aimer	to like
jouer	to play
regarder	to watch
surfer	to surf
tchatter	to chat

B
1. Tu télécharges de la musique?
   Je **télécharge** de la musique une fois par semaine.
2. Est-ce que tu **joues** sur ton ordinateur?
   Oui! Je joue tout le temps!
3. Est-ce que tu **tchattes** sur MSN?
   Oui, je tchatte sur MSN deux fois par semaine.
4. Est-ce que ta sœur surfe sur Internet?
   Oui, elle **surfe** souvent sur Internet.

C Je **joue** tous les soirs sur mon ordi. Je suis accro. J'**adore** les jeux, surtout Mario!
Ma sœur **aime** la musique. Elle **télécharge** de la musique tous les jours et elle **partage** avec moi. C'est génial!
Mon frère **tchatte** beaucoup sur MSN. Il **adore** ça!

D
1. Je joue **à la** pétanque avec mes amis.
2. On joue **aux** boules une fois par semaine.
3. Je joue **au** hockey avec mes copines.
4. Il joue tous les jours **au** tennis de table.

3 Qu'est-ce que tu fais? (Pupil Book pp. 54–55)

Mes passetemps 3

Learning objectives
- Talking about activities
- Using the verb *faire*

Framework objectives
1.4/Y7 Speaking – (b) using prompts: ex. 4
2.3/Y7 Reading – text features: ex. 6
3.1/Y7 Culture – aspects of everyday life: ex. 7
5.4 Strategies – working out meaning: ex. 6

Grammar
- *faire de* + a sport/activity

Key language
Qu'est-ce que tu fais?
Je fais du judo.
Je fais du parkour.
Je fais du patin à glace.
Je fais du roller.
Je fais du skate.
Je fais du vélo.
Je fais de la danse.
Je fais de la gymnastique
Je fais de la natation.
Je fais de l'équitation.
Je fais des promenades.
en été/en hiver
quand il fait beau/chaud/froid
quand il pleut

PLTS
R Reflective learners

Resources
CD 2, tracks 7–9
Accès Studio pages 8–9, 14–15 & 28–29
Cahier d'exercices A & B, page 24
ActiveTeach:
p.054 Flashcards
p.054 Thinking skills
p.055 Class activity
p.055 Grammar
p.055 Grammar practice
p.055 Grammar skills

Accès Studio Unit 6 (pp. 14–15) can be used to review or introduce sports vocabulary.

Accès Studio Unit 3 (pp. 8–9) can be used with this unit to review months.

Accès Studio Unit 13 (pp. 28–29) can be used to review or introduce weather vocabulary.

Starter 1
Aim
To introduce more language for talking about sports

Use exercises 1 and 2 on p. 54 of the Pupil Book as the Starter.

1 Associe les images et les phrases. (AT 3.1)
Reading. Pupils match the pictures and the sentences.

Answers
(See the audioscript for exercise 2: pupils listen to check their own answers.)

2 Écoute et vérifie. (1–6) (AT 1.1)
Listening. Pupils listen and check their answers to exercise 1.

Audioscript — CD 2 track 7
1 d – *Je fais de la natation.*
2 f – *Je fais des promenades.*
3 a – *Je fais du parkour.*
4 e – *Je fais de l'équitation.*
5 c – *Je fais du roller.*
6 b – *Je fais du patin à glace.*

R Discuss with pupils how they can note and learn the vocabulary for playing/doing sports from Units 2 and 3. For example, they could draw pictures to help the words stick in their mind, list items alphabetically, list items grammatically (e.g. all the *du* examples together, etc.). Ask them to think of ideas for remembering which sports take *jouer à* and which take *faire de*. For example, they could use different colours to note them, look for links between the sports in each category, look for links with English, etc.

3 Écoute. Copie et complète le tableau en anglais. (1–5) (AT 1.4)
Listening. Read through the key language box together. Pupils then copy out the table. They listen to five conversations about what people do in different seasons/types of weather and complete the table in English.

Audioscript — CD 2 track 8
1 – *Qu'est-ce que tu fais en été?*
  – *En été, je fais de la natation.*
  – *Et qu'est-ce que tu fais en hiver?*
  – *En hiver, je fais de la danse.*
2 – *Qu'est-ce que tu fais quand il fait beau?*
  – *Quand il fait beau, je fais des promenades.*
  – *Et quand il pleut?*
  – *Quand il pleut? Je fais du judo.*
3 – *Qu'est-ce que tu fais quand il fait chaud?*
  – *Euh … Quand il fait chaud, je fais de la natation.*
  – *Et quand il fait froid?*
  – *Quand il fait froid, je fais du roller.*

3 Mes passetemps 3 Qu'est-ce que tu fais?

4 – Qu'est-ce que tu fais en hiver?
– En hiver, je fais du patin à glace.
– Et en été?
– En été? Je fais de l'équitation.

5 – Qu'est-ce que tu fais quand il fait froid?
– Je fais du parkour. C'est génial!
– Et quand il fait beau?
– Je fais du skate. J'adore ça aussi!

Answers
a swimming **b** walking **c** roller-skating
d winter **e** summer **f** parkour **g** nice weather
h skateboarding

4 En tandem. Fais trois dialogues. Utilise les images. (AT 2.3)
Speaking. In pairs: using the pictures supplied, pupils make up three dialogues. A sample exchange is given.

Starter 2
Aim
To review the language for playing sports

Write up the following. Give pupils working in pairs three minutes to complete the table with as many sports as they can (from Units 2 and 3), writing each sport in the appropriate column. When the time is up, they swap answers with another pair to check. The pair with the most correct answers wins.

jouer au/à la/ à l'/aux	faire du/de la/ de l'/des

Alternative Starter 2:
Use ActiveTeach p. 054 Flashcards to review and practise the language for doing sports.

5 Écris une phrase pour chaque personne de l'exercice 3. (AT 4.3)
Writing. Using their completed table from exercise 3, pupils write a sentence for each person. An example is given.

Answers
1 En été, je fais de la natation, mais en hiver, je fais de la danse.
2 Quand il fait beau, je fais des promenades, mais quand il pleut, je fais du judo.
3 Quand il fait chaud, je fais de la natation, mais quand il fait froid, je fais du roller.
4 En hiver, je fais du patin à glace, mais en été, je fais de l'équitation.
5 Quand il fait froid, je fais du parkour, mais quand il fait beau, je fais du skate.

Studio Grammaire: *faire de* + a sport/ activity
Use the *Studio Grammaire* box to cover *faire du/ de la/de l'/des* with sports and activities and the singular forms of *faire*. There is more information and further practice on Pupil Book p. 64.

Ask pupils to translate the following sentences into French.
1 He goes swimming.
2 She goes walking.
3 Do you do judo?

6 Lis le texte de la chanson. Quels sont les mots qui manquent? Devine! (AT 3.4)
Reading. Pupils read and complete the gap-fill version of the song. Some vocabulary is glossed for support. Before they start, draw their attention to the tip box on reading strategies.

Answers
(For reference only: pupils listen to check their own answers in exercise 7.)
1 vélo **2** parkour **3** famille **4** fait **5** roller
6 très **7** skateboard **8** judo

7 Écoute et vérifie. Puis chante! (AT 1.4)
Listening. Pupils listen to the song and check their answers to exercise 6. They listen again and sing along.

Audioscript CD 2 track 9

Ma famille est très active.
Hé-oh, hé-oh, hé!
Elle est aussi très sportive.
Hé-oh, hé-oh, hé!

Mon père fait du **vélo** tous les jours,
Et ma mère fait souvent du **parkour**.
Du vélo, du parkour,
Ma famille adore le sport!
Ma **famille** est très active.
Hé-oh, hé-oh, hé!

Mon frère **fait** du patin en hiver,
Et ma grand-mère, elle fait du roller.
Du patin, du **roller**,
Ma famille, c'est un mystère!
Ma famille est **très** active.
Hé-oh, hé-oh, hé!

Mon chien fait du **skateboard** tout le temps,
Et mon chat fait du **judo**, c'est marrant!
Du skateboard, du judo,
C'est rigolo, c'est rigolo!
Ma famille est très active.
Hé-oh, hé-oh, hé!

3 Qu'est-ce que tu fais? Mes passetemps

Answers
(See exercise 6; also in bold in the audioscript.)

8 Imagine que ta famille est très active! Écris un paragraphe. (AT 4.4)

PLTS R

Writing. Pupils imagine that their own family is very active and write a paragraph about the sports activities they do. An example opening and a list of language features to include are supplied.

When they have finished, pupils swap with a partner and check each other's texts, awarding points for how well they have included the features listed (time and frequency expressions, opinions).

Plenary
Give pupils three minutes working in pairs to complete ActiveTeach p. 055 Grammar skills Worksheet 3.4 *Faire*, exercise C. Ask the class for answers.

Alternative Plenary:
Use ActiveTeach p. 055 Class activity to review the language for playing sports (from U2 and U3).

Workbook A, page 24

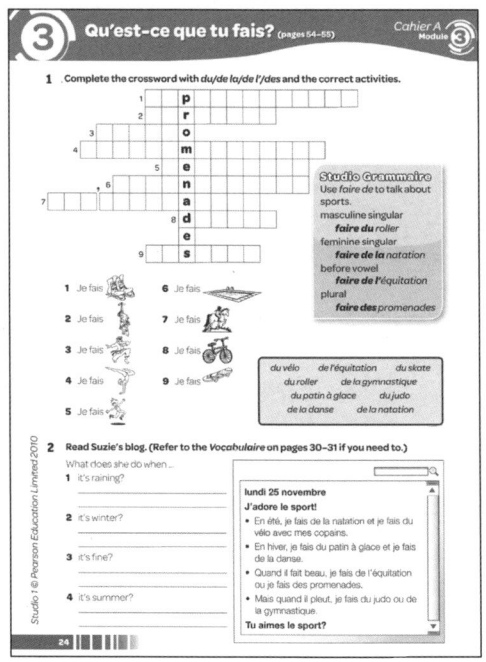

Answers
1. 1 du patin à glace 2 du roller 3 du judo
   4 de la gymnastique 5 de la danse
   6 de la natation 7 de l'équitation
   8 du vélo 9 du skate
2. 1 judo and gymnastics 2 ice-skating and dancing
   3 horse riding and walking
   4 swimming and cycling (with friends)

Workbook B, page 24

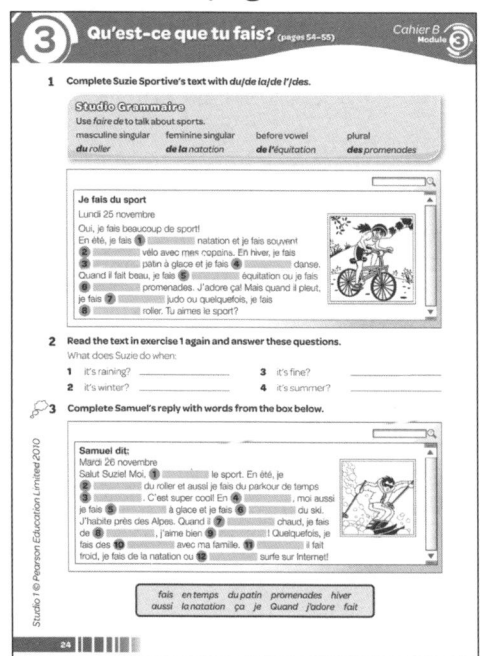

Answers
1. 1 de la 2 du 3 du 4 de la 5 de l' 6 des
   7 du 8 du
2. 1 judo or sometimes rollerblading
   2 ice-skating and dancing
   3 horse-riding or walking
   4 swimming and cycling (with friends)
3. 1 j'adore 2 fais 3 en temps 4 hiver
   5 du patin 6 aussi 7 fait 8 la natation
   9 ça 10 promenades 11 Quand 12 je

3 Mes passetemps 3 Qu'est-ce que tu fais?

Worksheet 3.3 Logic puzzle

Answers

B 1 Marie est **extrêmement sportive** et elle est fan de **l'Olympique de Marseille**.
2 Kévin est **assez sportif** et il est fan de **Nantes**.
3 Jamel est **très sportif** et il est fan de **Paris St-Germain**.
4 Coline **n'est pas du tout sportive** et elle est fan de **l'Olympique Lyonnais**.

Worksheet 3.4 *Faire*

Answers

A Ma copine Liza (1) **fait** du triathlon. Elle est championne.
Elle s'entraîne trois fois par semaine. D'abord, elle (2) **fait** du jogging. Ensuite, elle (3) **fait** du vélo. Quelquefois, je (4) **fais** du vélo avec elle. Puis elle (5) **fait** de la natation. Est-ce que tu (6) **fais** de la natation? Moi, je n'aime pas ça. L'entraînement, c'est fatigant, mais Liza adore.
Le soir, Liza aime écouter de la musique. Elle télécharge un peu de reggae et on (7) **fait** les devoirs dans sa chambre! Où est-ce que tu (8) **fais** tes devoirs?

B 1 Tu fais **de la** danse de temps en temps?
2 Moi, je fais **du** patin à glace tous les weekends.
3 Elodie fait **du** roller avec ses copines.
4 Ryan fait **de la** natation tous les jours.
5 Je fais **de l'**équitation. J'adore ça, c'est ma passion.
6 Moi, je fais **des** promenades avec ma famille.
7 On fait **du** vélo une fois par semaine.
8 Quand est-ce que tu fais **de la** gymnastique?

C 1 Quand il pleut, je fais du judo.
2 Quand il fait froid, je fais de la natation.
3 En hiver, je fais du patin à glace.
4 En été, je fais de l'équitation.

4 J'aime faire ça! (Pupil Book pp. 56–57)

Mes passetemps 3

Learning objectives
- Saying what you like doing
- Using *aimer* + the infinitive

Framework objectives
1.5/Y7 Speaking – (b) expression/non-verbal techniques: ex. 4

Grammar
- *aimer/adorer/détester* + infinitive

Key language
Qu'est-ce que tu aimes faire … ?
le soir/le weekend
le samedi/dimanche matin/après-midi/soir …
J'aime …
retrouver mes amies en ville.
regarder la télévision/la télé.
jouer sur ma PlayStation.
écouter de la musique.
faire les magasins.
faire du sport.
traîner avec mes copains.
téléphoner à mes copines.

PLTS
E Effective participators

Cross-curricular
ICT: e-mailing

Resources
CD 2, tracks 10–13
Cahier d'exercices A & B, page 25
ActiveTeach:
p.056 Video 6
p.056 Video worksheet 6
p.056 Flashcards
p.057 Learning skills

Starter 1
Aim
To review *aimer* + the infinitive

Give pupils three minutes to write six sentences using *j'aime* + a different infinitive. If necessary, model an example for support (e.g. *J'aime tchatter sur MSN.*).

Hear some answers. Explain that this unit will cover different verbs used to express likes/dislikes, all of which are followed by the infinitive.

1 Écoute et trouve la bonne image. (1–8) (AT 1.2)
Listening. Pupils listen to eight conversations and identify the correct picture and phrase for each, writing the appropriate letter.

Audioscript — CD 2 track 10

1 – Bonjour. Qu'est-ce que tu aimes faire le soir?
  – Euh … Le soir, j'aime écouter de la musique.
2 – Pardon. Qu'est-ce que tu aimes faire le weekend?
  – Le dimanche matin, j'aime faire du sport.
3 – Et toi? Qu'est-ce que tu aimes faire le weekend?
  – Moi? Le samedi après-midi, j'aime faire les magasins.
4 – Salut! Qu'est-ce que tu aimes faire le weekend?
  – Le samedi soir, j'aime regarder la télévision.
5 – Pardon. Qu'est-ce que tu aimes faire le weekend?
  – Le samedi matin, j'aime retrouver mes amies en ville.
6 – Bonjour. Qu'est-ce que tu aimes faire le soir?
  – Alors, le soir, j'aime jouer sur ma PlayStation.
7 – Et toi? Qu'est-ce que tu aimes faire le soir?
  – Le soir, j'aime téléphoner à mes copines.
8 – Salut! Qu'est-ce que tu aimes faire le weekend?
  – Euh … Le weekend, j'aime traîner avec mes copains.

Answers
1 d **2** f **3** e **4** b **5** a **6** c **7** h **8** g

2 Écoute à nouveau. Ils font ça quand? Note en anglais. (1–8) (AT 1.2)
Listening. Pupils listen to the recording from exercise 1 again and note in English when the speakers do the activities.

Audioscript — CD 2 track 11
As for exercise 1

Answers
1 in the evenings **2** on Sunday mornings
3 on Saturday afternoons **4** on Saturday evenings
5 on Saturday mornings **6** in the evenings
7 in the evenings **8** at the weekend

Use the pronunciation box to review and practise the sounds *en* and *in/ain*.

3 Écoute et répète. (AT 1.1)
Listening. Pupils listen to and repeat the examples featuring *en* and *in/ain*. The text is supplied.

Audioscript — CD 2 track 12

en: en ville, en été, en hiver
in: matin, patin, copain, Martin
Le matin, en hiver, mon copain Martin fait du patin en ville.

87

3 Mes passetemps 4 J'aime faire ça!

Studio Grammaire: *aimer* + infinitive
Use the *Studio Grammaire* box to cover *aimer/adorer/détester* + infinitive. There is more information and further practice on Pupil Book p. 65.

R Prompt with an activity from exercise 1, e.g. *Le weekend, je joue sur ma PlayStation.* Pupils respond with their opinion of it, e.g. *J'aime assez jouer sur ma PlayStation.*

4 En tandem. Interviewe ton/ta camarade. (AT 2.3–4)
Speaking. In pairs: pupils take it in turn to ask and answer questions about what they like to do in the evening and at the weekend, and what they don't like to do. A sample exchange is given. Encourage pupils to use expression to emphasise the activities that they like and those that they don't like.

Starter 2
Aim
To review *aimer/adorer/détester* + the infinitive

Write up the following, jumbling the order of the words in each sentence. Give pupils three minutes to write out each sentence in the correct order.

1 *J'aime assez faire du sport.*
2 *Je déteste faire les magasins.*
3 *J'aime beaucoup retrouver mes amies en ville.*
4 *Je n'aime pas téléphoner à mes copains.*

Alternative Starter 2:
Use ActiveTeach p. 056 Flashcards to review and practise the language for expressing likes and dislikes regarding leisure time activities.

5 Associe les phrases de l'exercice 1 et les phrases ci-dessous. Copie les paires de phrases. (AT 3.3)
Reading. Pupils match the sentences from exercise 1 with the sentences supplied here, copying out the pairs of sentences. *au centre-ville* is glossed for support. Before they start, draw their attention to the tip box on verb forms (*je joue/j'aime jouer*).

Answers
a J'aime retrouver mes amies en ville. – Je retrouve mes copines chez McDonald's.
b J'aime regarder la télévision/la télé. – Je regarde *Doctor Who* et *Les Simpson*.
c J'aime jouer sur ma PlayStation. – Je joue à *Final Fantasy*.
d J'aime écouter de la musique. – J'écoute du hip-hop et du rap.
e J'aime faire les magasins. – Je fais du shopping le samedi matin.
f J'aime faire du sport. – Je fais du sport le dimanche après-midi.
g J'aime traîner avec mes copains. – Je traîne avec mes copains au centre-ville.
h J'aime téléphoner à mes copines. – Je téléphone à mes copines sur mon portable.

Studio Grammaire: saying you *do* something vs saying you *like doing* something
Use the *Studio Grammaire* box to cover the difference between (for example) *je joue* and *j'aime jouer*. There is more information and further practice on Pupil Book p. 65.

6 Écoute et complète le texte de Yasmine. (AT 1.4, AT 3.4)
Listening. Pupils listen and complete the gap-fill version of Yasmine's text.

Audioscript   CD 2 track 13

*J'adore le weekend! Le samedi matin, j'aime **jouer** au basket avec ma sœur. Mais en été, je **joue** au tennis avec mon frère.*
*Le samedi après-midi, j'aime **retrouver** mes copines en ville. On traîne, on fait du shopping et quelquefois, on **mange** de la pizza. C'est chouette!*
*Le samedi soir, je **regarde** la télé, mais j'aime aussi **surfer** sur Internet.*
*Le dimanche matin, j'aime **faire** des promenades avec mon chien. L'après-midi, je fais mes devoirs. Je déteste ça parce que c'est ennuyeux!*
*Normalement, le dimanche soir, j'aime **écouter** de la musique.*
Et toi? Qu'est-ce que tu fais le weekend?

Answers
(Also in bold in the audioscript.)
1 *jouer* 2 *joue* 3 *retrouver* 4 *mange* 5 *regarde*
6 *surfer* 7 *faire* 8 *écouter*

4 J'aime faire ça! Mes passetemps

7 Prépare et dis six phrases sur ton weekend. Si possible, parle de mémoire.
(AT 2.3–4)

PLTS E

Speaking. Pupils prepare and say six sentences about their own weekend, three on what they do and three on what they like doing. Once they have prepared the sentences, they should try to say them from memory. If you have a partner school in France, pupils could exchange e-mails on the activities they like doing.

8 Écris une réponse à Yasmine.
(AT 4.3–4)

Writing. Pupils write a reply to Yasmine's text from exercise 6, giving details of what they do and what they like to do at the weekend.

> **Plenary**
> Ask pupils to summarise how verbs such as *aimer*, *adorer* and *détester* are used. Then say sentences from the unit using these verbs (including *beaucoup/assez/ne/n' ... pas* too). Make grammatical errors in some sentences – e.g. *j'adorer* or *j'aime pas* or *je déteste regarde*, etc. Pupils put up their hand to identify and correct an error.

Workbook A, page 25

Answers
1
  1 J'aime écouter de la musique.
  2 J'aime jouer sur ma PlayStation.
  3 J'aime regarder la télévision.
  4 J'aime retrouver mes copains en ville.
  5 J'aime faire les magasins.
  6 J'aime jouer au football.

Workbook B, page 25

Answers
1
  1 J'aime téléphoner à mes copines.
  2 J'aime traîner avec mes copains.
  3 J'aime retrouver mes copines en ville.
  4 J'aime faire les magasins.
  5 J'aime jouer au football.
  6 J'aime écouter de la musique.
2 (Example answers:)
  1 J'aime téléphoner à ma mère.
  2 J'aime traîner avec mes amis.
  3 J'aime retrouver mon frère en ville.
  4 J'aime faire du sport.
  5 J'aime jouer au basket.
  6 J'aime écouter du metal.
3 (Example answer:)
  J'aime retrouver mes copines en ville et j'aime faire les magasins. Le soir, j'aime écouter de la musique. Le weekend, j'aime jouer sur ma Wii et j'aime aussi traîner avec mes amis. Le samedi matin, j'aime regarder la télévision et le samedi après-midi, j'aime jouer au billard. Le dimanche matin, j'aime faire de la natation.

3 Mes passetemps 4 J'aime faire ça!

Worksheet 3.5 Building your vocabulary

Answers

A tous les jours
souvent
une ou deux fois par semaine
une fois par semaine
quelquefois
de temps en temps

B souvent – rarement
commencer – finir
intelligent – stupide
petit – grand
poli – impoli
bonjour – au revoir
en été – en hiver
patient – impatient
beaucoup – pas du tout
je déteste – j'adore
j'aime – je n'aime pas
nul – super
facile – difficile
il fait froid – il fait chaud

C (Answers will vary.)

Video

Episode 6: Les jeunes sapeurs pompiers

StudioFR is going to visit Verzenay fire station. Alex and Marielle are interviewing Charles, who trains with the young firemen of Verzenay. Video worksheet 6 can be used in conjunction with this episode.

Answers to video worksheet (ActiveTeach)

1 A The team is making a documentary about weekend activities – in this case, the Young Fire Brigade.
  B [PLTS T/E] She seems to be falling for the hunky fireman!
  C (Answers will vary.)
2 A She asks who he is and Alex introduces him. Even though he kisses her, it's just a French custom.
  B (His reasons are:) He likes sport and he likes helping people and saving lives. He doesn't like watching TV and he hates hanging around in town.
  C passion (passion)
  easy (facile)
  exercise (exercice)
  serious (sérieux)
  D lance à eau – hose pipe
  traîner en ville – hang around in town
  en pleine forme – on top form, fit
  E In winter as well as summer.
3 A [PLTS T/E] They are doing exercises about rescue equipment. He also mentions that it's the youngest members today.
  B It's an exam.
  C Simulating a mission
  D More boys. (Answers will vary.)
  E Are you ready?

5 Ils sont actifs! (Pupil Book pp. 58–59)

Mes passetemps 3

Learning objectives
- Describing what other people do
- Using *ils* and *elles*

Framework objectives
1.2/Y7 Listening – unfamiliar language: ex. 3
2.2/Y7 Reading – (a) unfamiliar language: ex. 4
4.5/Y7 Language – (a) set phrases about the past: ex. 3

Grammar
- *ils/elles* verb forms (regular *–er* verbs + *être, faire*)

Key language
Il fait de la lutte.
Elle fait du jogging.
Il a gagné le match.
Il est champion régional.
Elle est championne régionale.
Elle s'entraîne (trois) fois par semaine.
Ils font de la musculation.
Elles écoutent de la musique.
Ils jouent au foot.
Elles regardent la télé.
Ils sont des clowns.
Elles aiment le R&B.

PLTS
C Creative thinkers

Resources
CD 2, tracks 14–16
Cahier d'exercices A & B, page 26
ActiveTeach:
p.059 Class activity

Starter 1
PLTS C

Aim
To review present tense singular verbs

Write up the following. Give pupils three minutes working in pairs to identify the grammatical odd one out in each group, giving a reason for their choice.

1	fait	regarde	aime
2	parle	téléphones	joue
3	écouter	traîne	être
4	ai	est	suis
5	envoies	écoutes	télécharge

(Answers: **1** *fait* – irregular verb
2 *téléphones* – *tu* form
3 *traîne* – not an infinitive; or *être* – irregular verb
4 *est* – *il/elle* form; or *ai* – not part of *être*
5 *télécharge* – not a *tu* form; or *envoies* – has a spelling change)

1 Écoute et lis. Mets les images dans le bon ordre. (AT 1.4, AT 3.4)
Listening. Pupils listen to the information about Guillaume, reading the text at the same time. They then put the pictures into the order they are mentioned in the text.

Audioscript CD 2 track 14

Mon copain Guillaume a un passetemps original. Il fait de la lutte!
Il s'entraîne trois fois par semaine. D'abord, il fait du jogging. Ensuite, il fait de la musculation. Puis il fait de la natation. C'est fatigant, mais il adore faire de la lutte.
D'habitude, le samedi, il a un match. Samedi dernier, il a gagné le match. Il est champion régional.
Le soir, Guillaume aime regarder la télé. Qu'est-ce qu'il regarde? Il regarde la lutte, bien sûr!

Answers
c, b, e, d, a

2 Relis le texte et complète les phrases en anglais. (AT 3.4)
Reading. Pupils re-read the text in exercise 1 and complete the sentences summarising it in English.

Answers
1 Guillaume's hobby is **wrestling**.
2 He trains **three times** a week.
3 First of all he goes **jogging**.
4 Then he does **weight training**.
5 Then he goes **swimming**.
6 Usually on **Saturdays** he has a match.
7 Last Saturday Guillaume **won** the match.

R Pupils identify all the verbs in the text in exercise 1 and translate them into English.

3 Écoute la description du passetemps de Marie. Choisis la bonne réponse. (1–6) (AT 1.4)
Listening. Pupils listen to the description of Marie's hobby. They then complete each sentence, choosing from the two options each time.

3 Mes passetemps 5 Ils sont actifs!

Audioscript CD 2 track 15

1 *Ma copine Marie a un passetemps très dynamique. Elle fait de la gymnastique!*
2 *Elle s'entraîne quatre fois par semaine.*
3 *D'abord, elle fait du vélo.*
4 *Puis elle fait de la natation.*
5 *Dimanche dernier, elle a gagné une compétition. Elle est championne régionale!*
6 *Le soir, Marie aime écouter de la musique.*

Answers
1 *Marie fait **de la gymnastique**.*
2 *Elle s'entraîne **quatre** fois par semaine.*
3 *D'abord, elle fait **du vélo**.*
4 *Puis elle fait **de la natation**.*
5 *Dimanche dernier, elle a **gagné** une compétition. Elle est championne régionale!*
6 *Le soir, Marie aime **écouter de la musique**.*

Starter 2
Aim
To practise reading for gist; To use reading strategies

Give pupils 30 seconds to read the text in exercise 4. Ask them to summarise what it is about. Ask them which techniques are useful in this kind of task. Prompt as necessary to cover: using pictures, focusing on headings and the first sentence of each paragraph, looking for key words, using cognates and context.

Studio Grammaire: *ils/elles* verb forms (regular *–er* verbs + *être, faire*)
Use the *Studio Grammaire* box to cover *ils/elles* verb forms. There is more information and further practice on Pupil Book p. 65.

4 Lis le texte. Complète les phrases. (AT 3.4)
Reading. Pupils read the text about the circus school, then complete the gap-fill sentences summarising it by writing in the missing verbs.

Answers
(See the audioscript in exercise 5: pupils listen to check their own answers.)

5 Écoute et vérifie. (1–8) (AT 1.4)
Listening. Pupils listen to check their answers to exercise 4.

Audioscript CD 2 track 16

1 *Rémi et Dimitri **sont** des clowns.*
2 *Ils **adorent** la comédie.*
3 *Ils **font** de la musculation.*
4 *Le soir, ils **jouent** au foot ou ils **regardent** la télé.*
5 *Luna et Marina **sont** des funambules.*
6 *Elles **font** de la gymnastique et de la danse.*
7 *Le soir, elles **écoutent** de la musique.*
8 *Elles **aiment** le R&B.*

Answers
(Also in bold in the audioscript)
1 sont 2 adorent 3 font 4 jouent, regardent
5 sont 6 font 7 écoutent 8 aiment

6 Regarde les images et écris les phrases. (AT 4.4)
Writing. Pupils adapt the sentences given using *ils* or *elles* as appropriate to match the symbols shown, and using the *ils/elles* verb form.

Answers
1 *Ils aiment le sport.*
2 *Ils regardent la télé.*
3 *Elles écoutent de la musique.*
4 *Elles font du judo.*
5 *Ils jouent au tennis.*
6 *Ils sont sympas.*

7 Regarde les images. Décris le weekend de Thomas et Tariq ou de Claire et Clarisse. (AT 2.4)
Speaking. Using the picture prompts, pupils describe Thomas and Tariq's weekend or Claire and Clarisse's weekend. An example opening is supplied.

Answers
a *Le vendredi soir, Thomas et Tariq/Claire et Clarisse regardent la télé.*
b *Le samedi matin, ils/elles font de la natation.*
c *Le samedi après-midi, ils/elles jouent au foot(ball).*
d *Le samedi soir, ils/elles mangent de la pizza.*
e *Le dimanche matin, ils/elles font du vélo.*
f *Le dimanche après-midi, ils/elles jouent au basket.*
g *Le dimanche soir, ils/elles écoutent de la musique.*

Read together through the *Stratégie* on Pupil Book p. 67, covering high-frequency words. Pupils carry out the task given there (identifying high-frequency words in the *Vocabulaire* sections in Modules 1–3).

5 Ils sont actifs! Mes passetemps 3

Plenary

Play a team game to review the *ils/elles* form of present tense verbs. Prepare a sheet of paper for each team with the following prompts on it. Leave a space by each prompt for the *ils/elles* form to be written in.

ils/elles …

aimer   regarder   être   surfer   parler   téléphoner   faire   jouer   écouter   traîner   retrouver   tchatter

(Use just six prompts for a shorter game.)

Put the class into teams and put each team's sheet of paper with a pen at the front of the class in a place where the team can easily get to it. Each team member in turn comes to the front of the class and writes one of the verbs. The team with the most correct verbs at the end of the allotted time is the winner.

Alternative Plenary:
Use ActiveTeach p. 059 Class activity to review general grammar from the module.

Workbook A, page 26

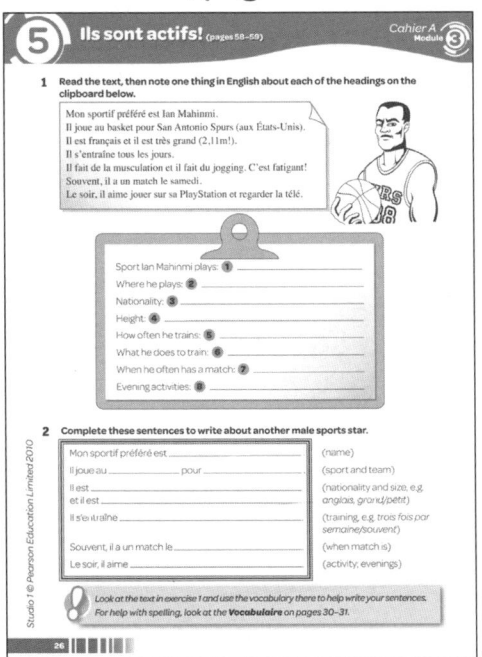

Answers
1 **1** basketball **2** America (for San Antonio Spurs)
   3 French **4** tall (2.11m) **5** every day
   6 weight lifting and jogging **7** Saturdays
   8 playing on his PlayStation and watching TV

Workbook B, page 26

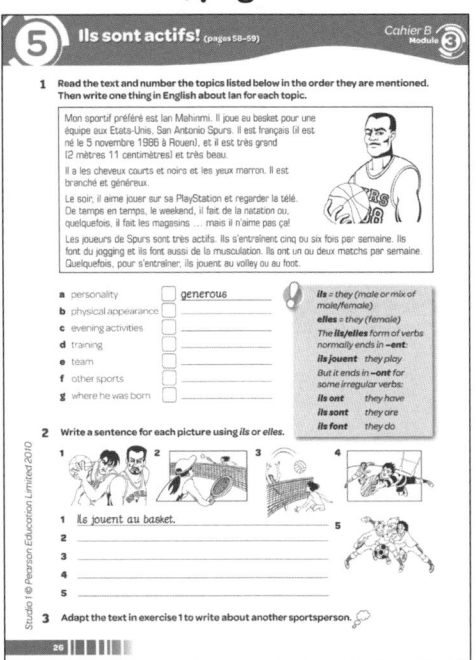

Answers
1 **a** 4 trendy/generous
   b 3 very tall and handsome; short, black hair and brown eyes
   c 5 plays on PlayStation and watches TV
   d 6 team trains five or six times a week; they jog and do weight training
   e 1 plays for San Antonio Spurs in USA
   f 7 team also plays volleyball or football
   g 2 born in Rouen on 5/11/86
2 **1** Ils jouent au basket.
   2 Elles jouent au tennis.
   3 Ils jouent au volley(ball).
   4 Ils jouent au rugby.
   5 Elles jouent au foot(ball).

Bilan et Révisions (Pupil Book pp. 60–61)

Mes passetemps 3

Bilan
Pupils use this checklist to review language covered in the module, working on it in pairs in class or on their own at home. Encourage them to follow up any areas of weakness they identify. There are Target Setting Sheets included in the Assessment Pack, and an opportunity for pupils to record their own levels and targets on the *J'avance* page in the Workbook, p. 29. You can also use the *Bilan* checklist as an end-of-module plenary option.

Révisions
These revision exercises can be used for assessment purposes or for pupils to practise before tackling the assessment tasks in the Resource & Assessment File.

Resources
CD 2, track 17
Cahier d'exercices A & B, pages 27 & 28

1 Écoute et note la bonne lettre. (1–6) (AT 1.3)
Listening. Pupils listen to six conversations and identify the pair of pictures for each one, writing the appropriate letter. You could extend the AT level of the activity to 1.4 by asking pupils to also note the expression of frequency used each time.

Audioscript CD 2 track 17

1 – Qu'est-ce que tu fais, le soir ou le weekend? Tu regardes la télévision?
 – Oui, tous les soirs, je regarde la télé.
 – Tu fais aussi du sport?
 – J'aime le tennis. En été, je joue au tennis.

2 – Qu'est-ce que tu fais, le soir ou le weekend? Tu envoies des SMS?
 – Ah, oui! J'envoie tout le temps des SMS.
 – Et qu'est-ce que tu fais aussi?
 – De temps en temps, je fais du vélo. J'aime faire du vélo!

3 – Qu'est-ce que tu fais, le soir ou le weekend?
 – Euh ... Quelquefois, je télécharge de la musique.
 – Ah bon? Tu télécharges de la musique? Et qu'est-ce que tu fais aussi?
 – Une fois par semaine, je joue au basket. C'est génial, le basket!

4 – Qu'est-ce que tu fais, le soir ou le weekend?
 – Quand il fait beau, je fais de l'équitation.
 – De l'équitation! Et quand il pleut?
 – Quand il pleut, je joue sur mon ordinateur. J'adore mon ordi!

5 – Qu'est-ce que tu fais, le soir ou le weekend?
 – Moi, j'adore la natation! Je fais tous les jours de la natation!
 – Et qu'est-ce que tu fais aussi?
 – Le samedi matin, je retrouve mes amis en ville. C'est cool!

6 – Qu'est-ce que tu fais, le soir ou le weekend?
 – D'habitude, je fais les magasins. J'adore faire les magasins!
 – Et à part ça, qu'est-ce que tu fais?
 – Souvent, je joue au volleyball. J'adore ça aussi!

Answers
1 d 2 a 3 c 4 f 5 b 6 e

2 En tandem. Interviewe ton/ta camarade. Change les mots soulignés. (AT 2.3)
Speaking. In pairs: pupils take it in turn to ask and answer questions about which activities they do in the evening and at the weekend. A sample exchange is supplied, with the details to be changed underlined. You could extend the AT level to 2.4 by asking pupils to add opinions and extra detail, such as when or how often they do things.

3 Lis le texte et trouve les quatre phrases correctes. (AT 3.4)
Reading. Pupils read the text and the eight English statements about it. They identify the four statements that are correct.

Answers
1, 3, 5, 8

4 Écris un court paragraphe sur tes passetemps. (AT 4.2–4)
Writing. Pupils write a short paragraph on their own leisure activities. A list of points to include is supplied. To achieve a higher AT level, pupils should also write about someone else.

… Bilan et Révisions   Mes passetemps 3

Workbook A, page 27

Answers
1 1 C2 2 F4 3 B3 4 E4 5 A6 6 D1
   7 C3 8 F2

Workbook A, page 28

Answers
1 a 4 b 2 c 5 d 6 e 1 f 3 g 7 h 4 i 8
2 1 Enzo is **19**.
   2 He does parkour on **Saturdays**.
   3 He does parkour with his **friends**.
   4 He lives in **Paris**.
   5 He **doesn't like** football and rugby.
   6 He likes parkour and **snowboarding**.
   7 In the **evenings**, he plays on his PlayStation.
   8 **At the weekend**, he likes hanging out with his friends.

95

3 Mes passetemps Bilan et Révisions

Workbook B, page 27

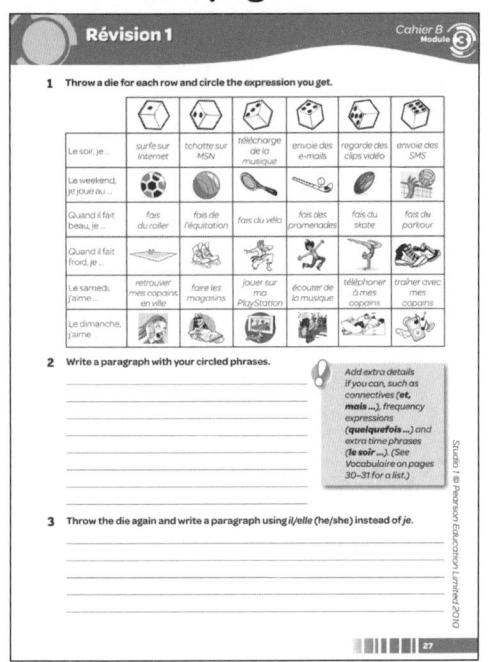

Workbook B, page 28

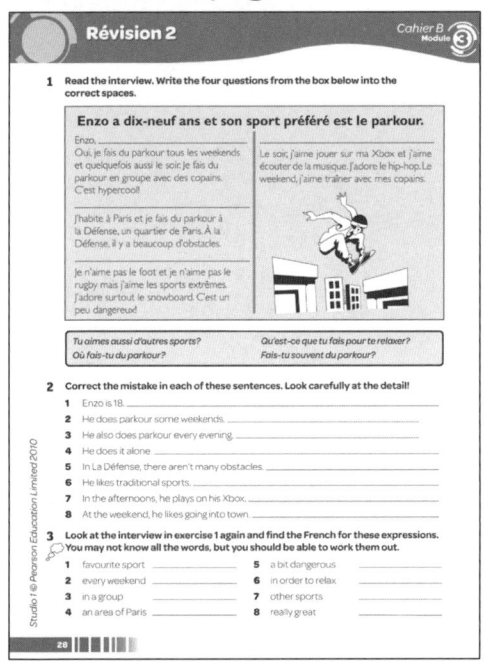

Answers
1–3 (Answers will vary.)

Answers
1 Fais-tu souvent du parkour?
Où fais-tu du parkour?
Tu aimes aussi d'autres sports?
Qu'est-ce que tu fais pour te relaxer?

2 1 Enzo is 19.
   2 He does parkour every weekend.
   3 He also does parkour sometimes in the evening.
   4 He does it with a group of friends.
   5 In La Défense, there are a lot of obstacles.
   6 He likes extreme sports.
   7 In the evening, he plays on his Xbox.
   8 At the weekend, he likes hanging out with his friends.

3 1 sport préféré **2** tous les weekends
   3 en groupe **4** un quartier de Paris
   5 un peu dangereux **6** pour te relaxer
   7 d'autres sports **8** hypercool

3 En plus: J'adore les sports extrêmes!
Mes passetemps
(Pupil Book pp. 62–63)

Learning objectives
- Talking about extreme sports
- Developing writing skills

Grammar
- possessive adjectives (*son/sa/ses*)

Key language
Review of language from the module
les sports extrêmes
j'adore faire du snowboard
C'est hypercool!
impressionnant(e)

PLTS
S Self-managers

Cross-curricular
ICT: word processing

Resources
ActiveTeach:
p.063 Assignment 3
p.063 Assignment 3: prep

Starter
Aim
To review the possessive pronouns *mon, ma, mes*

Write up the following. Pupils work in pairs. Give them two minutes to complete the table with their own preferences.

Mes sports préférés	
Mon sportif/Ma sportive préféré(e)	
Ma matière préférée	
Mon groupe préféré	

Hear some answers. Award a point to anyone who has an answer which no one else has come up with. Reward the pupils with the most points at the end.

1 Lis le blog en 30 secondes. Choisis le bon titre en anglais pour chaque paragraphe. (AT 3.4)
Reading. Give pupils 30 seconds to read the blog. They then choose the correct English heading for each paragraph. Draw pupils' attention to the tip box on reading for gist.

Answers
Paragraph 1: c   Paragraph 5: g
Paragraph 2: e   Paragraph 6: f
Paragraph 3: a   Paragraph 7: b
Paragraph 4: d

2 Trouve cinq mots nouveaux dans le texte. Devine ce que c'est en anglais et explique pourquoi. (AT 3.4)
Reading. Pupils identify five new words in the text in exercise 1 and try to work out what they mean, giving reasons for their deductions.

Studio Grammaire: possessive adjectives (*son/sa/ses*)
Use the *Studio Grammaire* box to cover the possessive adjectives *son, sa* and *ses*.

3 Relis le texte. Copie et complète les phrases. (AT 3.4)
Reading. Pupils re-read the text in exercise 1, then copy and complete the sentences summarising it in French.

Answers
1 Elle s'appelle **Maelys**.
2 Son groupe préféré s'appelle **les BB Brunes**.
3 En hiver, son sport préféré, c'est **le snowboard**.
4 En été, ses sports préférés sont **le skate et le roller**.
5 Sa ville s'appelle **Chamonix**.
6 Sa meilleure copine s'appelle **Natascha**.

4 Lis les phrases. Qui est-ce? Choisis la bonne réponse. (AT 3.4)
Reading. Pupils re-read the text in exercise 1. They then read the sentences and decide who is being described in each one. The answers are supplied in random order.

Answers
1 Maelys et sa famille   5 Charles Gagnon
2 Maelys   6 Julien Cudot
3 Maelys et ses copains   7 Maelys et Natascha
4 Maelys et son frère   8 les parents de Maelys

5 Copie et améliore le texte. (AT 4.4)
PLTS S

Writing. Read together through the tip box on language features used in an extended text. Encourage pupils to create and add to a checklist like this to refer to whenever they do a piece of extended writing. Pupils identify these features in the text in exercise 1. They rewrite the short text

3 Mes passetemps   En plus: J'adore les sports extrêmes!

supplied, improving it by using as many of the features listed as they can.

6 Écris un blog sur tes passetemps. (AT 4.4)

Writing. Pupils write a blog about their own leisure activities, using Maelys's text in exercise 1 as a model. A list of details to include is supplied. This task could be done on a computer. Also draw pupils' attention to the tip box on using a dictionary.

7 Vérifie et corrige ton texte. (AT 3.4)

Reading. Pupils check and correct their text, writing a second draft. A list of items to check is supplied for support.

Plenary

Ask the class to tell you the different forms of the French version of the possessive adjectives 'my' and 'his/her' (*mon/ma/mes* and *son/sa/ses*), saying when each one is used. Bring six pupils (a mixture of girls and boys) to the front of the class and give each of them a classroom item or school bag item to hold up. Ask the class to name the items (e.g. *un crayon*). The pupils holding the items then name them using the correct possessive form (e.g. *mon crayon*). The class then names them using *son/sa/ses* as appropriate (e.g. *son crayon*).

Worksheet 3.6 Les graphiques vivants

Worksheet 3.7 Les graphiques vivants. Prépa

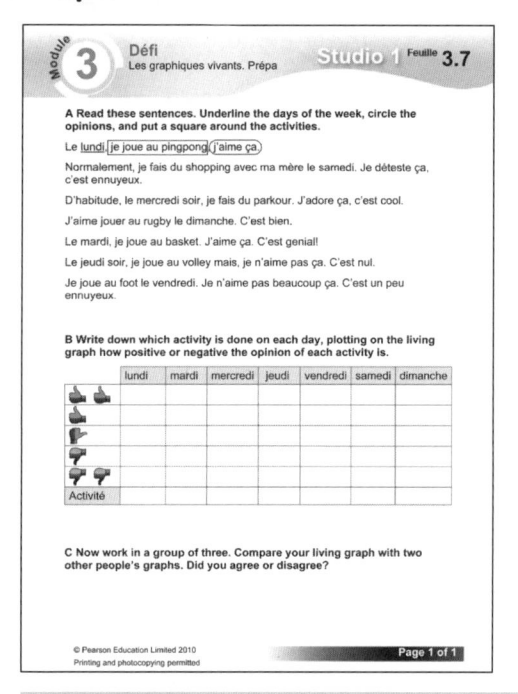

Answers

A Le lundi, je joue au ping-pong, j'aime ça.
Normalement, je fais du shopping avec ma mère le samedi. Je déteste ça, c'est ennuyeux.
D'habitude, le mercredi soir, je fais du parkour. J'adore ça, c'est cool.
J'aime jouer au rugby le dimanche. C'est bien.
Le mardi, je joue au basket. J'aime ça. C'est génial!
Le jeudi soir, je joue au volley, mais je n'aime pas ça. C'est nul.
Je joue au foot le vendredi. Je n'aime pas beaucoup ça. C'est un peu ennuyeux.

B & C (Answers will vary, as this is a personal interpretation.)

Studio Grammaire (Pupil Book pp. 64–65)

Mes passetemps 3

The *Studio Grammaire* section provides a more detailed summary of the key grammar covered in the module, along with further exercises to practise these points.

Grammar topics
- verbs – the present tense (regular –*er* verbs), *faire* (and *faire de* + a sport/activity), *jouer à* + a sport/game
- using verbs with nouns and infinitives
- saying 'they' in French

Verbs – the present tense

1 Find the parts of eleven –*er* verbs in the word snake. Then complete the sentences using the correct verbs.

Pupils identify the eleven present tense verbs in the word snake – there are some extra letters between words. They then complete the gap-fill sentences using the appropriate verbs.

Answers
parle, surfes, envoie, regarde, écoutes, télécharge, joue, tchatte, parles, envoies, regardes
1 Je **joue** sur ma PlayStation.
2 Tu **surfes** sur Internet tous les soirs!
3 Il **tchatte** sur MSN.
4 Elle **envoie** des e-mails.
5 Tu **regardes** un DVD?
6 Je **parle** avec mes copains sur mon portable.
7 Tu **écoutes** de la musique sur ton iPod?
8 On **regarde** des clips vidéo.

2 Write three sentences in French, each using one of the leftover verbs from exercise 1.

Pupils write three sentences, each using a different verb from those not used in the sentences from exercise 1. These are: *télécharge, parles, envoies*.

faire

3 Write six sentences in French, using the correct form of *faire de*.

Pupils use the picture and word prompts to write six sentences about sports, paying attention to the form of *faire* they need to use each time, as well as to the form of *de*.

Answers
1 Je fais du judo.
2 Il fait de la natation.
3 On fait de l'équitation.
4 Tu fais de la danse.
5 Mon frère fait du skate.
6 Ma sœur fait de la gymnastique.

jouer à

4 Translate the following sentences into French, using the correct form of *jouer à*.

Pupils translate the sentences into French, paying attention to the form of *jouer* they need to use each time, as well as to the form of *à*. Some of the sports and games are glossed for support.

Answers
1 Je joue au billard.
2 Est-ce que tu joues au tennis de table?/Tu joues au tennis de table?
3 Elle joue au golf.
4 Il joue aux cartes.
5 Je joue aux échecs.
6 On joue à la bataille.

Using verbs with nouns and infinitives

5 Copy and complete the grid.

Pupils copy and complete the grid with the correct verb forms.

Answers

j'aime + noun	*j'aime* + infinitive	present tense verb
J'aime le tennis.	J'aime jouer au tennis.	Je joue au tennis.
J'aime la natation.	J'aime faire de la natation.	Je fais de la natation.
J'aime la télé.	J'aime regarder la télé.	Je regarde la télé.
J'aime la radio.	J'aime écouter la radio.	J'écoute la radio.
J'aime mes copains.	J'aime retrouver mes copains.	Je retrouve mes copains en ville.

3 Mes passetemps   Studio Grammaire

6 Write six sentences about the activities you do. Use the three ways of talking about activities.

Pupils write six sentences about their own leisure activities, using the three different ways covered in this section: present tense verb; *j'aime* + noun, *j'aime* +infinitive.

Saying 'they' in French

7 Write sentences using the pictures and the *ils/elles* form of the verb.

Using the picture prompts, pupils write sentences with the *ils/elles* form of the verb and using *ils* or *elles* as appropriate.

Answers
1 Ils jouent au rugby.
2 Elles font de la gymnastique.
3 Ils regardent la télé(vision).
4 Elles écoutent de la musique.
5 Ils font de la natation.

Mes passetemps 3 — À toi (Pupil Book pages 122–123)

Self-access reading and writing

A Reinforcement

1 Complète les phrases. (AT 3.2)
Reading. Pupils match the sentence halves.

Answers
1 Je regarde des clips vidéo.
2 Je parle avec mes amis.
3 J'envoie des e-mails.
4 Je joue au rugby.
5 Je fais du vélo.
6 J'envoie des SMS avec mon portable.

2 Regarde la chambre de Zahra. Trouve les deux phrases fausses. (AT 3.3)
Reading. Pupils look at the picture of Zahra's bedroom. They then read the eight sentences about it and identify the two sentences that are false (i.e. which mention items not shown in the picture).

Answers
3 and 6

3 Regarde la chambre de Jamel. Écris six phrases pour Jamel. (AT 4.3)
Writing. Pupils write six sentences describing Jamel's hobbies, based on the picture supplied.

Answers
(Any six from:)
Je joue sur ma PlayStation.
Je joue au foot(ball).
Je joue au billard.
Je fais du judo.
Je fais du patin à glace.
Je fais du skate.
Je joue de la guitare.

B Extension

1 Trouve un copain/une copine anglais(e) pour chaque Français(e). (AT 3.4)
Reading. Pupils read about the activities that the people on the penpal site like, then match each French person to an appropriate English penpal.

Answers
Axelle et Tom
Rémi et Natasha
Tariq et Nassim
Clémence et Zoe
Laurine et Emma

2 Relis les textes français de l'exercice 1. C'est quelle(s) personne(s)? (AT 3.4)
Reading. Pupils read the French texts again and identify the person/people being described in each of the six sentences.

Answers
1 Laurine 2 Rémi 3 Clémence 4 Rémi et Tariq
5 Axelle et Clémence 6 Axelle et Tariq

3 Écris des e-mails à *trouvedesamis.fr* pour Nadia, Max et toi. (AT 4.4)
Writing. Using the picture prompts, pupils write e-mails on behalf of Nadia and Max to the penpal site in exercise 1. They then write an e-mail presenting themselves on the site.

Answers
(Possible answers:)
Nadia: J'aime/J'adore jouer au basket et faire du patin à glace. J'aime aussi envoyer des SMS. Je n'aime pas jouer au foot(ball).
Max: J'aime/J'adore jouer sur ma PlayStation, faire du vélo et jouer au rugby, mais je n'aime pas nager/faire de la natation.

Module 4: Ma zone (Pupil Book pp. 68–87)

Unit & Learning objectives	PoS & Framework objectives	Key language	Grammar and other language features
1 Là où j'habite (pp. 70–71) Talking about your town/village Using *il y a …/il n'y a pas de …*	**2.1b** memorising **2.1d** previous knowledge **2.2a** listen for gist **2.2c** respond appropriately **2.2f** initiate/sustain conversations **2.2h** redraft to improve writing **2.1/Y7** Reading – main points and detail **2.4/Y7** Writing – (b) building text	*Qu'est-ce qu'il y a … ? Il y a … un café, une patinoire, des magasins, etc. C'est … bien, super, ennuyeux, trop petit, etc. Je pense que … À mon avis … Tu es d'accord? Oui, je suis d'accord. Non, je ne suis pas d'accord.*	**G** *il y a …/il n'y a pas de …*
2 Perdu dans le parc d'attractions! (pp. 72–73) Giving directions Understanding when to use *tu* and *vous*	**2.1c** knowledge of language **2.2a** listen for gist **2.2c** respond appropriately **2.2e** ask and answer questions **4f** language for interest/enjoyment **4g** language for a range of purposes **1.5/Y7** Speaking – (b) expression/non-verbal techniques	*Où est/sont … ? C'est … à gauche, tout droit, etc. entre, derrière, devant le manège, la soucoupe volante, les autos tamponneuses, etc.*	**G** *tu* and *vous* – *Où est … ?/Où sont … ?*
3 Le weekend (pp. 74–75) Talking about where you go Using *à* + the definite article	**2.2a** listen for gist **2.2f** initiate/sustain conversations **2.2j** adapt previously learned language **4b** communicate in pairs, etc. **4e** use a range of resources **4f** language for interest/enjoyment **4.4/Y7** Language – sentence formation	Review of vocabulary for places in town (from Unit 2) *d'habitude normalement quelquefois tous les weekends*	**G** *à* + the definite article **G** *aller* (present tense) – speaking/writing skills: using expressions of frequency and opinions to extend sentences
4 Coucou! (pp. 76–77) Asking someone to go somewhere Using *je veux/tu veux* + infinitive	**2.1d** previous knowledge **2.2d** pronunciation and intonation **2.2f** initiate/sustain conversations **2.2g** write clearly and coherently **2.2i** reuse language they have met **3c** apply grammar **1.3/Y7** Listening – (a) interpreting intonation and tone **1.3/Y7** Speaking – (b) using intonation and tone **2.3/Y7** Reading – text features **2.5/Y7** Writing – different text types **4.5/Y7** Language – (b) modal verbs	*je veux, tu veux, etc. Tu veux aller (au cinéma) (samedi soir)? Bonne idée! C'est super top. etc. Oui, je veux bien. Non, je n'ai pas envie. Si tu veux. Non merci.*	**G** *vouloir* + infinitive

Ma zone 4

Unit & Learning objectives	PoS & Framework objectives	Key language	Grammar and other language features
5 Qu'est-ce qu'on peut faire à …? (pp. 78–79) Saying what you can do in town Using *on peut* + infinitive	**2.1b** memorising **2.1d** previous knowledge **2.1e** use reference materials **2.2e** ask and answer questions **2.2i** reuse language they have met **4e** use a range of resources **1.2/Y7** Listening – unfamiliar language **1.4/Y7** Speaking – (b) using prompts **4.5/Y7** Language – (b) modal verbs **5.2** Strategies – memorising **5.8** Strategies – evaluating and improving	*Qu'est-ce qu'on peut faire à … ? je peux, tu peux, on peut … aller au concert faire du bowling manger au restaurant* etc.	**G** *pouvoir* + infinitive – speaking skills: using model texts as a source of language; including connectives and opinions – writing skills: avoiding complicated language; using a dictionary
Bilan et Révisions (pp. 80–81) Pupils' checklist and practice exercises			
En plus: Destination France (pp. 82–83) Facts about France Researching a region of France	**2.2a** listen for gist **3e** different countries/cultures **4a** use language in the classroom, etc. **4c** use more complex language **4e** use a range of resources **4f** language for interest/enjoyment **3.2/Y7** Culture – (b) challenging stereotypes	Review of language from the module *Il y a … des montagnes, des rivières, des plateaux,* etc. *Les villes principales sont …*	– listening skills: anticipating what you might hear – writing skills: using *si* clauses to extend sentences
Studio Grammaire (pp. 84–85) Detailed grammar summary and practice exercises			**G** *aller* **G** looking for patterns in language **G** modal verbs
À toi (pp. 124–125) Self-access reading and writing at two levels			

Ma Zone 4 — 1 Là où j'habite (Pupil Book pp. 70–71)

Learning objectives
- Talking about your town/village
- Using *il y a …/il n'y a pas de …*

Framework objectives
2.1/Y7 Reading – main points and detail: ex. 5
2.4/Y7 Writing – (b) building text: ex. 7

Grammar
- *il y a …/il n'y a pas de …*

Key language
Qu'est-ce qu'il y a … ?
Il y a …
un café
un centre commercial
un centre de loisirs
un château
un cinéma
un hôtel
un marché
un parc
un restaurant
un stade
une église
une patinoire
une piscine
des magasins
des musées
Il n'y a pas de (café).
Tu aimes ta ville/ton village?
Je pense que …
À mon avis, …
c'est …
bien/super/joli/intéressant/ennuyeux
vraiment nul/trop petit
Tu es d'accord?
Oui, je suis d'accord.
Non, je ne suis pas d'accord.

PLTS
T Team workers

Resources
CD 2, tracks 18–20
Accès Studio pages 22–23
Cahier d'exercices A & B, page 32
ActiveTeach:
p.070 Flashcards
p.070 Thinking skills
p.071 Learning skills

Accès Studio Unit 10 (pp. 22–23) can be used with this unit to review or introduce vocabulary to talk about where you live.

Starter 1
Aim
To practise reading strategies; To review the indefinite article

Write up the following, jumbling the order of the second column. Give pupils three minutes to match up the French and English.

un centre commercial	a shopping centre
un centre de loisirs	a leisure centre
un château	a castle
un marché	a market
un stade	a stadium
un parc	a park
une piscine	a swimming pool
des magasins	some shops
des musées	some museums

Check answers, asking pupils how they worked them out. Ask pupils to tell you what *un*, *une* and *des* mean and when they are used.

1 Écoute. Qu'est-ce qu'il y a dans la ville/le village? Écris la bonne lettre. (1–10) (AT 1.2)
Listening. Pupils listen to ten conversations and identify the place mentioned in each, writing the appropriate letter.

Audioscript CD 2 track 18
1 – Qu'est-ce qu'il y a dans ton village?
  – Dans mon village, il y a une église.
2 – Qu'est-ce qu'il y a dans ta ville?
  – Dans ma ville, il y a un stade.
3 – Qu'est-ce qu'il y a dans ton village?
  – Dans mon village, il y a une piscine.
4 – Qu'est-ce qu'il y a dans ta ville?
  – Dans ma ville, il y a un marché.
5 – Qu'est-ce qu'il y a dans ta ville?
  – Dans ma ville, il y a un château.
6 – Qu'est-ce qu'il y a dans ta ville?
  – Dans ma ville, il y a des musées.
7 – Qu'est-ce qu'il y a dans ta ville?
  – Dans ma ville, il y a une patinoire.
8 – Qu'est-ce qu'il y a dans ta ville?
  – Dans ma ville, il y a un centre de loisirs.
9 – Qu'est-ce qu'il y a dans ta ville?
  – Dans ma ville, il y a un centre commercial.
10 – Qu'est-ce qu'il y a dans ta ville?
  – Dans ma ville, il y a des magasins.

Answers
1 f 2 e 3 g 4 d 5 a 6 j 7 h 8 b 9 c
10 i

Studio Grammaire: *il y a … /il n'y a pas de …*
Use the *Studio Grammaire* box to cover *il y a (un/une/des)…* and *il n'y a pas de …*

1 Là où j'habite   **Ma zone 4**

2 Écoute. Qu'est-ce qu'il y a? Qu'est-ce qu'il n'y a pas? Note les informations en anglais. (1–5) (AT 1.2)

Listening. Pupils listen to the descriptions of towns and identify which amenities each town has and doesn't have.

Audioscript   CD 2 track 19

1 *Il y a une piscine, mais il n'y a pas de patinoire.*
2 *Il y a des magasins, mais il n'y a pas de centre de loisirs.*
3 *Il y a un centre commercial, mais il n'y a pas de stade.*
4 *Il y a un marché, mais il n'y a pas de musée.*
5 *Il y a un château, mais il n'y a pas d'église.*

Answers
1 swimming pool, no ice rink
2 shops, no sports centre
3 shopping centre, no stadium
4 market, no museum
5 castle, no church

3 En tandem. Décris une ville. Ton/ta camarade dit la bonne lettre. (AT 2.2)

Speaking. In pairs: pupils take it in turn to describe a town using the picture prompts supplied. The other pupil identifies the town by giving the appropriate letter. An example dialogue is given.

Starter 2
Aim
To review the language for places in town

Prompt with places in town (*piscine, musées, église, château, stade, magasins, patinoire, centre de loisirs, centre commercial, marché*), e.g. *Il y a … piscine.* Pupils respond with the complete sentence. (*Il y a une piscine.*) Include negative prompts, e.g. *Il n'y a pas … piscine.*

Alternative Starter 2:
Use ActiveTeach p. 070 Flashcards to review and practise the language for buildings in town.

4 Écoute et écris la bonne lettre/les bonnes lettres. (1–5) (AT 1.4)

Listening. Pupils listen to five conversations about towns and identify the opinion given in each, writing the appropriate letter.

Audioscript   CD 2 track 20

1 – *Tu aimes ta ville?*
 – *Oui, à mon avis, c'est bien.*
2 – *Tu aimes ton village?*
 – *Non, je pense que c'est ennuyeux.*
3 – *Aimes-tu ton village?*
 – *Oui, à mon avis, c'est un endroit intéressant.*
4 – *Tu aimes ta ville?*
 – *Oui, je pense que c'est super et intéressant aussi.*
5 – *Aimes-tu ta ville?*
 – *Non, à mon avis, c'est trop petit. C'est vraiment nul. Tu es d'accord?*
 – *Ben non, je ne suis pas d'accord, je pense que c'est bien.*

Answers
1 a   2 d   3 c   4 b, c   5 f, e; a

R Pupils working in pairs take it in turn to prompt with one of the expressions from exercise 4 and to draw the appropriate face symbol (smiley or sad).

5 Lis et note: vrai (V) ou faux (F)? (AT 3.4)

Reading. Pupils read the four chatroom entries. They then read the six sentences in English about the entries and write V if the sentence is true or F if it is false. *joli* is glossed for support.

Answers
1 V   2 F   3 F   4 V   5 V   6 F

6 En tandem. Fais quatre conversations: une *très* positive, une *assez* positive, une *assez* négative et une *très* négative. (AT 2.4)

PLTS T

Speaking. In pairs: pupils put together four conversations about towns – one very positive, one quite positive, one quite negative and one very negative. A key language box is supplied.

7 Écris un paragraphe sur ta ville/ton village. (AT 4.4)

Writing. Pupils write a paragraph about their own town or village. A writing frame is supplied for support. When pupils have finished their work, ask them to check it for errors and to identify two ways they could improve the content (e.g. using connectives, intensifiers, adjectives, etc.). They then do a second draft.

4 Ma zone — 1 Là où j'habite

Plenary

Ask the class: *Tu aimes ta ville/ton village?* Pupils respond using the opinion phrases from exercise 6. Prompt them to say whether they agree with one another and to justify their opinions with *Il y a …* and *Il n'y a pas de …* to review the vocabulary of the unit. Encourage them to include intensifiers in their opinions.

Workbook A, page 32

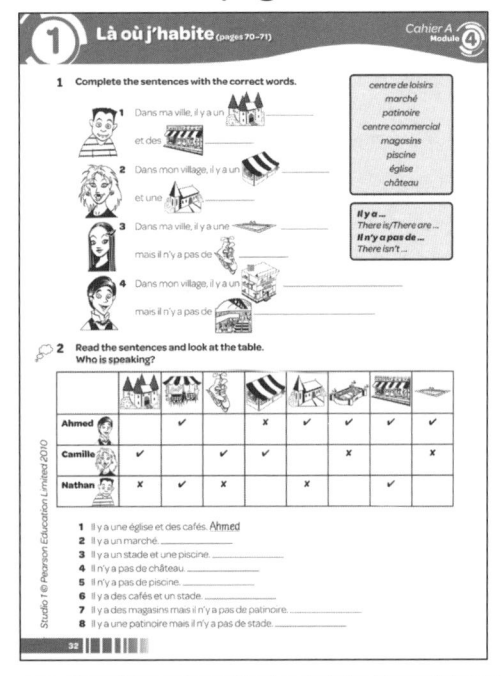

Answers

1.
   1. château; magasins
   2. marché; église
   3. piscine; patinoire
   4. centre de loisirs; centre commercial
2.
   1. Ahmed 2. Camille 3. Ahmed 4. Nathan
   5. Camille 6. Ahmed 7. Nathan 8. Camille

Workbook B, page 32

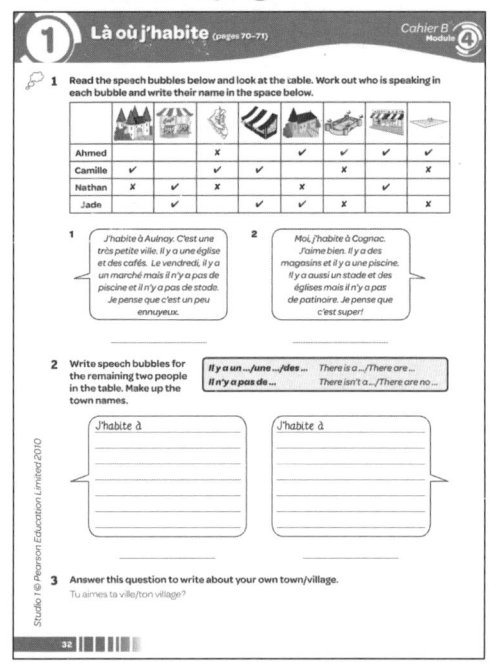

Answers

1. **1** Jade **2** Ahmed
2. (Example answers:)
   Camille: J'habite à Montargis. C'est une petite ville. Il y a un château, une patinoire et un marché mais il n'y a pas de stade et il n'y a pas de piscine.
   Nathan: J'habite à Néré. C'est un village. Il y a un café et des magasins mais il n'y a pas de château, il n'y a pas d'église et il n'y a pas de patinoire. C'est nul!

Worksheet 4.1 Mnemonics

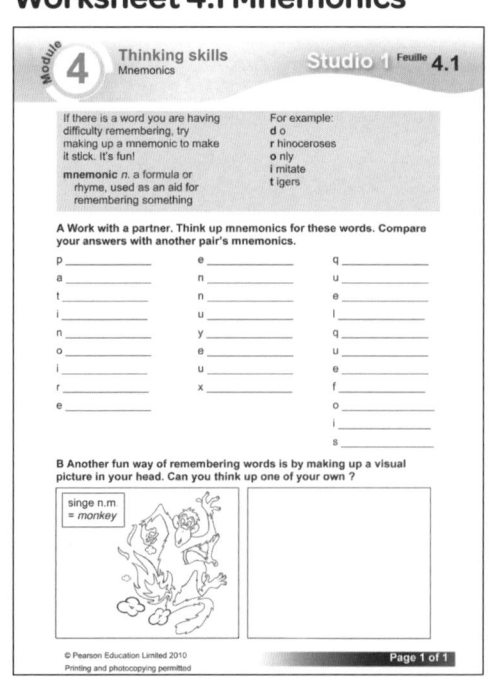

Answers

A & **B** (Answers will vary.)

Worksheet 4.2 Using a dictionary (ii)

Answers

A 1 baguette (f.)   stick (often stick of French bread), baton
    2 couverture (f.)   blanket
    3 siège (m.)   seat
    4 clavier (m.)   keyboard
    5 truite (f.)   trout
    6 manège (m.)   merry-go-round

B 1 door   n. porte f.
    2 branch   n. branche f.
    3 window   n. fenêtre f.
    4 squirrel   n. écureuil m.

C 1 a Did you enjoy your stay?   noun   séjour
    b I can't stay long.   verb   rester
    2 a You are very kind.   adjective   gentil
    b What kind of racket do you use?   noun   sorte
    3 a It was an excellent play.   noun   pièce
    b Does she play tennis?   verb   jouer
    4 a I watch TV every night.   verb   regarder
    b Do you like my new watch?   noun   montre

2 Perdu dans le parc d'attractions!

(Pupil Book pp. 72–73)

Ma Zone 4

Learning objectives
- Giving directions
- Understanding when to use *tu* and *vous*

Framework objectives
1.5/Y7 Speaking – (b) expression/non-verbal techniques: ex. 3

Grammar
tu and *vous*

Key language
Pardon…
Où est…?
Où sont…?

C'est…
à gauche
à droite
tout droit
au carrefour
entre
derrière
devant
le bateau pirate
le café
le Cheval de Troie
le manège
le restaurant
le petit train
le toboggan géant
le trampoline magique
la grotte mystérieuse

la rivière enchantée
la soucoupe volante
l'hôtel
les autos tamponneuses
les chaises volantes

PLTS
R Reflective learners

Resources
CD 2, tracks 21–22
Cahier d'exercices A & B, page 33
ActiveTeach:
p.073 Class activity
p.074 Video 7
p.074 Video worksheet 7

Starter 1
Aim
To review *être*

Write up the following. Give pupils three minutes to unscramble the parts of the verb *être* and to translate the verbs into English.

1 ej ussi **2** leel ste **3** lis nots **4** li tes
5 selle tons

Answers: **1** *je suis* – I am **2** *elle est* – she is
3 *ils sont* – they are (male) **4** *il est* – he is
5 *elles sont* – they are (female)

Check answers. Ask pupils to confirm which subjects are used with *est* and *sont*.

1 Écoute. Écris la bonne lettre et la bonne direction. (1–8) (AT 1.2)
Listening. Pupils listen to eight conversations in which people are asking for directions in a theme park. For each conversation, they identify the correct picture (writing the appropriate letter) and draw the appropriate direction symbol.

Audioscript — CD 2 track 21

1 – Où est le petit train?
– C'est à gauche.
2 – Où est la rivière enchantée?
– Tout droit.
3 – Où sont les chaises volantes?
– À droite.
4 – Où est le restaurant?
– À droite.
5 – Où est l'hôtel?
– L'hôtel? Au carrefour.
6 – Où sont les autos tamponneuses?
– À gauche.
7 – Où est le manège?
– À gauche.
8 – Où est la soucoupe volante?
– Tout droit.

Answers
1 b ⇐ **2** e ⇑ **3** h ⇒ **4** a ⇒ **5** d ✽
6 g ⇐ **7** c ⇐ **8** f ⇑

2 En tandem. Quelle est la question? Demande le chemin pour chaque attraction. (AT 2.2)
Speaking. In pairs: pupils take it in turn to ask directions to the theme park attractions in exercise 1, using *Où est…* or *Où sont…?* as appropriate.

Studio Grammaire: *tu/vous*
Use the *Studio Grammaire* box to cover the difference between *tu* and *vous*.

3 En tandem. Fais deux conversations avec *tu* et deux avec *vous* au parc d'attractions. Change les détails soulignés. (AT 2.3)
Speaking. In pairs: pupils make up four conversations at the theme park, two using *tu* and two using *vous*. Two model conversations, with the details to be changed underlined, are supplied. Draw pupils' attention to the cultural note on the use of *monsieur/madame/mademoiselle*. You could suggest that pupils use gestures to reinforce the directions they give (pointing to the left for *à gauche*, etc.).

2 Perdu dans le parc d'attractions! Ma zone 4

Starter 2
Aim
To review vocabulary from the unit

Write up only the bold letters in the following, leaving a gap or drawing an underline for the text to be supplied by the pupils. Explain that these are the starting letters of the eight theme park features introduced in the last lesson. Give pupils three minutes working in pairs to write them all out, including the correct definite article for each. Then check answers.

[les] **a**[utos] **t**[amponneuses] [le] **r**[estaurant]
[la] **r**[ivière] **e**[nchantée] [le] **m**[anège]
[la] **s**[oucoupe] [volante] [l'] **h**[ôtel]
[les] **c**[haises] **v**[olantes] [le] **p**[etit] **t**[rain]

(Where there are two words, you can omit the initial letter of the second word to make it slightly more challenging.)

Alternative Starter 2:
Use ActiveTeach p. 073 Class activity to review and practise general sentences about town.

4 Écris le message en anglais. (AT 3.3)
Reading. Pupils translate the message into English, writing it out.

Answer
The restaurant is between the dodgems and the flying chairs, behind the merry-go-round, but in front of the little train.

5 Où vont-ils? Écoute et écris la bonne lettre. (1–8) (AT 1.3)
Listening. Pupils listen to eight conversations. For each conversation they identify the picture of the place being discussed, writing the appropriate letter.

Audioscript CD 2 track 22

1 – Où est (...), s'il vous plaît?
   – C'est devant le toboggan géant.
   – Merci, monsieur.
2 – S'il vous plaît, où est (...)?
   – C'est derrière le bateau pirate.
3 – Où est (...)?
   – Là voilà. Entre le bateau pirate et le café.
4 – Et où est (...)?
   – Devant le Cheval de Troie.
5 – Où est (...)?
   – C'est derrière le trampoline magique.
6 – S'il vous plaît, où est (...)?
   – C'est derrière le Cheval de Troie.
7 – Où est (...)?
   – Entre le toboggan géant et le Cheval de Troie. Derrière la grotte mystérieuse et devant l'hôtel.
   – Ah oui, génial. On y va?
8 – S'il vous plaît, où est (...)?
   – C'est derrière le café et devant le restaurant.
   – Merci, madame.

Answers
1 d 2 a 3 g 4 h 5 b 6 c 7 e 8 f

6 Regarde le plan et lis le message. C'est quelle attraction? (AT 3.4)
Reading. Pupils read the text message and, using the map in exercise 5, they follow the directions and work out which attraction they end up at.

Answer
le Cheval de Troie

R Pupils play a memory game in pairs. The first pupil closes his/her Pupil Book. The other says a letter from a to f and the first pupil tries to remember which theme park feature on the map in exercise 5 this letter represents. After four prompts, they change roles.

7 Tu es dans le parc d'attractions. Écris des SMS pour tes copains. (AT 4.3)
Writing. Pupils imagine they are in the theme park. Using the picture prompts supplied, they write texts to their friends to give them directions.

Answers
1 *Tu vas tout droit, puis tu tournes à gauche. Au carrefour, tu vas tout droit, puis tu tournes à droite. À tout de suite!*
2 *Tu tournes à gauche. Au carrefour, tu tournes à droite. Puis tu tournes à droite et ensuite, tu vas tout droit. À tout de suite!*
3 *Tu tournes à droite. Au carrefour, tu vas tout droit. Tu vas tout droit et puis tu tournes à gauche.*
4 *Tu vas tout droit. Au carrefour, tu tournes à gauche. Puis tu tournes à droite et ensuite, tu tournes à gauche.*

+ If you have a partner school in France, pupils could exchange brochures for local theme parks. Ask pupils to summarise what rides there are in the French theme park.

4 Ma zone 2 Perdu dans le parc d'attractions!

Plenary

PLTS R

Ask the class for ideas on what they think they could usefully spend time reviewing from Units 1 and 2 (vocabulary/grammar). Make a list of their suggestions and then get them to write down two areas covered in the list to focus on at home.

Then ask pupils to tell you the difference between the two words for 'you' in French, and when each is used. As a class, work out what the formal instructions would be for the first set of prompts in exercise 7, reminding them as necessary of the verb forms *allez* and *tournez*. Continue with the other three sets of prompts, this time allowing pupils to do more of the work. They should not refer to their answers to exercise 7, but work just from the prompts.

Answers

1

Le château, c'est C.

2 **1** droite **2** derrière **3** devant **4** gauche **5** tout **6** carrefour

Workbook A, page 33

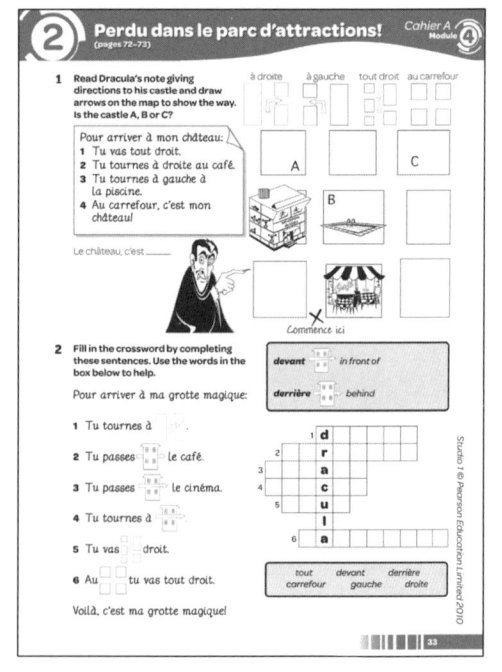

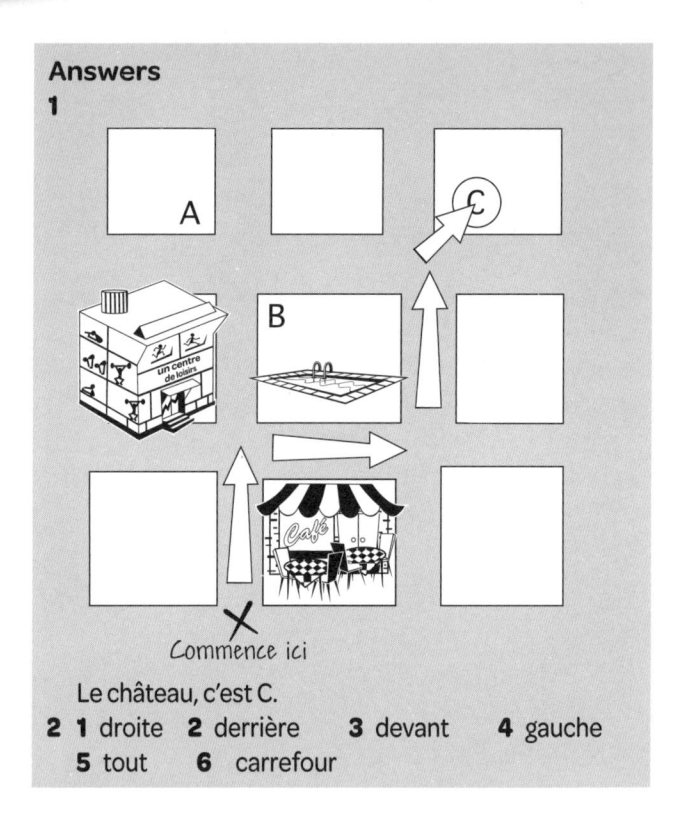

Workbook B, page 33

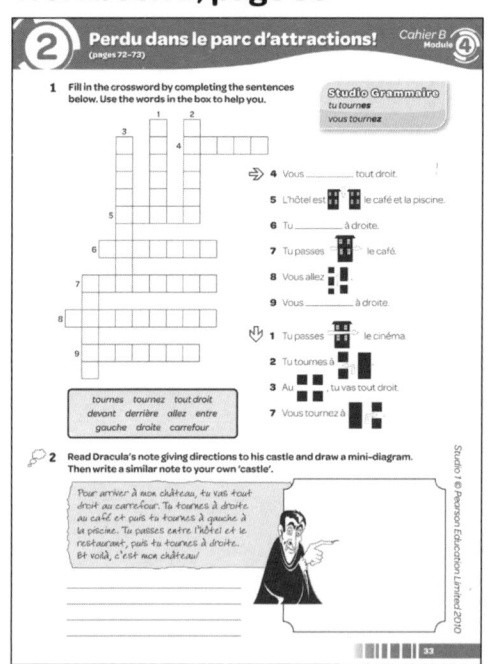

Answers

1 ➡ **4** allez **5** entre **6** tournes **7** derrière **8** tout droit **9** tournez

⬆ **1** devant **2** gauche **3** carrefour **4** droite

2 Perdu dans le parc d'attractions! — Ma zone 4

Video
Episode 7: Perdu dans la ville!
Samira and Hugo are working in StudioFR headquarters. Samira is wondering where Alex and Marielle are. Video worksheet 7 can be used in conjunction with this episode.

Answers to video worksheet (ActiveTeach)

1 A We learn about asking for directions and understanding them. But the original intention was to make a video about the town – it only turned out this way because Marielle got lost!
  B She is increasingly exasperated by Marielle's behaviour. She shakes her head, tuts and looks scornful.
  C [F3.1/2.2] (Examples of things that might come up:)
   – It seems very historic.
   – The pedestrian facilities seem very good.
   – It seems very 'green'.
   – The close-ups reveal that it is a bit dilapidated.

2 A [PLTS T/E] She thinks she's dippy and unreliable.
   – She says 'Of course it's you. I phoned you!'
   – She tuts when she hears she is lost.
   – She shakes her head when she hears she has lost Alex as well.
   – She is exasperated when she hears Marielle has no credit on her phone.
  B 'jar' is the abbreviation for 'jardin public' – park. Alex uses it.
  C à gauche, à droite, tout droit
  D – I don't know
   – Where are you?
   – Stay there.

3 A Because by the time Marielle gets to the park, Alex has already left.
  B Ils sont impossibles!
  C There are several cafés there and Marielle doesn't know which one Alex is in.
  D Tous les deux: au studio! Maintenant! – Both of you, get back to the studio! Now!

4 (Answers will vary.)

Ma zone 4

3 Le weekend (Pupil Book pp. 74–75)

Learning objectives
- Talking about where you go
- Using *à* + the definite article

Framework objectives
4.4/Y7 Language – sentence formation: ex. 3

Grammar
- *à* + the definite article
- *aller* (present tense)

Key language
Review of vocabulary for places in town (from Unit 2)
d'habitude
normalement
quelquefois
tous les weekends
J'aime ça./J'adore ça.

PLTS
I Independent enquirers

Cross-curricular
ICT: drawing a graph to show survey results

Resources
CD 2, track 23
Cahier d'exercices A & B, page 34
ActiveTeach:
p.074 Grammar
p.074 Grammar practice
p.074 Grammar skills
p.075 Grammar skills

Starter 1
Aim
To review *à* + the definite article

Write up the following as a model. Score through *le* and write *au* above it (*au cinéma*).

Le weekend, je vais …
le cinéma.

Ask pupils to translate the sentence. Then write up the following. Give pupils three minutes working in pairs to change all the definite articles to *à* + definite article. If necessary, go through and/or write up the different forms for reference.

Le weekend, je vais …
le café   *la piscine*
les magasins   *l'église*
la patinoire   *le centre de loisirs*
les musées   *le marché*

Alternative Starter 1:
Use ActiveTeach p. 074 Grammar practice to review and practise *à* + the definite article.

1 Lis les textes et réponds aux questions. (AT 3.3)
Reading. Pupils read the three texts and then answer the questions on them, giving the appropriate names.

Answers
1 *Emma and Alice* 2 *Magali* 3 *Emma and Alice*
4 *Magali* 5 *Magali* 6 *Nino* 7 *Nino*
8 *Emma and Alice*

Studio Grammaire: *à* + the definite article
Use the *Studio Grammaire* box to cover *à* + the definite article. There is more information and further practice on Pupil Book p. 84.

2 Écoute. Copie et complète le tableau. (1–4) (AT 1.3)
Listening. Pupils copy out the table. They listen to four conversations and complete the table with the details of where each person goes and who with.

Audioscript CD 2 track 23

1 – *Tu vas où, le weekend, Lara?*
  – *Le weekend, je vais au centre commercial avec mes copines.*
2 – *Et toi, Aurélien, tu vas où, le weekend?*
  – *Euh … Normalement, le weekend, je vais à la piscine avec mes copains.*
3 – *Tu vas où le weekend, Sarah?*
  – *Je vais au marché avec mes parents.*
4 – *Et toi, Youssuf? Tu vas où, le weekend?*
  – *Le weekend, je vais au centre de loisirs avec mon frère et ma sœur.*

Answers

	Où?	Avec qui?
Lara	centre commercial	copines
Aurélien	piscine	copains
Sarah	marché	parents
Youssuf	centre de loisirs	frère et sœur

112

3 Le weekend   Ma zone 4

> **Studio Grammaire:** *aller* (present tense)
> Use the *Studio Grammaire* box to cover the irregular verb *aller* (present tense). There is more information and further practice on Pupil Book p. 84.

3 En tandem. Fais des dialogues. (AT 2.4)
Speaking. In pairs: pupils make up dialogues using the picture prompts. They take it in turn to ask and say what they do at the weekend and who with. Key language is supplied. Before they start, draw their attention to the tip box on including expressions of frequency and opinions.

Starter 2
Aim
To review talking about going to places in town

Write up the following, jumbling the order of the words in each sentence. Give pupils three minutes to write out each sentence in the right order. You can include capital letters and punctuation for support, if necessary.

1 *je vais au stade avec mon frère*
2 *il va à la piscine avec son copain*
3 *elle va aux magasins avec ses parents*

Check answers, asking pupils to translate the sentences into English.

4 Lis le texte et fais un graphique. (AT 3.4)
Reading. Pupils read the text on the findings of a survey and draw a graph of the results. This could be done on a computer. *voici* is glossed for support.

5 Fais le même sondage dans ta classe. (AT 2.4)
PLTS
Speaking. Pupils carry out the survey from exercise 4, asking other members of the class where they go at the weekend.

6 Écris une description de tes résultats. (AT 4.4)
Writing. Pupils write a description of their survey results, using the text in exercise 4 as a model.

7 À trois. Jeu du Weekend. (AT 2.4)
Speaking. In threes: pupils play the board game. The rules and the instructions to use while playing are supplied. Some vocabulary is glossed for support.

Plenary
Play a chain game round the class to practise *à* + the definite article. Start it off: *Le weekend, je vais au cinéma.* The next person repeats what you have said and adds a different place (e.g. *... et je vais à la piscine.*). Continue round the class. If someone can't remember the chain, makes a mistake or can't think of anything to add, he/she sits down and the chain starts again. If you have time, play it again, using *on va ...*

Alternative Plenary:
Use ActiveTeach p. 074 Grammar practice to review and practise *aller* and *faire*.

Workbook A, page 34

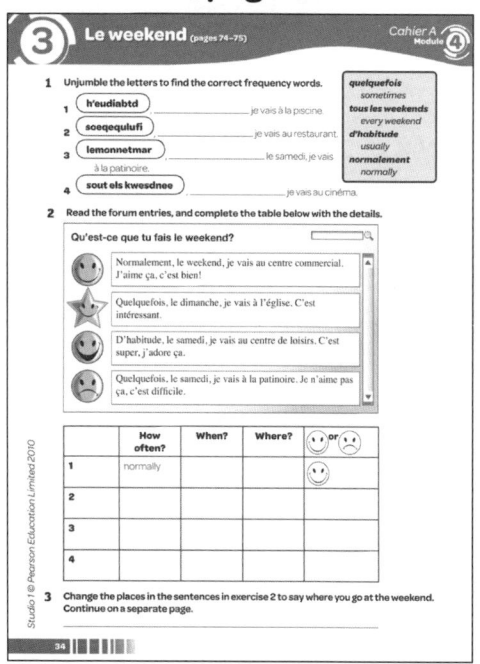

Answers
1 1 D'habitude 2 Quelquefois 3 Normalement 4 Tous les weekends

2

	How often?	When?	Where?	☺ ☹
1	normally	the weekend	shopping centre	☺
2	sometimes	Sundays	church	☺
3	usually	Saturdays	leisure centre	☺
4	sometimes	Saturdays	ice rink	☹

4 Ma zone 3 Le weekend

Workbook B, page 34

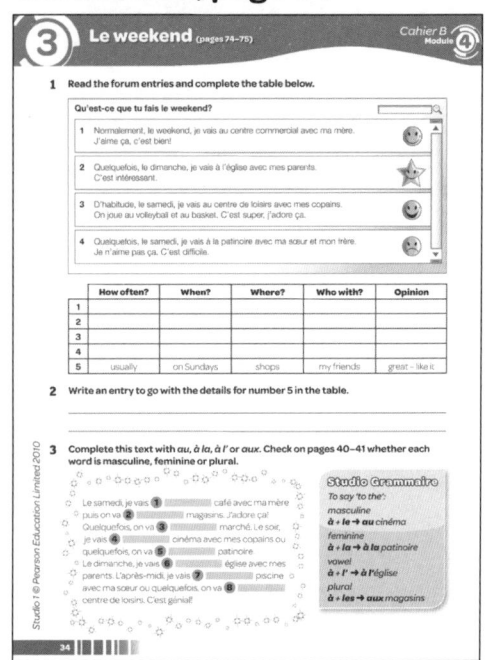

Answers

1

	How often?	When?	Where?	Who with?	Opinion?
1	normally	at the weekend	shopping centre	my mum	good – like it
2	sometimes	on Sundays	church	my parents	interesting
3	usually	on Saturdays	leisure centre	my friends	great – love it
4	sometimes	on Saturdays	ice rink	my sister and brother	don't like it – difficult

2 D'habitude, le dimanche, je vais aux magasins avec mes copains/mes copines/mes amis. C'est génial, j'aime ça.

3 1 au 2 aux 3 au 4 au 5 à la 6 à l' 7 à la 8 au

Worksheet 4.3 *Aller*

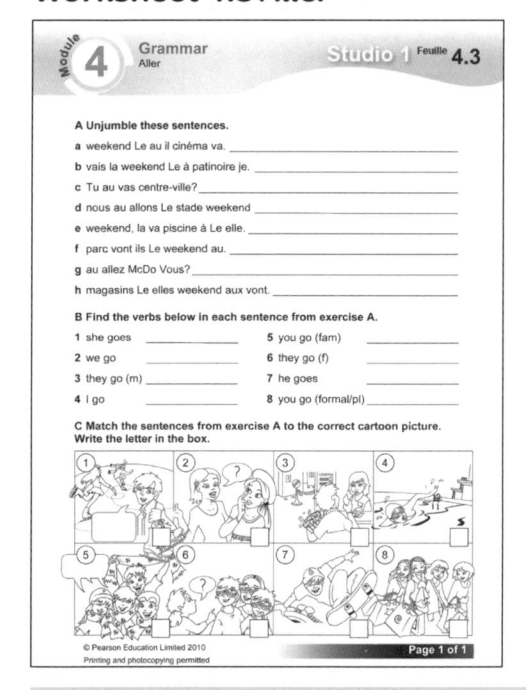

Answers

A
a Le weekend, il va au cinéma.
b Le weekend, je vais à la patinoire.
c Tu vas au centre-ville?
d Le weekend, nous allons au stade.
e Le weekend, elle va à la piscine.
f Le weekend, ils vont au parc.
g Vous allez au McDo?
h Le weekend, elles vont aux magasins.

B
1 elle va
2 nous allons
3 ils vont
4 je vais
5 tu vas
6 elles vont
7 il va
8 vous allez

C 1 b 2 c 3 a 4 e 5 d 6 g 7 f 8 h

Worksheet 4.4 Negatives

Module 4 Grammar – Negatives — Studio 1 Feuille 4.4

- **ne … pas** makes a sentence negative. It forms a sandwich around the verb in the sentence. **ne** becomes **n'** before a noun or a silent 'h'.
- When you use **ne … pas**, **j'** becomes **je** again, **c'** becomes **ce** e.g.
  j'aime → je n'aime pas
  c'est → ce n'est pas

A Underline the verb in each of these sentences. Rewrite the sentences using *ne* and *pas*.

1 Je vais au musée.
2 Il va en ville.
3 J'aime ma ville.
4 Je suis d'accord.
5 C'est ennuyeux.
6 Tu vas au MacDo?
7 Elle surfe sur Internet.
8 Il joue au foot.

B Unjumble these sentences.

1 n' l'injustice je pas aime
2 pas elle les aime insectes n'
3 ? pas tu aimes la n' musique
4 je sœur n' pas ai de
5 on va au pas ne cinéma
6 n' ils pas animaux aiment les

il y a = there is … / there are …
il n'y a pas de … = there is not a … / there are no …
With the negative, the article disappears and is replaced by 'de':
il y a une patinoire → il n'y a pas de patinoire
il y a des musées → il n'y a pas de musées

C Make each of these sentences negative.

1 Il y a des cafés.
2 Il y a des restaurants.
3 Il y a un centre commercial.
4 Il y a un centre de loisirs.
5 Il y a un stade.
6 Il y a un parc d'attractions

© Pearson Education Limited 2010
Printing and photocopying permitted
Page 1 of 1

Answers

A 1 Je ne <u>vais</u> pas au musée.
2 Il ne <u>va</u> pas en ville.
3 Je n'<u>aime</u> pas ma ville.
4 Je ne <u>suis</u> pas d'accord.
5 Ce n'<u>est</u> pas ennuyeux.
6 Tu ne <u>vas</u> pas au MacDo?
7 Elle ne <u>surfe</u> pas sur Internet.
8 Il ne <u>joue</u> pas au foot.

B 1 Je n'aime pas l'injustice.
2 Elle n'aime pas les insectes.
3 Tu n'aimes pas la musique?
4 Je n'ai pas de sœur.
5 On ne va pas au cinéma
6 Ils n'aiment pas les animaux.

C 1 Il n'y a pas de café.
2 Il n'y a pas de restaurant.
3 Il n'y a pas de centre commercial.
4 Il n'y a pas de centre de loisirs.
5 Il n'y a pas de stade.
6 Il n'y a pas de parc d'attractions.

4 Coucou! (Pupil Book pp. 76–77)

Learning objectives
- Asking someone to go somewhere
- Using *je veux/tu veux* + infinitive

Framework objectives
1.3/Y7 Listening – (a) interpreting intonation and tone: ex. 1 (reinforcement suggestion)
1.3/Y7 Speaking – (b) using intonation and tone: ex. 6
2.3/Y7 Reading – text features: ex. 5
2.5/Y7 Writing – different text types: ex. 7
4.5/Y7 Language – (b) modal verbs: ex. 1

Grammar
- *vouloir* + infinitive

Key language
je veux, tu veux, il/elle/on veut
Tu veux aller (au cinéma) (samedi soir)?
Bonne idée!
Super!
Génial!
D'accord.
Oui, c'est super top.
Oui, je veux bien.
Non, je n'ai pas envie.
Si tu veux.
Non merci.
C'est vraiment nul!
C'est ennuyeux.

PLTS
C Creative thinkers

Cross-curricular
English: grammatical terms

Resources
CD 2, tracks 24–26
Accès Studio pages 8–9
Cahier d'exercices A & B, page 35

AccèsS tudio Unit 3 (pp. 8–9) can be used with this unit to review days of the week.

Starter 1
Aim
To review infinitives; To review grammatical terms

Write up the following, omitting the underline (which denotes correct answers). Ask pupils working in pairs to write down all the infinitives and to put up their hand when they finish. Note the first three or four pairs to complete the task.

<u>aller</u> sont <u>avoir</u> sur <u>retrouver</u> <u>tchatter</u>
allons soir jour <u>finir</u> <u>commencer</u> <u>être</u>
<u>jouer</u> sœur par <u>traîner</u> au ils gourde

Check answers. Award a prize to the first pair to finish with all the answers correct. Ask pupils to identify what kind of words the remaining words are.

(Answers: *sont* – verb (they), *sur* – preposition, *allons* – verb (we), *soir* – noun, *jour* – noun, *sœur* – noun, *par* – preposition, *au* – preposition + definite article, *ils* – pronoun, *gourde* – noun)

1 Écoute et lis. Associe les dialogues et les bonnes images. (1–6) (AT 1.3)
Listening. Pupils listen to six conversations, reading the text at the same time. They match each conversation to the correct picture, writing the appropriate letter.

Audioscript CD 2 track 24
1 – *Tu veux aller au centre-ville dimanche après-midi?*
  – *Non merci, je n'ai pas envie.*
2 – *Tu veux aller au cinéma vendredi soir?*
  – *Non merci, c'est ennuyeux.*
3 – *Tu veux aller au MacDo dimanche matin?*
  – *D'accord, si tu veux.*
4 – *Tu veux aller à la patinoire samedi soir?*
  – *Ben non, c'est vraiment nul.*
5 – *Tu veux aller au parc samedi après-midi?*
  – *Oui, je veux bien.*
6 – *Tu veux aller aux magasins samedi matin?*
  – *Ah oui, super.*

Answers
1 b **2** f **3** c **4** e **5** a **6** d

R Pupils read the text in exercise 1 again and note whether the invitation is accepted or refused each time. Remind them that listening for intonation will help them to work out whether the response is positive or negative.

Studio Grammaire: *vouloir* + infinitive
Use the *Studio Grammaire* box to cover *vouloir* (singular) + infinitive. There is more information and further practice on Pupil Book p. 85.

2 Écoute et chante. (AT 1.4)
Listening. Pupils listen to the song and sing along. *franchement* is glossed for support.

4 Coucou! Ma zone 4

Audioscript CD 2 track 25

- Veux-tu sortir aujourd'hui?
- Oui, peut-être cet après-midi.
- Veux-tu aller au parc avec ma sœur?
- Mouais, c'est ennuyeux, mais si tu veux.
- Je ne suis pas d'accord, c'est super!
  Je m'appelle Aline, je suis sa sœur!
- Veux-tu aller plus tard au centre-ville?
- Oui, je veux bien. Génial!
- Veux-tu aller à la patinoire demain soir?
- Ben, non merci, j'ai beaucoup de devoirs.
- Veux-tu aller à la piscine avec moi mardi?
- Euh, non merci, je n'ai pas envie.
- Jeudi après-midi, veux-tu aller au ciné?
- Aller au ciné? Oui! Bonne idée!
- Veux-tu aller au café Pénélope?
  C'est génial. C'est super top.
- Aller au café? Je n'aime pas ça.
  Franchement, je préfère rester chez moi.

Starter 2

PLTS C

Aim
To review the days of the week

Write up the following, using a different symbol for each vowel. Give pupils three minutes to break the code, working out what ●, □, ☆ and ✚ mean, and writing out the words in full. If they need help to get started, tell them to think about which set of words would come in a group of seven.

l✚nd☆   v□ndr□d☆
m●rd☆   s●m□d☆
m●rcr□d☆   d☆m●nch□
j□✚d☆

(Answers: ● = a, □ = e, ☆ = i, ✚ = u)

Read together through the pronunciation box on *eux* and fillers to help pupils sound French.

3 Écoute et répète. (AT 1.1)
Listening. Pupils listen and repeat the pronunciation examples. The pronunciation box explains how to make the sounds needed, and when to use these fillers.

Audioscript CD 2 track 26

Tu veux … ennuyeux …
Euh, ben, mouais

4 Mets les images dans l'ordre de la chanson. (AT 3.4)
Reading. Pupils re-read the text of the song in exercise 2, then put the pictures of places in the order they are mentioned.

Answers
f, e, c, a, b, d

5 Relis la chanson. Trouve ces phrases en français. (AT 3.4)
Reading. Pupils re-read the song in exercise 2 and find in the text the French versions of the English phrases listed.

Answers
1 aujourd'hui   2 cet après-midi
3 jeudi après-midi   4 peut-être
5 je ne suis pas d'accord   6 j'ai beaucoup de devoirs
7 je préfère   8 je n'aime pas ça

6 À trois. Fais un dialogue. (AT 2.4)
Speaking. In threes: two of the pupils make up a conversation, one suggests an outing and the other responds to the invitation; the third pupil comments on their pronunciation, intonation and the language used. All pupils should have a turn at each of the three roles. Key language is supplied.

7 Écris une chanson ou un poème. (AT 4.4)
Writing. Pupils write a five-verse song or poem about an invitation to go on an outing and the response to the invitation. Details of what to include are supplied.

Plenary
Ask pupils to summarise how *vouloir* is used to say what you want to do. Go round the class. Pupils take it in turn to give an invitation (e.g. *Tu veux aller à la piscine lundi soir?*) and to respond (e.g. *Bonne idée!*).

4 Ma zone   4 Coucou!

Workbook A, page 35

Answers

1 1 f 2 b 3 c 4 a 5 e 6 d

2 (Other suitable answers may also be accepted.)
  1 Marine: Tu veux aller à la piscine samedi?
     Tom: Non, je n'ai pas envie.
  2 Marine: Tu veux aller au cinéma samedi après-midi?
     Tom: Non merci.
  3 Marine: Tu veux aller à la patinoire samedi soir?
     Tom: Non, c'est ennuyeux!
  4 Marine: Alors, tu veux surfer sur Internet?
     Tom: Oui, je veux bien.

Workbook B, page 35

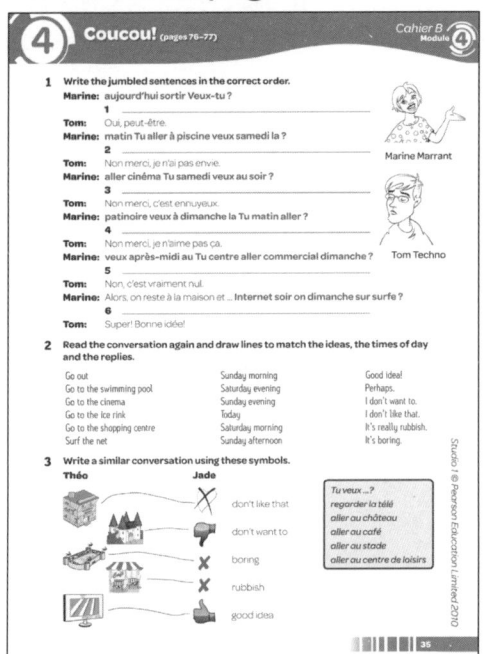

Answers

1 1 Veux-tu sortir aujourd'hui?
   2 Tu veux aller à la piscine samedi matin?
   3 Tu veux aller au cinéma samedi soir?
   4 Tu veux aller à la patinoire dimanche matin?
   5 Tu veux aller au centre commercial dimanche après-midi?
   6 Alors, on reste à la maison et on surfe sur Internet dimanche soir?

2 Go out–Today–Perhaps
   Go to the swimming pool–Saturday morning–I don't want to
   Go to the cinema–Saturday evening–It's boring
   Go to the ice rink–Sunday morning–I don't like that
   Go to the shopping centre–Sunday afternoon–It's really rubbish
   Surf the net–Sunday evening–Good idea!

3 Théo: Tu veux aller au centre de loisirs aujourd'hui?
   Jade: Non merci, je n'aime pas ça.
   Théo: Tu veux aller au château samedi matin?
   Jade: Non merci, je n'ai pas envie.
   Théo: Tu veux aller au stade samedi soir?
   Jade: Non merci, c'est ennuyeux.
   Théo: Tu veux aller au café dimanche après-midi?
   Jade: Non, c'est vraiment nul.
   Théo: Tu veux regarder la télé?
   Jade: Oui, bonne idée!

5 Qu'est-ce qu'on peut faire à … ?

MaZone 4 (Pupil Book pp. 78–79)

Learning objectives
- Saying what you can do in town
- Using *on peut* + infinitive

Framework objectives
1.2/Y7 Listening – unfamiliar language: ex. 4
1.4/Y7 Speaking – (b) using prompts: ex. 2
4.5/Y7 Language – (b) modal verbs: ex. 1
5.2 Strategies – memorising: ex. 6 (extension)
5.8 Strategies – evaluating and improving: ex. 5

Grammar
- *pouvoir* + infinitive

Key language
Qu'est-ce qu'on peut faire à … ?
je peux, tu peux, il/elle/on peut
aller au concert
faire du bowling
faire du roller ou du skate
faire du vélo
faire une promenade en barque
jouer au babyfoot et au flipper au café
manger au restaurant
visiter les jardins/les monuments/les musées

PLTS
S Self-managers

Cross-curricular
ICT: word processing/DTP, scanning/using a drawing package

Resources
CD 2, tracks 27–28
Cahier d'exercices A & B, page 36
ActiveTeach:
p.078 Video 8
p.078 Video worksheet 8
p.078 Flashcards
p.078 Grammar
p.078 Grammar practice
p.079 Learning skills
p.079 Class activity

Starter 1
Aim
To review verb structures

Write up the following, omitting the text in brackets. Give pupils three minutes to correct the grammatical error in each sentence.

1. *Je veux allez au concert.* [aller]
2. *J'aime visite les musées.* [visiter]
3. *Je manger au restaurant.* [mange]
4. *Tu veux joue au babyfoot?* [jouer]
5. *Je n'aime faire du bowling.* [n'aime pas]
6. *Il veut fais du vélo.* [faire]

Check answers. Ask pupils to tell you which verbs are often followed by an infinitive: verbs of opinion (*aimer, adorer, détester*) and the modal verb *vouloir*. Explain that in this unit they will learn another modal verb – *pouvoir* – which is also followed by an infinitive.

1 Écoute et écris les bonnes lettres. (1–4) (AT 1.2)
Listening. Pupils listen to four conversations about what you can do in Châlons-en-Champagne and identify the pictures of the activities mentioned, writing the appropriate letters.

Audioscript CD 2 track 27

1. – *Qu'est-ce qu'on peut faire à Châlons-en-Champagne?*
   – *On peut jouer au babyfoot et au flipper au café. On peut aussi faire du bowling.*

2. – *Qu'est-ce qu'on peut faire à Châlons-en-Champagne?*
   – *À Châlons-en-Champagne, on peut visiter les monuments. Si on veut, on peut faire du roller ou du skate.*

3. – *Qu'est-ce qu'on peut faire à Châlons-en-Champagne?*
   – *On peut visiter les jardins, faire une promenade en barque et faire du vélo.*

4. – *Qu'est-ce qu'on peut faire à Châlons-en-Champagne?*
   – *On peut visiter les musées, aller au concert et manger au restaurant.*

Answers
1 f, j **2** b, h **3** c, g, i **4** a, e, d

Studio Grammaire: *pouvoir* + infinitive
Use the *Studio Grammaire* box to cover *pouvoir* + infinitive. There is more information and further practice on Pupil Book p. 85.

2 En tandem. Décris les villes. Quelle ville préfères-tu? (AT 2.4)
Speaking. In pairs: pupils make up dialogues about what there is to do in each of four French towns, using the picture prompts supplied. A framework is given for support.

4 Ma zone 5 Qu'est-ce qu'on peut faire à ...?

Starter 2
Aim
To review vocabulary for activities in town; To practise using grammar to make connections

Write up the following, jumbling the order of the second column. Give pupils three minutes to match and write out the phrases.

1	visiter	les monuments
2	faire une	promenade en barque
3	jouer au	flipper au café
4	faire du roller	ou du skate
5	manger	au restaurant
6	aller au	concert
7	faire	du bowling
8	visiter les	jardins

Check answers, asking pupils to translate each completed phrase into English.

Alternative Starter 2:
Use ActiveTeach p. 078 Flashcards to review and practise the language for activities in town.

3 Lis l'e-mail de Thibault. Corrige les phrases. (AT 3.4)
Reading. Pupils read Thibault's e-mail and then read the eight sentences about it. They rewrite the sentences, correcting the error in each one. Some vocabulary is glossed for support.

Answers
1 Thibault habite à **Toulouse**.
2 Il y a des magasins, des **musées** et des monuments.
3 Il y a beaucoup de restaurants.
4 Il n'y a **pas** de patinoire.
5 Thibault **adore** le bowling.
6 D'habitude, au café, il joue au **babyfoot**.
7 Tous les weekends, il va **au parc** avec son frère.
8 Thibault **aime** sa ville.

Pupils read aloud and translate Thibault's text into English round the class, a sentence each.

4 Écoute. Comment est Villandraut? Note les informations en anglais. (AT 1.4)
Listening. Pupils listen to someone describing Villandraut and note the details in English.

Audioscript CD 2 track 28

J'habite à Villandraut. C'est un petit village. À Villandraut, il y a un château. Il y a aussi un musée, il y a des restaurants et des cafés, mais il n'y a pas de patinoire, il n'y a pas de centre commercial et il n'y a pas de centre de loisirs.
On peut faire du canoë-kayak, mais c'est tout. Moi, je vais au café. J'aime ça. C'est bien. D'habitude, je joue au flipper avec mes copains. Quelquefois, je vais au château.
Tous les weekends, je vais au marché avec ma mère. Je déteste ça.
Je n'aime pas habiter ici. À mon avis, c'est nul. C'est très ennuyeux.

Answers
Villandraut – small village
a castle, a museum, restaurants and cafés
no ice rink, shopping centre or leisure centre
You can go canoeing.
Speaker goes to café, plays pinball; sometimes goes to the castle
Goes to the market every weekend – hates it
Doesn't like living there – thinks it's boring

5 Prépare un exposé sur ta ville/ton village. (AT 2.4)
Speaking. Pupils prepare and give a presentation on their town or village. A framework is supplied for support. Read through the tip box and encourage pupils to use earlier units in the module as well as Thibault's text in exercise 3 to identify how to work in connectives and opinions.

When pupils have given their presentation, ask the rest of the class to give constructive feedback. Details of how to do this are supplied.

6 Écris une description de ta ville virtuelle idéale. Cherche les mots inconnus dans un dictionnaire. (AT 4.4)

Writing. Pupils write a description of their own ideal virtual town, using a dictionary to look up words they don't know. Draw pupils' attention to the tip box on avoiding language which is too complicated at this stage. The writing could be done using word processing or DTP to produce a brochure: pupils could add scanned in sketches or, if you have a drawing package, a layout/map done on screen.

PLTS S

Read together through the *Stratégie* on Pupil Book p. 87, covering mnemonics. Set pupils the task of choosing and learning five words using this approach, either in the classroom or at home.

5 Qu'est-ce qu'on peut faire à …?

Ma zone 4

Plenary
Ask pupils to give you examples of verbs usually followed by an infinitive, prompting as necessary to review *aimer, adorer, détester, vouloir* and *pouvoir*. Then ask what there is to do in the pupils' own town/village and/or a larger city nearby: *Qu'est-ce qu'on peut faire à … ?* Encourage as many pupils as possible to answer using *On peut* + infinitive.

Alternative Plenary:
Use ActiveTeach p. 079 Class activity to review and practise general vocabulary from the module.

Workbook A, page 36

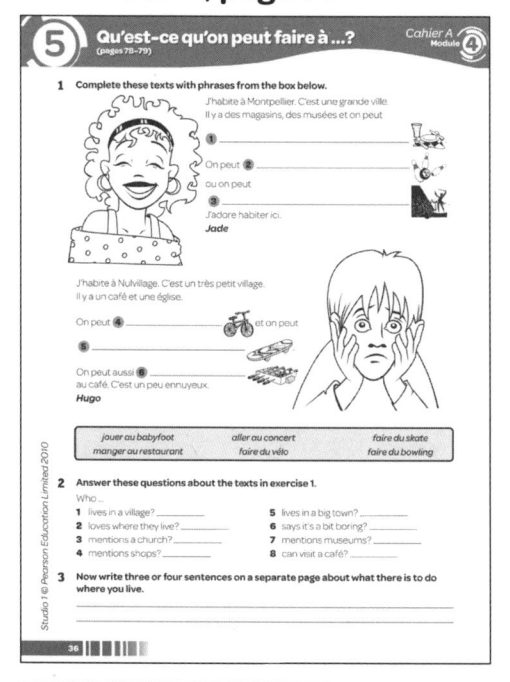

Answers
1. 1 manger au restaurant 2 faire du bowling
   3 aller au concert 4 faire du vélo
   5 faire du skate 6 jouer au babyfoot
2. 1 Hugo 2 Jade 3 Hugo 4 Jade 5 Jade
   6 Hugo 7 Jade 8 Hugo

Workbook B, page 36

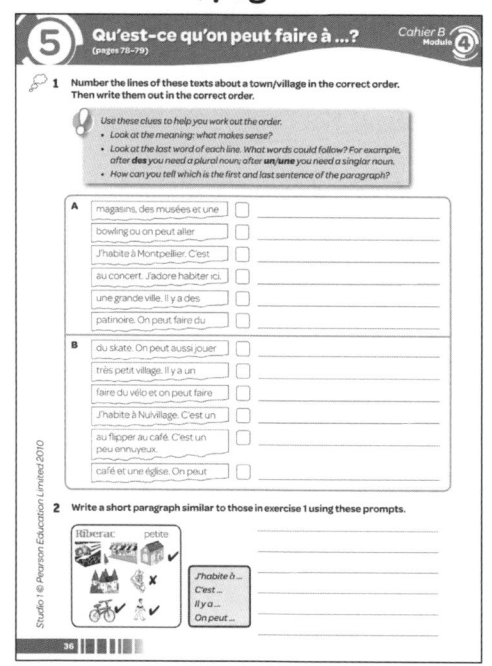

Answers
1. **A** 3, 5, 1, 6, 2, 4
   J'habite à Montpellier. C'est une grande ville. Il y a des magasins, des musées et une patinoire. On peut faire du bowling ou on peut aller au concert. J'adore habiter ici.

   B 5, 2, 4, 1, 6, 3
   J'habite à Nulvillage. C'est un très petit village. Il y a un café et une église. On peut faire du vélo et on peut faire du skate. On peut aussi jouer au flipper au café. C'est un peu ennuyeux.

2. (Example answer:)
   J'habite à Riberac. C'est une petite ville. Il y a un cinéma, des magasins et des musées mais il n'y a pas de château et il n'y a pas de patinoire. On peut faire du vélo ou on peut faire des promenades. J'adore habiter ici.

4 Ma zone   5 Qu'est-ce qu'on peut faire à ...?

Worksheet 4.5 Summarising

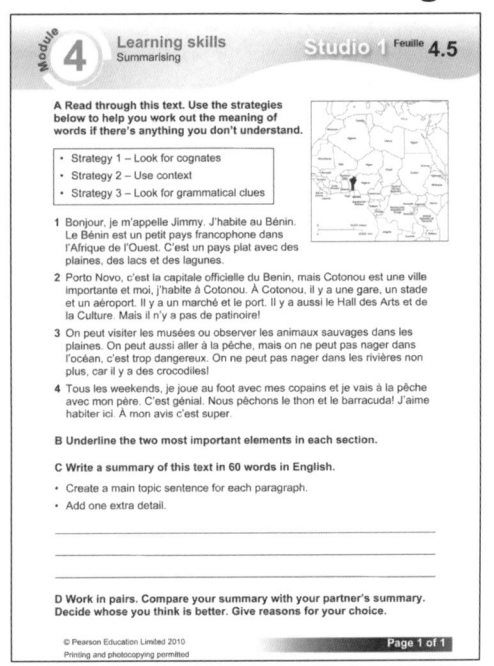

Answers

B 1 Bonjour, je m'appelle <u>Jimmy</u>. J'habite au Bénin. Le <u>Bénin</u> est un petit pays francophone dans <u>l'Afrique de l'Ouest</u>. C'est un pays plat avec des plaines, des lacs et des lagunes.

2 Porto Novo, c'est la capitale officielle du Benin, mais Cotonou est une ville importante et moi, <u>j'habite à Cotonou. À Cotonou, il y a une gare, un stade et un aéroport. Il y a un marché et le port</u>. Il y a aussi le Hall des Arts et de la Culture. Mais il n'y a pas de patinoire!

3 <u>On peut</u> visiter les musées ou <u>observer les animaux sauvages</u> dans les plaines. On peut aussi aller à la pêche, mais <u>on ne peut pas nager dans l'océan, c'est trop dangereux</u>. On ne peut pas nager dans les rivières non plus, car il y a des crocodiles!

4 Tous les weekends, je joue au foot avec mes copains et je vais à la pêche avec mon père. C'est génial. <u>Nous pêchons le thon et le barracuda! J'aime habiter ici</u>. À mon avis, c'est super.

C & D (Answers will vary.)

Video

Episode 8: Voici Châlons-en-Champagne

The StudioFR team are in their headquarters brainstorming ideas for a piece about their town, Châlons-en-Champagne. Video worksheet 8 can be used in conjunction with this episode.

Answers

1 A Things already experienced and which might be included are the school, the cinema, the square and the park.
  B market, shops, flats, town hall, museum, ice rink, bowling alley
  C il y a ... (there is ...), on peut ... (you can ...)
2 A Because, as usual, she is trying to hog the limelight.
  B go shopping, go on a boat trip, visit the gardens
  C Positive: génial. Negative: c'est nul, ennuyeux, pas intéressant
  D – Let's get to work!
     – everyone
     – in my opinion
  E [PLTS T/E] shops, flats, museum – boring, not very interesting
3 A intéressant (interesting), vieux (old), moderne (modern)
  B visit the gardens, go on a boat trip, go to a restaurant, do some sport
  C sensationnelle!
  D They are unimpressed.
  E [F3.1/3.2]
4 (Answers will vary.)

Ma zone 4 Bilan et Révisions (Pupil Book pp. 80–81)

Bilan
Pupils use this checklist to review language covered in the module, working on it in pairs in class or on their own at home. Encourage them to follow up any areas of weakness they identify. There are Target Setting Sheets included in the Assessment Pack, and an opportunity for pupils to record their own levels and targets on the *J'avance* page in the Workbook, p. 39. You can also use the *Bilan* checklist as an end-of-module plenary option.

Révisions
These revision exercises can be used for assessment purposes or for pupils to practise before tackling the assessment tasks in the Resource & Assessment File.

Resources
CD 2, track 29
Cahier d'exercices A & B, pages 37 & 38

1 Écoute. Copie et complète le tableau en anglais. (1–4) (AT 1.4)
Listening. Pupils copy the table. They then listen to four conversations about different towns and what people do there, and complete the table with the details in English.

Audioscript CD 2 track 29

1 Romain
J'habite à Strasbourg. C'est une grande ville et c'est joli. On peut visiter les musées ou les monuments. C'est bien. Moi, je vais au parc avec mes copains. Le weekend, je vais au cinéma. J'aime Strasbourg. J'aime beaucoup habiter ici.

2 Yara
J'habite à Avèze. C'est un petit village. Il y a un camping et un hôtel, et c'est tout. Moi, je vais au café et je joue au flipper. Mais c'est vraiment nul. Je déteste habiter ici.

3 Bianca
J'habite à Limoges. C'est une ville. Il y a une piscine et une patinoire. Moi, je vais au stade tous les weekends avec mon père. Et quelquefois, je vais au centre de loisirs. C'est joli, Limoges. J'aime habiter ici.

4 Younis
J'habite à Pontivy. C'est une ville et j'aime bien. On peut faire une promenade en bateau sur la rivière. C'est génial. Moi, je vais tous les jours au café et quelquefois, je vais au château. Tous les weekends, je vais au musée. J'aime habiter ici. À mon avis, c'est bien.

Answers

	things to do in town	where they go	opinion
Romain	museums, monuments	park, cinema	likes it a lot
Yara	campsite, hotel	café, pinball	hates it – it's rubbish
Bianca	swimming pool, ice rink	stadium, leisure centre	likes it – it's pretty
Younis	boat trip on river	café, castle, museum	likes it – it's good

2 En tandem. Fais des dialogues. (AT 2.3)
Speaking. In pairs: pupils make up conversations using the picture prompts supplied. A sample exchange is given.

3 Lis l'e-mail et corrige les phrases. (AT 3.4)
Reading. Pupils read the e-mail and then read the six sentences about it. They rewrite the sentences, correcting the errors in them.

Answers
1 Dinan, c'est une **petite** ville.
2 À Dinan, il y a des magasins, un château et un **musée**.
3 On peut faire **de la natation** ou du vélo.
4 Laura va tous les **weekends** au centre-ville.
5 Elle fait les magasins avec sa **copine**.
6 Laura **aime** habiter à Dinan.

4 Propose une sortie pour chaque jour de la semaine. Donne ton opinion sur chaque destination. (AT 4.4)
Writing. Pupils write seven pairs of sentences, each pair suggesting an outing for a different day of the week and giving an opinion of the place/activity they suggest. An example is given.

4 Ma zone — Bilan et Révisions

Workbook A, page 37

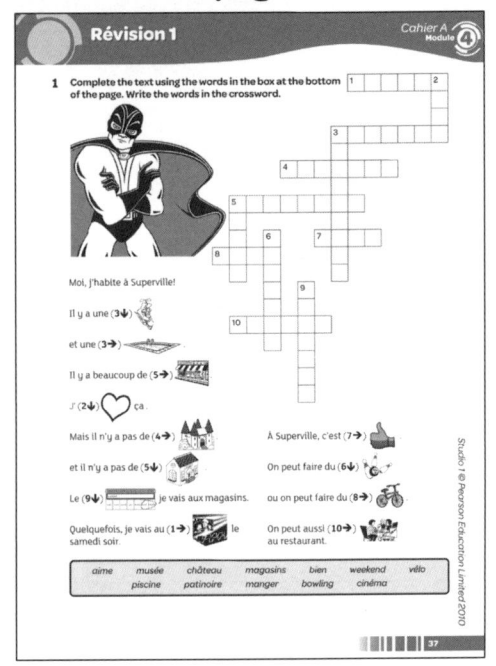

Answers
1 cinéma   2 aime   3 → piscine   3 ↓ patinoire
4 château   5 → magasins   5 ↓ musée
6 bowling   7 bien   8 vélo   9 weekend   10 manger

Workbook A, page 38

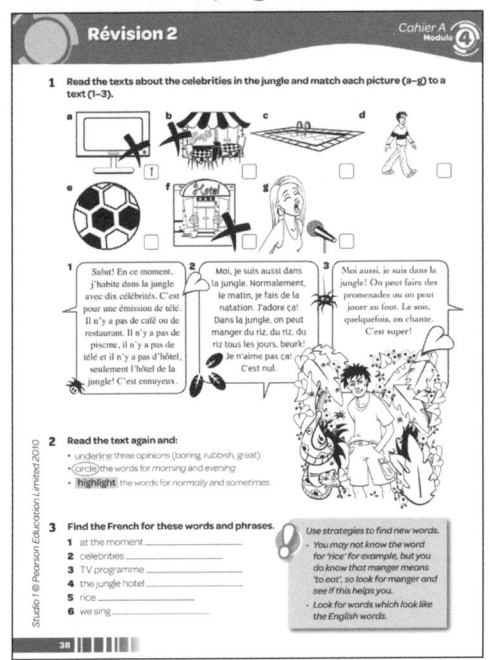

Answers
1 a 1   b 1   c 2   d 3   e 3   f 1   g 3
2 (Three underlined from:) C'est ennuyeux, J'adore ça, Je n'aime pas ça, C'est nul, C'est super!
(Circled:) le matin, le soir
(Highlighted:) normalement, quelquefois
3 1 en ce moment   2 célébrités
  3 une émission de télé   4 l'hôtel de la jungle
  5 du riz   6 on chante

Workbook B, page 37

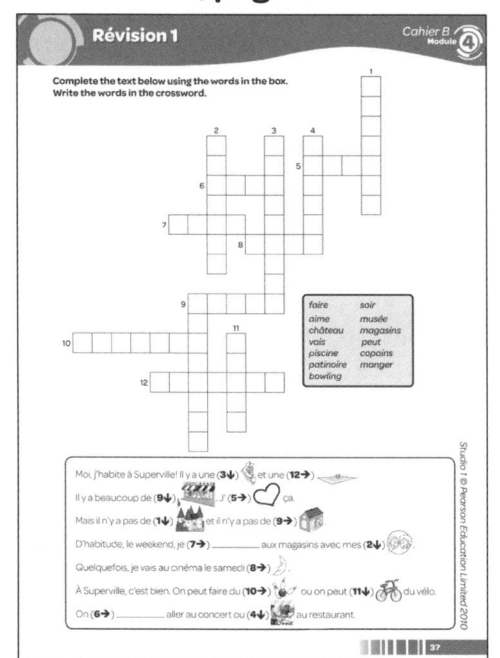

Answers
1 château 2 copains 3 patinoire 4 manger
5 aime 6 peut 7 vais 8 soir **9 across** musée
9 down magasins 10 bowling 11 faire 12 piscine

Workbook B, page 38

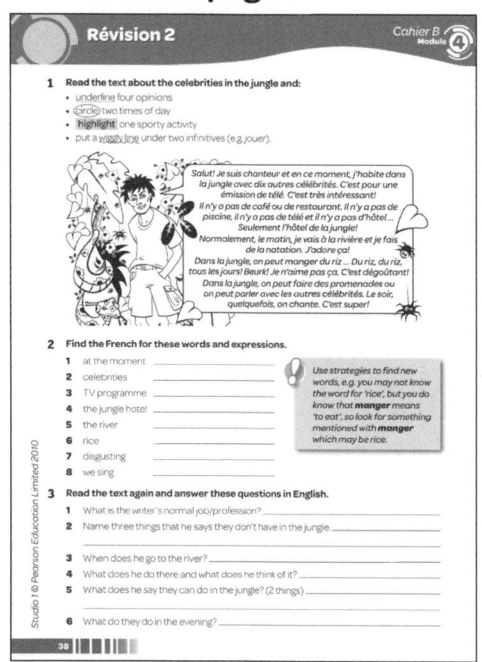

Answers
1 (four underlined from:) C'est très intéressant! J'adore ça! Je n'aime pas ça. C'est dégoûtant! C'est super!
(circled:) le matin, Le soir
(highlighted:) je fais de la natation
(wiggly line under two from:) manger, faire, parler
2 1 en ce moment 2 célébrités 3 émission de télé
   4 l'hôtel de la jungle 5 la rivière 6 (du) riz
   7 dégoûtant 8 on chante
3 1 He's a singer.
   2 Café, restaurant, swimming pool, TV, hotel
   3 He normally goes in the morning.
   4 He swims; he thinks it's great.
   5 Eat rice, go for walks, talk to the other celebrities
   6 They sing.

Ma Zone 4 — En plus: Destination France
(Pupil Book pp. 82–83)

Learning objectives
- Facts about France
- Researching a region of France

Framework objective
3.2/Y7 Culture – (b) challenging stereotypes: Alternative plenary

Key language
Review of language from the module
un pays
la région
diverse
au nord-ouest, au sud, à l'ouest
la mer du Nord, la Manche, la Méditerranée, l'océan Atlantique
la Belgique, le Luxembourg, l'Allemagne, la Suisse, l'Italie, l'Espagne
le Rhône, la Loire, la Seine, la Garonne
les Pyrénées, les Alpes
Les villes principales sont …
Il y a …
des plateaux/des plaines/des forêts/des lacs/des fleuves/des rivières/des montagnes/des plages

PLTS
E Effective participators

Cross-curricular
ICT: Internet research
Geography: France

Resources
CD 2, tracks 30–32
ActiveTeach:
p.083 Assignment 4
p.083 Assignment 4: prep

Starter
Aim
To introduce key places in France

Bring in or prepare a map of France with the places listed below clearly shown on it.

In pairs: pupils quickly sketch an outline map of France (one for each pair), copying the one on p. 82 of the Pupil Book. Write up the following. Give pupils three minutes working in their pairs to mark the places/features on their map.

- Paris, Marseille, Toulouse, Châlons-en-Champagne
- the Alps, the Pyrenees, the Seine
- Normandy, Brittany
- at least one other place they know in France

1 Sylvain va parler de sa ville, Besançon. Prédis ce que tu vas entendre. Copie et remplis le tableau. (AT 4.2)
Writing. Read together through the tip box on the listening skill of anticipating what you might hear. Pupils then copy the table and complete it by predicting the language that might come up in the recording about Sylvain's town in each of the specified categories.

Answers
(Answers will vary.)

2 Écoute et vérifie le vocabulaire que tu as noté. (AT 1.5)
Listening. Pupils listen to Sylvain talking about his town, Besançon, and check whether their predictions in exercise 1 were correct.

Audioscript — CD 2 track 30

Bonjour, je m'appelle Sylvain. J'habite à Besançon, dans l'est de la France. J'aime habiter ici. C'est bien. C'est très joli. À Besançon, il y a un centre commercial et un cinéma. Il y a aussi un aquarium. J'adore l'aquarium, c'est intéressant. Il y a aussi beaucoup de jardins.

Ici, on peut jouer au basket ou au foot. On peut faire du bowling ou de la natation. On peut aussi jouer au mini-golf. Il y a un très beau musée, le musée du Temps.

On peut visiter la citadelle de Vauban. On peut faire une promenade en bateau si on veut, c'est super. J'aime ça. Samedi dernier, j'ai fait du canoë-kayak avec mon frère. C'était génial.

Answers

nouns	un centre commercial, un cinéma, un aquarium, jardins, un musée, la citadelle de Vauban
activities	basket, foot, bowling, natation, mini-golf, promenade en bateau, canoë-kayak
verbs (infinitive form)	habiter, jouer, faire, visiter
other structures	il y a, j'aime + infinitive, on peut + infinitive, faire de, jouer à
connectives	et, aussi, ou
intensifiers	très

En plus: Destination France **Ma zone 4**

3 Écoute à nouveau et choisis la bonne réponse. (AT 1.4)

Listening. Pupils listen to the recording from exercise 2 again and complete the six sentences about it, choosing from the two options given each time.

Audioscript — CD 2 track 31

As for exercise 2

Answers
1 Besançon est dans **l'est** de la France.
2 À Besançon, il y a **un centre commercial** et un cinéma.
3 Sylvain adore **l'aquarium**.
4 À Besançon, on peut jouer **au mini-golf**.
5 Le musée s'appelle **le musée du Temps**.
6 Le weekend dernier, Sylvain a fait du canoë-kayak avec **son frère**.

4 Écoute et lis le texte. (AT 1.4)

Listening. Pupils listen to the information about France, reading the text at the same time.

After playing the recording, draw pupils' attention to the tip box on extending sentences using *si* clauses. Ask them to identify the *si* clauses used in the text. Encourage them to use this structure in their own writing. Some vocabulary is glossed for support.

Audioscript — CD 2 track 32

Je découvre la France ...
La mer du Nord et la Manche bordent la France au nord-ouest. La Méditerranée borde la France au sud, et à l'ouest il y a l'océan Atlantique.
Six pays importants touchent la France: la Belgique, le Luxembourg, l'Allemagne, la Suisse, l'Italie et l'Espagne.
Paris est la capitale de la France. Ici, on peut visiter des monuments. Il y a 80 musées et 200 galeries d'art.
Les régions de la France sont très diverses. Si tu aimes l'histoire, tu peux visiter les châteaux de la Loire. Si tu préfères le grand air, tu peux faire des randonnées dans les Pyrénées ou les Alpes. Et en hiver, on peut faire du ski. Génial!
Le Rhône, la Loire, la Seine et la Garonne sont des fleuves très importants. On peut faire une promenade en barque sur le Canal du Midi. Au bord de la mer, on peut faire du surf. Cool!
En France, il y a des plateaux et des plaines, des forêts, des lacs, des fleuves et des rivières. On t'attend chez nous!

5 Donne les informations suivantes mentionnées dans le texte. (AT 3.4)

Reading. Pupils re-read the text in exercise 4 and identify the places and features specified.

Answers
(six countries bordering France:) Belgium, Luxembourg, Germany, Switzerland, Italy, Spain
(four rivers that flow into the sea:) the Rhône, the Loire, the Seine, the Garonne
(four seas/oceans:) the North Sea, the English Channel, the Mediterranean, the Atlantic Ocean
(two mountain ranges:) the Pyrenees, the Alps
(five geographical features:) plateaux, plains, forests, lakes, rivers

6 Choisis une région de France et fais des recherches. Prépare un exposé pour ta classe. (AT 2.3–4)

PLTS E

Speaking. Pupils research a region of France, then prepare and give a presentation on it. Headings for notes and a framework for speaking are supplied.

Plenary
Challenge the class to a quiz on France. As well as the information in this unit, you can use facts that pupils have read in the module openers in Modules 1–4. Pupils close their books. Use the headings in exercise 5 as prompts. If they can remember all the features of France specified there, they win. Otherwise you win.

Alternative Plenary:
Remind the class of your discussion on French stereotypes at the start of the year. Discuss what they have learned since then and their opinions of France and French people now.

4 Ma zone — En plus: Destination France

Worksheet 4.6 Mon royaume à moi

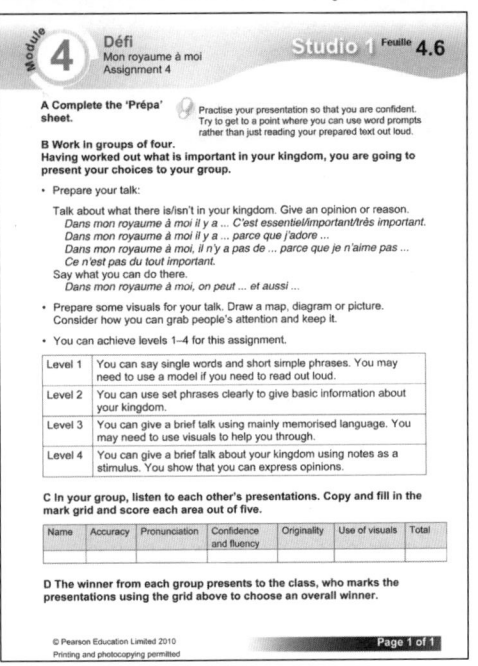

Module 4 — Défi
Mon royaume à moi
Assignment 4
Studio 1 Feuille 4.6

A Complete the 'Prépa' sheet.

Practise your presentation so that you are confident. Try to get to a point where you can use word prompts rather than just reading your prepared text out loud.

B Work in groups of four.
Having worked out what is important in your kingdom, you are going to present your choices to your group.

- Prepare your talk:
  Talk about what there is/isn't in your kingdom. Give an opinion or reason.
    Dans mon royaume à moi il y a … C'est essentiel/important/très important.
    Dans mon royaume à moi il y a … parce que j'adore …
    Dans mon royaume à moi, il n'y a pas de … parce que je n'aime pas …
    Ce n'est pas du tout important.
  Say what you can do there.
    Dans mon royaume à moi, on peut … et aussi …
- Prepare some visuals for your talk. Draw a map, diagram or picture. Consider how you can grab people's attention and keep it.
- You can achieve levels 1–4 for this assignment.

Level 1	You can say single words and short simple phrases. You may need to use a model if you need to read out loud.
Level 2	You can use set phrases clearly to give basic information about your kingdom.
Level 3	You can give a brief talk using mainly memorised language. You may need to use visuals to help you through.
Level 4	You can give a brief talk about your kingdom using notes as a stimulus. You show that you can express opinions.

C In your group, listen to each other's presentations. Copy and fill in the mark grid and score each area out of five.

| Name | Accuracy | Pronunciation | Confidence and fluency | Originality | Use of visuals | Total |

D The winner from each group presents to the class, who marks the presentations using the grid above to choose an overall winner.

Worksheet 4.7 Mon royaume à moi. Prépa

Module 4 — Défi
Mon royaume à moi Prépa
Studio 1 Feuille 4.7

You are going to design your own kingdom. Look at this grid. First, think about what is important to you. Note for each thing mentioned whether it is:

essentiel = e
très important = ti
assez important = ai
pas du tout important = pdti

La géographie	Les activités	Les endroits en ville
un océan	aller à la pêche	un château
des plateaux	faire du surf	un amphithéâtre
des plaines	faire du parkour	un bowling
des forêts	faire du patin à glace	un théâtre
des lacs	faire du roller	un cinéma
des rivières	faire du vélo	un parc d'attractions
des montagnes	faire du shopping	un MacDo
des lagunes	faire du yoga	un centre commercial
	faire de la gymnastique	un circuit de karting
	faire de l'équitation	un centre de loisirs
	faire des promenades	un stade
	traîner au centre-ville	une halle de glisse
	visiter les jardins	une salle de concerts
		une patinoire
		des parcs
		des restaurants
		des magasins
		des monuments

Studio Grammaire (Pupil Book pp. 84–85)

Ma Zone 4

The *Studio Grammaire* section provides a more detailed summary of the key grammar covered in the module, along with further exercises to practise these points.

Grammar topics
- *aller*
- looking for patterns in language
- modal verbs

aller

1 Choose the correct verb, then translate the sentences into English.
Pupils write out the completed sentences, choosing the correct form of *aller* from the two options given each time. They then translate the sentences into English.

Answers
1 Elle **va** à la piscine. – She goes/is going to the swimming pool.
2 Six personnes **vont** au stade. – Six people go/are going to the stadium.
3 Je **vais** souvent au cinéma. – I often go to the cinema.
4 Tu **vas** à la patinoire. – You go/are gong to the ice rink.
5 Elles **vont** au centre commercial tous les jours. – They go to the shopping centre every day.
6 Vous **allez** au centre de loisirs? – Do you go/Are you going to the leisure centre?
7 Il **va** au café avec son frère. – He goes/is going to the café with his brother.
8 On **va** au parc tous les weekends. – We go to the park every weekend.
9 Nous **allons** au château. – We go/are going to the castle.

Looking for patterns in language

2 Correct the mistakes in the sentences.
Pupils rewrite the sentences, correcting the grammatical errors in them.

Answers
1 J'aime **les** maths.
2 Je vais **au** stade ce soir.
3 Tu aimes **les** magazines?
4 Mon frère joue **au** foot tous les soirs.
5 J'adore **le** tennis.

3 *au, à la, à l'* or *aux*? Complete the messages.
Pupils complete the gap-fill sentences with the appropriate form of *à* + definite article.

Answers
1 Je vais **au** parc.
2 On va **au** café.
3 Tu vas **au** stade?
4 Elle va **à l'**hôtel
5 Il va **à la** patinoire.
6 Nous allons **à la** piscine.

4 Complete the text.
Pupils complete the gap-fill text with the correct form of the definite article, the indefinite article or *à* + definite article, as appropriate.

Answers
1 les 2 au 3 un 4 des 5 au 6 le 7 au 8 au

Modal verbs

5 Find five sentences in this word snake. Write them out, then translate them into English.
Pupils write out the five sentences contained in the word snake, then translate them into English.

Answers
Je peux aller au parc. – I can go to the park.
Il veut sortir. – He wants to go out.
Tu veux aller au stade. – You want to go to the stadium.
On peut aller au café. – We/You can go to the café.
Elle veut aller au cinéma. – She wants to go to the cinema.

6 Choose the correct option to complete each sentence.
Pupils write out the completed sentences, choosing the correct verb form from the three options given each time.

Answers
1 visiter 2 manger 3 aller 4 faire 5 surfer 6 jouer 7 faire 8 jouer

4 Ma zone — Studio Grammaire

7 Translate the sentences into French.
Pupils translate into French the eight sentences featuring the modal verb + infinitive structure.

Answers
1 Il peut aller à la patinoire.
2 Elle veut jouer au foot.
3 Tu veux aller au centre commercial?
4 On peut aller au parc.
5 Je veux jouer à des jeux vidéo.
6 Je ne veux pas sortir.
7 Il ne veut pas jouer au tennis.
8 Je peux aller au concert.

Ma Zone 4 À toi (Pupil Book pages 124–125)

Self-access reading and writing

A Reinforcement

1 Écris chaque endroit correctement et note la bonne lettre. (AT 3.2)
Reading. Pupils unscramble the anagrams and write out the places. They match each place to the correct picture, writing the appropriate letter.

Answers
1 une piscine – f
2 une patinoire – i
3 des magasins – b
4 un centre commercial – e
5 un château – c
6 un centre de loisirs – h
7 un stade – a
8 un marché – d
9 une église – j
10 des musées – g

2 Lis les textes. Écris la bonne lettre. (AT 3.3)
Reading. Pupils read the three speech bubbles and match each to the correct picture, writing the appropriate letter.

Answers
1 a 2 c 3 b

3 Décris la semaine de Romain. (AT 4.3)
Writing. Using the information in the diary, pupils describe Romain's week, writing a sentence for each day.

Answers
Lundi, il va au centre de loisirs avec Samir.
Mardi, il va à la piscine avec Régine.
Mercredi, il va à la patinoire avec Grégoire.
Jeudi, il va au cinéma avec Fatima.
Vendredi, il va au centre commercial avec Jamel.

B Extension

1 Prends un élément de chaque case et écris cinq phrases. Ensuite, traduis les phrases en anglais. (AT 4.3)
Writing. Pupils write five sentences, each containing one element from each box. They then translate their sentences into English.

Answers
(Answers will vary.)

2 Lis et note: vrai (V) ou faux (F)? (AT 3.4)
Reading. Pupils read Laura's text. They then read the six sentences about it and decide whether each is true (writing V) or false (writing F).

Answers
1 F 2 F 3 V 4 V 5 F 6 F

3 Dans le texte, retrouve: (AT 3.3)
Reading. Pupils re-read the text in exercise 2 and identify: three opinions, eleven places in town, two frequency expressions and three infinitives.

Answers
(opinions:) à mon avis, c'est génial; J'adore habiter à Nîmes; Je pense que c'est top.
(endroits:) des magasins, des musées, des monuments, un amphithéâtre, des restaurants, des cafés, des hôtels, un stade, un théâtre, un parc, une piscine
(expressions de fréquence:) tous les weekends, quelquefois
(infinitifs:) faire, aller, habiter

4 Écris une conversation sur ta ville. Voici des mots pour t'aider. (AT 4.3–4)
Writing. Pupils write a conversation about their own town. A list of useful words is supplied for support.

Module 5: 3 ... 2 ... 1 Partez! (Pupil Book pp. 88–107)

Unit & Learning objectives	PoS & Framework objectives	Key language	Grammar and other language features
1 Les vacances, mode d'emploi (pp. 90–91) Using *nous* to say 'we' Talking about your holidays	**2.2a** listen for gist **2.2c** respond appropriately **2.2g** write clearly and coherently **2.2h** redraft to improve writing **4b** communicate in pairs, etc. **4e** use a range of resources **2.2/Y7** Reading – (a) unfamiliar language **4.5/Y7** Language – (a) set phrases about the past	*Tous les ans, ...* *Normalement, ...* *nous allons ...* *nous restons ...* *en France, au Portugal, aux Etats-Unis*, etc. *à la campagne* *à la mer* *à la montagne* *Nous visitons des monuments.* *Nous faisons de la rando.* etc.	**G** *nous* forms (regular –*er* verbs + *aller, faire*) – writing skills: attaining a higher level by including a reason
2 Je me prépare ... (pp. 92–93) Talking about getting ready to go out Using reflexive verbs (singular)	**2.1a** identify patterns **2.1d** previous knowledge **2.2g** write clearly and coherently **3c** apply grammar **4e** use a range of resources **4f** language for interest/enjoyment **4.2/Y7** Language – high-frequency words **5.6** Strategies – reading aloud	*Je me douche.* *Je m'habille.* *Je me regarde dans la glace.* etc.	**G** reflexive verbs (singular) – using *ne ... pas* with reflexive verbs – writing skills: using expressions of time and frequency to improve sentences
3 Au Café de la Plage (pp. 94–95) Buying drinks and snacks Using higher numbers	**2.1a** identify patterns **2.2a** listen for gist **2.2c** respond appropriately **2.2f** initiate/sustain conversations **2.2i** reuse language they have met **2.2k** deal with unfamiliar language	Numbers: *quarante* to *quatre-vingt-quinze* *Tu as combien d'argent?* *J'ai (dix euros cinquante).* *Je voudrais ...* *un café-crème* *un sandwich au fromage* *une crêpe* *une glace à la vanille* etc.	– reading strategies: using what you know
4 Je vais aller en colo! (pp. 96–97) Talking about holiday plans Using the near future tense	**2.2a** listen for gist **2.2c** respond appropriately **2.2e** ask and answer questions **2.2g** write clearly and coherently **2.2h** redraft to improve writing **3c** apply grammar **4.5/Y7** Language – (a) set phrases about the future	*Qu'est-ce que tu vas faire pendant les vacances?* *Je vais ...* *aller à la pêche* *danser* *faire de la voile* *rester au lit* etc.	**G** the near future tense

3 ... 2 ... 1 Partez! 5

Unit & Learning objectives	PoS & Framework objectives	Key language	Grammar and other language features
5 Mes rêves (pp. 98–99) Saying what you would like to do Using *je voudrais* + infinitive	**2.2d** pronunciation and intonation **2.2j** adapt previously learned language **3a** spoken and written language **3b** sounds and writing **3c** apply grammar **3d** use a range of vocab/structures **4.5/Y7** Language – (a) set phrases about the future	*Quels sont tes rêves? Je voudrais aller ... à Paris en Australie au Canada Je voudrais ... être footballeur professionnel faire le tour du monde* etc.	**G** *je voudrais* + infinitive **G** 'to'/'in' a place or country
Bilan et Révisions (pp. 100–101) Pupils' checklist and practice exercises			
En plus: Tu vas aller où? (pp. 102–103) Talking about where people go on holiday Finding out about holidays in France	**2.1d** previous knowledge **2.1e** use reference materials **3f** compare experiences **4c** use more complex language **4e** use a range of resources **4f** language for interest/enjoyment **2.2/Y7** Reading – (b) text selection **5.5** Strategies – reference materials	Review of language from the module *le canoë-kayak, la randonnée, l'équitation,* etc.	– using a dictionary to find out gender – speaking skills: personalising a response by including opinions and reactions
Studio Grammaire (pp. 104–105) Detailed grammar summary and practice exercises			**G** regular *–er* verbs in the present tense **G** using *nous* in the present tense **G** reflexive verbs **G** *je voudrais* + infinitive **G** the near future tense
À toi (pp. 126–127) Self-access reading and writing at two levels			

5 1 Les vacances, mode d'emploi
(Pupil Book pp. 90–91)

Learning objectives
- Using *nous* to say 'we'
- Talking about your holidays

Framework objectives
2.2/Y7 Reading – (a) unfamiliar language: ex. 5
4.5/Y7 Language – (a) set phrases about the past: ex. 6, 7, 8

Grammar
- *nous* forms (regular *–er* verbs + *aller*, *faire*)

Key language
Tous les ans, …
Normalement, …
nous allons/restons …
en France/Espagne/Grèce/Italie
au Portugal
aux États-Unis
à la mer
à la montagne
à la campagne
Nous faisons du camping.
Nous faisons de la rando.
Nous faisons de la natation.
Nous faisons des activités sportives.
Nous allons au restaurant.
Nous visitons des monuments.

PLTS
I Independent enquirers

Cross-curricular
ICT: collate and present survey results

Resources
CD 3, tracks 2–5
Cahier d'exercices A & B, page 42
Accès Studio pages 26–27
ActiveTeach:
p.090 Flashcards
p.091 Flashcards
p.091 Thinking skills

Accès Studio Unit 12 (pp. 26–27) can be used with this unit to review countries.

Starter 1
Aim
To review subject pronouns

Say aloud a series of sentences in English using the subject pronouns 'I', 'you', 'he', 'she', 'we' and 'they' (e.g. 'They went to the park.'). For each sentence, pupils say (or write) the corresponding subject pronoun in French. Prompt as necessary to review both *tu* and *vous*. Explain that, in addition to *on*, French has another word for 'we', which will be covered in this unit.

1 Écoute et écris la bonne lettre. (1–5) (AT 1.2)
Listening. Pupils listen to five people talking about where they normally go on holiday. They identify the picture of each place mentioned, writing the appropriate letter. You might want to warn them that there are two answers for one of the people.

Audioscript CD 3 track 2

1 *Tous les ans, nous allons en Espagne. Nous allons à la mer. J'aime bien.*
2 *Normalement, nous allons aux États-Unis. C'est super. Nous allons à la montagne. J'adore ça. C'est super.*
3 *Tous les ans, nous allons en Italie, à la campagne. C'est cool.*
4 *Tous les ans, nous restons en France, mais nous allons à la mer et c'est génial.*
5 *Normalement, nous allons en Grèce ou au Portugal. Nous allons tous les jours à la mer. C'est top.*

Answers
1 b 2 e 3 d 4 a 5 c, f

R Pupils working in pairs take it in turn to prompt with one of the country names from exercise 1 and to respond with the correct word for 'to'/'in' (*en*, *au* or *aux*).

2 Écoute à nouveau. À la campagne, à la montagne ou à la mer? Écris la bonne lettre. (1–5) (AT 1.2)
Listening. Pupils listen to the recording from exercise 1 again. They identify whether each speaker is talking about going to the countryside, the mountains or the seaside, writing the letter of the appropriate picture.

Audioscript CD 3 track 3

As for exercise 1

Answers
1 c 2 b 3 a 4 c 5 c

Studio Grammaire: *nous* forms (regular *–er* verbs + *aller*, *faire*)
Use the *Studio Grammaire* box to cover *nous* forms (regular *–er* verbs + *aller*, *faire*). There is more information and further practice on Pupil Book p. 104.

1 Les vacances, mode d'emploi 3 ... 2 ... 1 Partez! 5

3 Fais un sondage dans la classe. Fais un graphique des résultats. (AT 2.2)

PLTS

Speaking. Pupils carry out a survey on where people in the class normally go on holiday (country and location). A sample exchange is given. Pupils then make a graph of their results. This could be done on a computer.

Starter 2
Aim
To review present tense *nous* forms

Write up the following, jumbling the order of the words in each phrase. Give pupils three minutes to write them out as sentences, using capitals and inserting punctuation where needed.

1 *nous restons en France*
2 *nous allons à la mer*
3 *nous visitons des monuments*
4 *nous faisons de la natation*

Alternative Starter 2:
Use ActiveTeach p. 090 Flashcards to review and practise the language for holiday destinations.

4 Écoute et écris les bonnes lettres. (1–3) (AT 1.2)

Listening. Pupils listen to three people talking about what they normally do on holiday. They identify the two activities mentioned by each person, writing the letters of the appropriate pictures.

Audioscript CD 3 track 4

1 *Normalement, nous faisons de la rando et des activités sportives.*
2 *D'habitude, nous faisons du camping et nous faisons tous les jours de la natation.*
3 *Normalement, nous visitons des monuments et quelquefois, nous allons au restaurant.*

Answers
1 d, f **2** c, e **3** a, b

5 Lis les textes et réponds aux questions en anglais. (AT 3.5)

Reading. Pupils read the two e-mails from Adélaïde and Damien and identify which of them is described in each of the questions in English. Some vocabulary is glossed for support.

Answers
1 Adélaïde **2** Damien **3** Adélaïde **4** Damien
5 Adélaïde **6** Damien

6 Écoute. Que fait William pendant les grandes vacances? Prends des notes en anglais. (AT 1.5)

Listening. Pupils listen to William talking about what he and his family do during the summer holidays and note the main details in English.

Audioscript CD 3 track 5

L'année dernière, nous sommes allés en Espagne, mais normalement, nous allons au Portugal. Nous allons à la mer, à la plage. Nous faisons de la natation et des activités sportives. Quelquefois, nous allons au restaurant ou nous visitons des monuments. C'est génial.

Answers
last year, they went to Spain; usually go to Portugal, to the beach; swim and do sports activities; sometimes go to a restaurant or visit monuments

7 Que fait ta famille pendant les vacances? Prépare un exposé. (AT 2.5)

Speaking. Pupils prepare and give a presentation on what their family does on holiday. A list of details to include and a framework are supplied.

8 Écris ton exposé. (AT 4.5)

Writing. Pupils adapt their presentation from exercise 7 and write it out. When they have finished, they should check and correct their text and produce a second draft. Draw pupils' attention to the tip box on how they can attain a higher level by including a reason.

Plenary
Put the class into teams. Teams take it in turn (with a different team member speaking each time) to say a sentence about their holidays. Explain that accurate sentences will score points as follows: any sentence using *nous* in the present tense wins 1 point; a sentence using *nous sommes allés* wins 2 points; and a sentence using both forms of *nous* (e.g. *L'année dernière, nous sommes allés en France, mais normalement, nous allons au Portugal.*) wins 3 points. The team with most points wins.

Alternative Plenary:
Use ActiveTeach p. 091 Flashcards to review and practise the language for activities on holiday.

5   3…2…1 Partez!   1 Les vacances, mode d'emploi

Workbook A, page 42

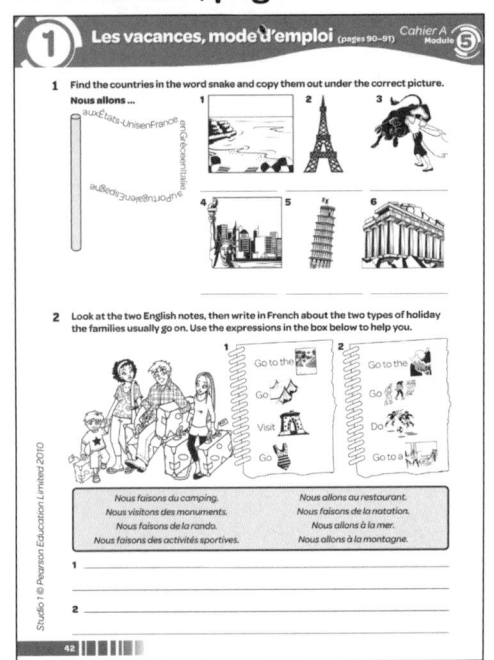

Answers

1 1 au Portugal   2 en France   3 en Espagne
   4 aux États-Unis   5 en Italie   6 en Grèce
2 1 Nous allons à la mer.
     Nous faisons du camping.
     Nous visitons des monuments.
     Nous faisons de la natation.
   2 Nous allons à la montagne.
     Nous faisons de la rando.
     Nous faisons des activités sportives.
     Nous allons au restaurant.

Workbook B, page 42

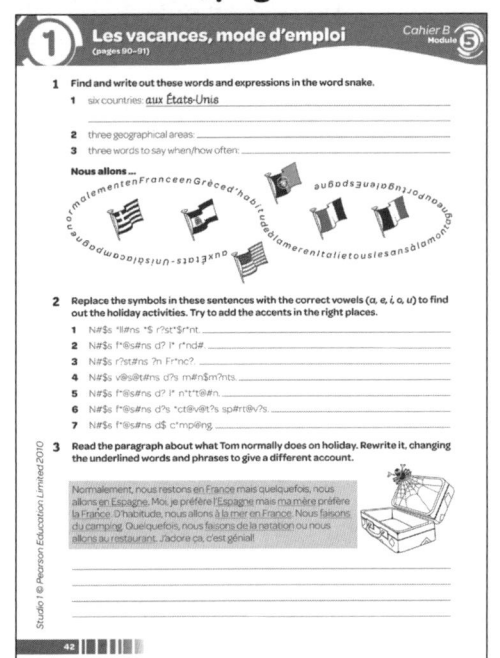

Answers

1 1 aux États-Unis, en France, en Grèce, en Italie, au Portugal, en Espagne
   2 à la campagne, à la mer, à la montagne
   3 normalement, d'habitude, tous les ans
2 1 Nous allons au restaurant.
   2 Nous faisons de la rando.
   3 Nous restons en France.
   4 Nous visitons des monuments.
   5 Nous faisons de la natation.
   6 Nous faisons des activités sportives.
   7 Nous faisons du camping.

Worksheet 5.1 Sound patterns

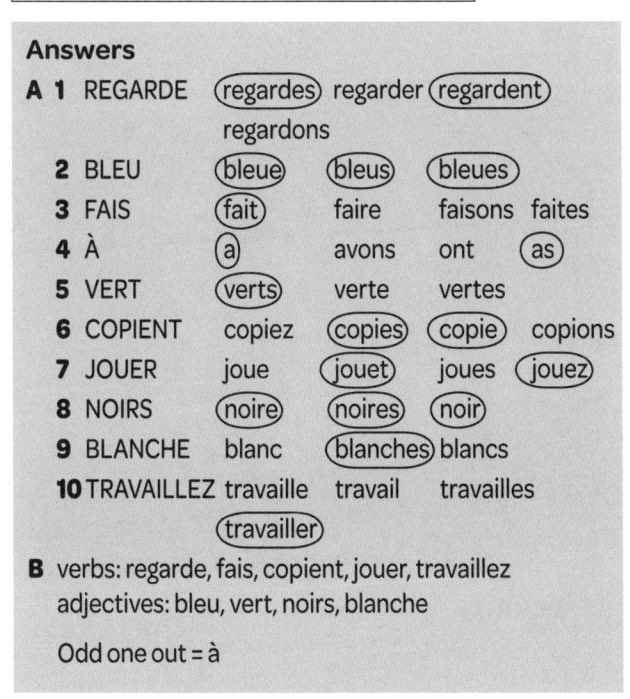

Module 5 — Thinking skills — Sound patterns — Studio 1 Feuille 5.1

A Work with a partner. Each set of words has a key word. Circle all the other words in that set which sound the same as the key word when read aloud.

#	Key word				
1	REGARDE	regardes	regarder	regardent	regardons
2	BLEU	bleue	bleus	bleues	
3	FAIS	fait	faire	faisons	faites
4	À	a	avons	ont	as
5	VERT	verts	verte	vertes	
6	COPIENT	copiez	copies	copie	copions
7	JOUER	joue	jouet	joues	jouez
8	NOIRS	noire	noires	noir	
9	BLANCHE	blanc	blanches	blancs	
10	TRAVAILLEZ	travaille	travail	travailles	travailler

B Classify the key words into one of the following groups. One of the key words is the 'odd one out' and does not belong to either group.

verbs	adjectives

Odd one out: _____

© Pearson Education Limited 2010
Printing and photocopying permitted
Page 1 of 1

Answers

A
1. REGARDE — (regardes) regarder (regardent) regardons
2. BLEU — (bleue) (bleus) (bleues)
3. FAIS — (fait) faire faisons faites
4. À — (a) avons ont (as)
5. VERT — (verts) verte vertes
6. COPIENT — copiez (copies) (copie) copions
7. JOUER — joue (jouet) joues (jouez)
8. NOIRS — (noire) (noires) (noir)
9. BLANCHE — blanc (blanches) blancs
10. TRAVAILLEZ — travaille travail travailles (travailler)

B verbs: regarde, fais, copient, jouer, travaillez
adjectives: bleu, vert, noirs, blanche

Odd one out = à

5 Partez! 2 Je me prépare ... (Pupil Book pp. 92–93)

Learning objectives
- Talking about getting ready to go out
- Using reflexive verbs (singular)

Framework objectives
4.2/Y7 Language – high-frequency words: ex. 6
5.6 Strategies – reading aloud: ex. 3

Grammar
- reflexive verbs (singular)

Key language
Je me douche.
Je me fais une crête.
Je me parfume.
Je m'habille.
Je me brosse les cheveux.
Je me lave les dents.
Je me regarde dans la glace.
Je me prépare.
Je me maquille.
Je me rase.

PLTS
E Effective participators

Cross-curricular
ICT: word processing

Resources
CD 3, tracks 6–7
Cahier d'exercices A & B, page 43
ActiveTeach:
p.092 Flashcards
p.092 Grammar
p.092 Grammar practice
p.092 Learning skills
p.093 Class activity
p.093 Grammar skills

Starter 1
Aim
To review *s'appeler* (singular) to introduce reflexive verbs

Write up the following, leaving the second column of the table blank. Give pupils two minutes to read the text and complete the table with the correct French versions of the verbs.

Salut! Je m'appelle Luc. J'habite à Marseille avec ma famille. Ma mère s'appelle Mathilde. Elle a quarante ans. J'ai une sœur et deux frères. Ils s'appellent Thérèse, Marc et Kévin. J'ai aussi un chien. Il est très grand. Il s'appelle Obélix! Comment t'appelles-tu? Tu as des frères et des sœurs?

I'm called	je m'appelle
you're called	tu t'appelles
he's called	il s'appelle
she's called	elle s'appelle

Check answers. Ask pupils what the difference is between the verb *s'appeler* and a verb like *aimer*. Prompt as necessary to cover the reflexive pronoun forms. Explain that this kind of verb is called a reflexive verb and that these will be covered in detail in this unit.

1 Écoute et écris la bonne lettre. (1–10) (AT 1.2)
Listening. Pupils listen to people describing their morning routine and identify the picture for each activity mentioned, writing the appropriate letter.

Audioscript — CD 3 track 6
1 *Je me douche.*
2 *Je me maquille.*
3 *Je me brosse les cheveux.*
4 *Je me parfume.*
5 *Je m'habille.*
6 *Je me prépare.*
7 *Je me rase.*
8 *Je me fais une crête.*
9 *Je me lave les dents.*
10 *Je me regarde dans la glace.*

Answers
1 a **2** i **3** e **4** c **5** d **6** h **7** j **8** b **9** f
10 g

Studio Grammaire: reflexive verbs (singular)
Use the *Studio Grammaire* box to cover reflexive verbs (singular). Draw pupils' attention to the way the pronoun contracts before a vowel sound (e.g. *il s'habille, elle s'appelle*). There is more information and further practice on Pupil Book pp. 104–105.

2 En tandem. Réponds à ces questions par une phrase affirmative ou une phrase négative. (AT 2.3)
Speaking. In pairs: pupils take it in turn to ask and answer the six questions supplied, either negatively or positively. A sample response is given. Draw pupils' attention to the tip box, which explains how to make reflexive verbs negative.

2 Je me prépare... 3...2...1 Partez! 5

+ Pupils write out negative responses to the six questions to practise using *ne ... pas* with reflexive verbs.

3 Écoute et chante. (AT 1.3)
Listening. Pupils listen to the song and sing along.

Audioscript CD 3 track 7

Que fais-tu quand tu te prépares ...
Que fais-tu quand tu te prépares ...
Que fais-tu quand tu te prépares ...
Pour sortir le soir?

Je me douche et je me maquille.
Je me douche et je me maquille.
Je me douche et je me maquille.
Ensuite, je m'habille.

Je me rase et je me lave les dents.
Je me rase et je me lave les dents.
Je me rase et je me lave les dents.
Se préparer, c'est amusant!

Que fais-tu quand tu te prépares ...
Que fais-tu quand tu te prépares ...
Que fais-tu quand tu te prépares ...
Pour sortir le soir?

Starter 2
Aim
To review reflexive verbs

Write up *je m'appelle* as a model. Give pupils three minutes working in pairs to list the *je* form of as many different reflexive verbs as they can.

Check answers. Ask pupils to give you the *tu, il* and *elle* forms of some of the verbs.

Alternative Starter 2:
Use ActiveTeach p. 092 Flashcards to review and practise reflexive verbs.

4 Trouve ces phrases en français dans la chanson. (AT 3.3)
Reading. Pupils re-read the song in exercise 3 and identify the French versions of the English sentences listed.

Answers
1 Que fais-tu quand tu te prépares?
2 Ensuite, je m'habille.
3 Je me lave les dents.
4 Se préparer, c'est amusant!
5 Pour sortir le soir.

5 Lis et note: vrai (V) ou faux (F)? (AT 3.4)
Reading. Pupils read the two texts, then read the eight sentences about them. They decide whether each sentence is true (writing V) or false (writing F). Some vocabulary is glossed for support.

Answers
1 V 2 V 3 V 4 F 5 F 6 V 7 F 8 F

6 Que fais-tu quand tu te prépares pour sortir? (AT 4.4)

Writing. Pupils write a paragraph about how they get ready to go out. A framework is supplied. Draw pupils' attention to the tip box on using expressions of time and frequency to improve their sentences. This work could be done on computers, with pupils checking each other's texts and then producing a second draft.

Plenary
PLTS E
Construct sentences about going out, going round the class. Ask the class to stand. Pupils take it in turn to add a word each time, e.g. Pupil 1 *D'abord*, Pupil 2 *je*, Pupil 3 *me*, etc. If a sentence is complete, the next pupil starts a new one. If a pupil makes a mistake or can't think of a word to add, he/she sits down and the game continues.

Alternative Plenary:
Use ActiveTeach p. 093 Class activity to review and practise reflexive verbs.

5 3...2...1 Partez! 2 Je me prépare...

Workbook A, page 43

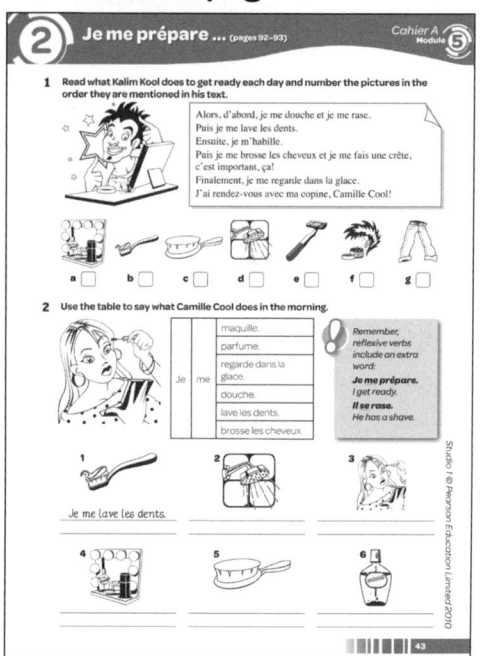

Answers

1 **a** 7 **b** 3 **c** 5 **d** 1 **e** 2 **f** 6 **g** 4

2 1 Je me lave les dents.
  2 Je me douche.
  3 Je me maquille.
  4 Je me regarde dans la glace.
  5 Je me brosse les cheveux.
  6 Je me parfume.

Workbook B, page 43

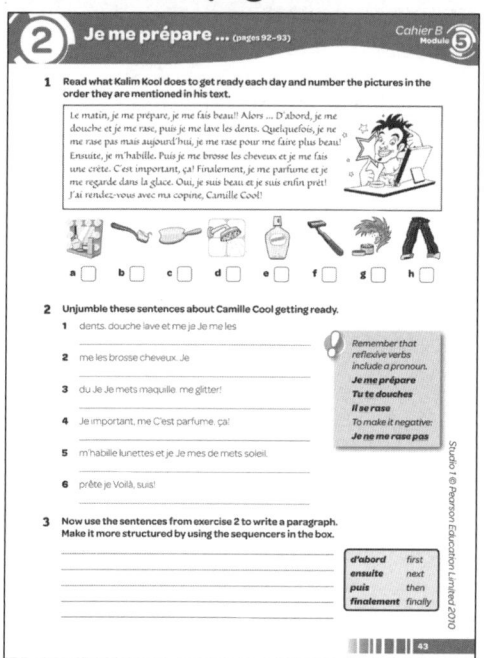

Answers

1 **a** 8 **b** 3 **c** 5 **d** 1 **e** 7 **f** 2 **g** 6 **h** 4

2 1 Je me douche et je me lave les dents.
  2 Je me brosse les cheveux.
  3 Je me maquille. Je mets du glitter!
  4 Je me parfume. C'est important, ça!
  5 Je m'habille et je mets mes lunettes de soleil.
  6 Voilà, je suis prête!

Worksheet 5.2 Using connectives, intensifiers and time expressions

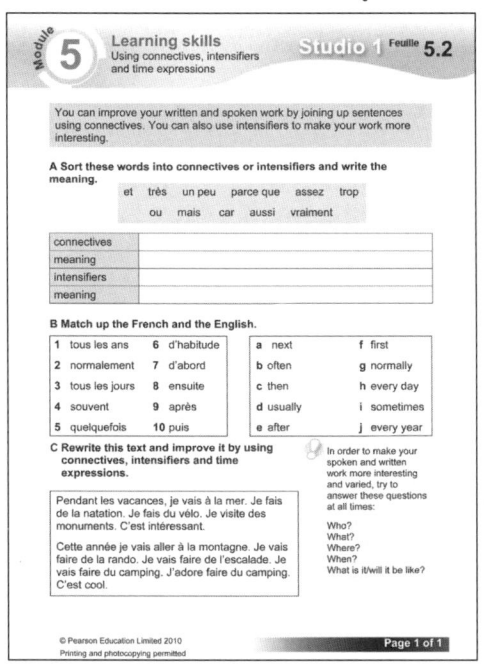

Answers

A

connectives	meaning	intensifiers	meaning
et	and	très	very
parce que	because	un peu	a bit
ou	or	assez	quite
mais	but	trop	too
car	because	vraiment	really
aussi	also		

B
1. tous les ans — j
2. normalement — g
3. tous les jours — h
4. souvent — b
5. quelquefois — i
6. d'habitude — d
7. d'abord — f
8. ensuite — a
9. après — e
10. puis — c

C (Example answer:)
Pendant les vacances, **normalement**, je vais à la mer. **Tous les jours**, je fais de la natation **ou** je fais du vélo. Je visite des monuments. C'est **assez** intéressant.
Cette année, je vais aller à la montagne **et** je vais faire de la rando. Je vais faire aussi de l'escalade **et** je vais faire du camping. J'adore faire du camping parce que c'est cool.

Worksheet 5.3 Reflexive verbs

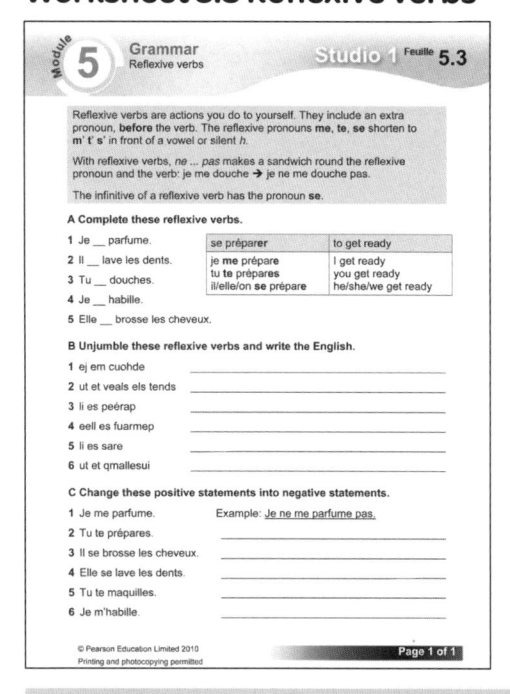

Answers

A
1. Je **me** parfume.
2. Il **se** lave les dents.
3. Tu **te** douches.
4. Je **m'**habille.
5. Elle **se** brosse les cheveux.

B
1. je me douche — I have a shower
2. tu te laves les dents — you brush your teeth
3. il se prépare — he gets himself ready
4. elle se parfume — she puts on perfume
5. il se rase — he shaves
6. tu te maquilles — you put on make-up

C
1. Je ne me parfume pas.
2. Tu ne te prépares pas.
3. Il ne se brosse pas les cheveux.
4. Elle ne se lave pas les dents.
5. Tu ne te maquilles pas.
6. Je ne m'habille pas.

3 Au Café de la Plage (Pupil Book pp. 94–95)

Learning objectives
- Buying drinks and snacks
- Using higher numbers

Key language
quarante
quarante-cinq
cinquante
cinquante-cinq
soixante
soixante-cinq
soixante-dix
soixante-quinze
quatre-vingts
quatre-vingt-cinq
quatre-vingt-dix
quatre-vingt-quinze
Tu as combien d'argent?
J'ai (dix euros cinquante).
J'ai faim et j'ai soif.
Vous désirez, monsieur/mademoiselle?
Je voudrais ...
un café
un café-crème
un thé (au lait/au citron)
un chocolat chaud
un coca
un jus d'orange
un Orangina
une limonade
un sandwich au fromage
un sandwich au jambon
un croquemonsieur
une crêpe
une glace (à la vanille/à la fraise/au chocolat)

PLTS
C Creative thinkers

Cross-curricular
Maths: number sequences

Resources
CD 3, tracks 8–10
Accès Studio pages 6–7, 8–9 & 24–25
Cahier d'exercices A & B, page 44
ActiveTeach:
p.094 Flashcards
p.095 Video 9
p.095 Video worksheet 9
p.095 Flashcards
p.095 Class activity

Accès Studio Units 2 & 3 (pp. 6–9) can be used with this unit to review numbers to 31.
Accès Studio Unit 11 (pp. 24–25) can be used with this unit to review food vocabulary.

Starter 1
Aim
To review numbers 1–30

Write up the following. Give pupils three minutes to add two more numbers to continue each sequence (answers shown in brackets).

1 *trente, vingt-six, vingt-deux, ...* (*dix-huit, quatorze* – minus 4 each time)
2 *trois, six, neuf, ...* (*douze, quinze* – 3 times table)
3 *un, quatre, neuf, ...* (*seize, vingt-cinq* – square numbers)
4 *un, deux, quatre, sept, ...* (*onze, seize* – add 1 more each time, so add 1, then 2, then 3, etc.)

1 Associe les chiffres et les mots. (AT 3.1)
PLTS C
Reading. Pupils match the numbers to the words. Draw their attention to the tip box on reading strategies and remind them, if necessary, to look for cognates and patterns.

Answers
(See the audioscript for exercise 2: pupils listen to check their own answers.)

2 Écoute et vérifie. (AT 1.1)
Listening. Pupils listen and check their answers to exercise 1.

Audioscript   CD 3 track 8

40 quarante
45 quarante-cinq
50 cinquante
55 cinquante-cinq
60 soixante
65 soixante-cinq
70 soixante-dix
75 soixante-quinze
80 quatre-vingts
85 quatre-vingt-cinq
90 quatre-vingt-dix
85 quatre-vingt-quinze

3 À quatre. Joue au loto! (AT 2.1)
Speaking. In fours: pupils play bingo. The instructions are given in English.

4 Écoute. Ils ont combien d'argent? (1–5) (AT 1.4)
Listening. Pupils listen to five conversations about money and note how much money each person has. Some vocabulary is glossed for support.

3 Au Café de la Plage 3 … 2 … 1 Partez! 5

Audioscript CD 3 track 9

1 – *Tu as combien d'argent?*
 – *J'ai huit …, neuf …, dix euros cinquante.*
 – *Dix euros cinquante? OK. On va au café?*
 – *D'accord. Allons-y!*

2 – *Tu as combien d'argent?*
 – *Euh, attends … sept euros et … cinquante … soixante. J'ai sept euros soixante. Pourquoi?*
 – *On va au café. D'accord?*

3 – *Tu as soif?*
 – *Oui, j'ai soif. On va au café?*
 – *Tu as combien d'argent?*
 – *Pas beaucoup. J'ai cinq euros quarante-cinq.*
 – *Cinq euros quarante-cinq! C'est tout?*

4 – *Oh, j'ai faim! Et toi, tu as faim?*
 – *Oui, j'ai faim. Tu as combien d'argent?*
 – *Je suis riche! J'ai neuf euros quatre-vingts!*
 – *Neuf euros quatre-vingts! D'accord. On va au café!*

5 – *Oh, il fait chaud! Tu as faim?*
 – *J'ai faim et j'ai soif! On va au café?*
 – *Tu as combien d'argent?*
 – *Alors, j'ai … douze euros soixante-dix.*
 – *Ça va. Allons-y!*

Answers
1 10,50€ **2** 7,60€ **3** 5,45€ **4** 9,80€ **5** 12,70€

5 En tandem. Mets les phrases dans le bon ordre et fais un dialogue. (AT 2.3)

Speaking. In pairs: pupils put the sentences into the correct order to make a dialogue. They take it in turn to play each part. The opening is supplied for support.

Answers
● *Tu as soif?*
■ *Oui, j'ai faim et j'ai soif!*
● *On va au café?*
■ *Tu as combien d'argent?*
● *J'ai 12,80€. Et toi, tu as combien?*
■ *Pas beaucoup. J'ai 3,70€.*
● *D'accord. Allons-y!*

Starter 2
Aim
To review prices

Write up the following, with the first one as a model. Give pupils three minutes to write out each price in words.

1 8,60€ – *huit euros soixante*
2 5,80€ **3** 3,40€ **4** 12,75€ **5** 30,55€
6 20,95€

Alternative Starter 2:
Use ActiveTeach p. 094 Flashcards to review and practise numbers.

6 Regarde le menu et les photos. Complète les prix sur le menu. (AT 3.3)

Reading. Pupils use the prices from the photos to fill in the missing prices in the menu.

Answers
1 1,50€ **2** 2,50€ **3** 2,50€ **4** 3,00€ **5** 2,60€
6 2,50€ **7** 4,50€ **8** 2,60€

R Pupils working in pairs take it in turn to prompt with one of the items of food/drink pictured and to give the price in French.

7 Écoute. Qu'est-ce qu'ils commandent au Café de la Plage? Note en anglais. (1–5) (AT 1.4)

Listening. Pupils listen to five conversations in which people are ordering food/drink in a café and note in English the details of what each person orders.

Audioscript CD 3 track 10

1 – *Vous désirez, monsieur?*
 – *Je voudrais une limonade et un sandwich au jambon, s'il vous plaît.*

2 – *Mademoiselle, vous désirez?*
 – *Euh … je voudrais un jus d'orange et une glace à la vanille, s'il vous plaît.*

3 – *Et pour vous, monsieur?*
 – *Pour moi, un croquemonsieur et un café-crème, s'il vous plaît.*

4 – *Mademoiselle, que désirez-vous?*
 – *J'ai faim, moi! Je voudrais une crêpe, s'il vous plaît.*
 – *Et comme boisson?*
 – *Heu … un chocolat chaud, s'il vous plaît.*

5 – *Et pour vous, mademoiselle?*
 – *Moi, je voudrais un thé au lait et un sandwich au fromage, s'il vous plaît.*

5 3...2...1 Partez!   3 Au Café de la Plage

Answers
1. lemonade and ham sandwich
2. orange juice and vanilla ice-cream
3. toasted cheese and ham sandwich and white coffee
4. pancake and hot chocolate
5. tea with milk and cheese sandwich

8 En groupe. Imagine que tu vas au Café de la Plage avec tes copains. (AT 2.4)

Speaking. In groups: pupils make up conversations at *Café de la Plage*. One pupil plays the waiter/waitress; the others play the part of customers ordering food and drinks. A framework is supplied. Each pupil should take a turn as the waiter/waitress.

9 Écris un menu pour le Café Fou! Ensuite, écris un dialogue. (AT 4.4)

Writing. Pupils write a menu for *Café Fou* – the Mad Café – which specialises in strange food. An example is given. They then write a dialogue in which some customers order food at *Café Fou*.

Plenary

Ask groups of pupils to perform their dialogues from exercise 8. The rest of the class gives constructive feedback. If you want to structure this, ask the class to identify the two things they thought were best about the performance and one thing the group could improve on. (You could make this more challenging – and funnier – by having pupils use the details from the menus they wrote for *Café Fou* in exercise 9.)

Alternative Plenary:
Use ActiveTeach p. 095 Class activity to review and practise numbers and the language for food and drink.

Workbook A, page 44

Answers
1. 1 une glace 2 un chocolat chaud
   3 un sandwich au fromage 4 un croquemonsieur
   5 un jus d'orange 6 un thé 7 une crêpe
   8 un café
2. 1 un sandwich au fromage 2 une glace
   3 un café 4 un croquemonsieur 5 une crêpe
   6 un jus d'orange

3 Au Café de la Plage 3 ... 2 ... 1 Partez! 5

Workbook B, page 44

Answers
1 1 une glace 2 un thé 3 un sandwich au fromage
4 un croquemonsieur 5 un jus d'orange
6 une limonade 7 une crêpe
8 un chocolat chaud

2 Bonjour monsieur, vous désirez?
Je voudrais un croquemonsieur, s'il vous plaît.
Et comme boisson?
Un café-crème, s'il vous plaît
Et pour vous, mademoiselle?
Pour moi, une crêpe et un jus d'orange, s'il vous plaît.

3 12,85€ (douze euros quatre-vingt-cinq)

Video
Episode 9: J'ai faim!
The StudioFR team are in a treetop adventure park. Samira is ready to film but Hugo is too hungry and Marielle is too thirsty to start so they go to the snack bar. Video worksheet 9 can be used in conjunction with this episode.

Answers to video worksheet (ActiveTeach)
1 **A** French food.
  B They actually want to film the treetop adventure attraction in this leisure park.
  C [PLTS T/E] Not at all, as they start eating and drinking instead.
2 **A** They are hungry and thirsty.
  B Ham sandwich, cheese sandwich, croquemonsieur (toasted cheese and ham sandwich), pancakes, waffles
  C Vanilla ice-cream, chocolate ice-cream, strawberry ice-cream
  D On the board there are: cola, Orangina, lemonade, coffee, tea, hot chocolate
3 **A** She tries to order a salad – presumably to maintain her appearance.
  B He seems shocked that it's so much. (He has to take more money out of his pocket.)
  C Marielle ordered a pancake but gets a ham sandwich.
  D Samira starts out with a sweatshirt but ends up wearing a coat.
  E He starts to fall asleep, but she says it's out of the question.
  F Alex should prepare the camera, Hugo the questions and Marielle ... herself!
4 [F3.1/3.2]

4 Je vais aller en colo! (Pupil Book pp. 96–97)

Learning objectives
- Talking about holiday plans
- Using the near future tense

Framework objectives
4.5/Y7 Language – (a) set phrases about the future: ex. 1

Grammar
- the near future tense

Key language
Qu'est-ce que tu vas faire pendant les vacances?
Je vais ...
aller à la pêche
danser
faire de l'accrobranche
faire du karaoké
faire de la voile
faire de la planche à voile
nager dans la mer
rester au lit
retrouver mes copains/copines
Normalement, ...
Cette année, ...

PLTS
R Reflective learners

Resources
CD 3, tracks 11–12
Cahier d'exercices A & B, page 45
ActiveTeach:
p.096 Flashcards
p.096 Grammar
p.096 Grammar practice
p.097 Video 10
p.097 Video worksheet 10
p.097 Thinking skills
p.099 Grammar skills, exercise B

Starter 1
Aim
To review infinitive forms

Write up the following (omitting the answers given in brackets). Give pupils three minutes to write the infinitive form of each of the verbs listed.

1 nages (nager)
2 fais (faire)
3 retrouve (retrouver)
4 dansons (danser)
5 restent (rester)
6 ai (avoir)
7 aime (aimer)
8 vont (aller)

Check answers. Ask pupils for examples of sentences using these infinitives, prompting as necessary to cover structures such as *j'aime/je peux/je veux* + infinitive. Remind pupils that the infinitive is the verb form used in a dictionary. Explain that this unit covers another use of the infinitive: with the verb *aller*, to talk about the future.

1 Écoute. Qu'est-ce qu'ils vont faire pendant les vacances? Écris la bonne lettre. (1–6) (AT 1.3)
Listening. Pupils listen to six conversations and identify the picture of the activity that each person is going to do in the holidays, writing the appropriate letter.

Audioscript CD 3 track 11

1 – Bonjour. Qu'est-ce que tu vas faire pendant les vacances?
 – Pendant les vacances? Je vais aller à la pêche avec mon frère. C'est top!
2 – Et toi? Qu'est-ce que tu vas faire pendant les vacances?
 – Moi? Je vais faire de la voile avec ma famille.
3 – Pardon. Qu'est-ce que tu vas faire pendant les vacances?
 – Je vais nager dans la mer! J'adore nager!
4 – Et toi, qu'est-ce que tu vas faire?
 – Pendant les vacances, je vais faire de la planche à voile.
 – De la planche à voile?
 – Oui. C'est ma première fois!
 – Alors, bonne chance!
5 – Salut! Qu'est-ce que tu vas faire pendant les vacances?
 – Moi, je vais danser! Je vais danser avec mes copines!
6 – Excuse-moi. Qu'est-ce que tu vas faire pendant les vacances?
 – Je vais rester au lit!
 – Tu vas rester au lit?
 – Oui. Je suis très fatiguée!

Answers
1 c 2 b 3 a 4 e 5 f 6 d

Studio Grammaire: the near future tense
Use the *Studio Grammaire* box to introduce the near future tense. There is more information and further practice on Pupil Book p. 105.

2 Lis le texte et réponds aux questions. (AT 3.3)
Reading. Pupils read the three texts, then identify who is being described in each of the six questions in English.

146

4 Je vais aller en colo! 3 ... 2 ... 1 Partez! 5

Answers
1 Hugo 2 Éloïse 3 Medhi 4 Éloïse 5 Medhi
6 Éloïse

3 En tandem. Fais un dialogue. Utilise les images A, B ou C. (AT 2.3)

Speaking. In pairs: pupils take it in turn to ask what they are going to do on holiday and answer using the picture prompts A, B or C. A sample conversation is given.

Starter 2
Aim
To review the near future tense

Give pupils three minutes working in pairs to complete ActiveTeach p. 099 Grammar skills, Worksheet 5.5 Using two tenses together, exercise B. Ask the class for answers. (See p. 153 of this Teacher's Guide for the answers.)

4 Lis le texte. Regarde les images: Nathan fait ça normalement ou il va faire ça en colo? (AT 3.5)

Reading. Pupils read Nathan's text and look at the pictures of activities below. They identify which activities he normally does and which he is going to do at holiday camp, writing the appropriate letters. Some vocabulary is glossed for support.

Answers
Normalement: e, g, d
En colo: a, c, h, f, b

➕ Pupils work in pairs with their books closed. Between them they try to recall the three activities Nathan normally does (using *Normalement* + the present tense) and the five activities he's going to do this year (using *Cette année* + the near future tense).

5 Écoute. C'est au présent ou au futur? Écris P ou F. (1–10) (AT 1.5)

Listening. Pupils listen to ten sentences about activities and note whether each one uses the present tense (writing P) or the near future tense (writing F).

Audioscript CD 3 track 12
1 Je fais du camping.
2 Je vais faire du VTT.
3 Je vais rester au lit.
4 Je vais aller à la pêche.
5 Je retrouve mes copains en ville.
6 Je vais jouer au tennis.
7 Je vais nager dans la mer.
8 Je joue au basket.
9 Je vais danser avec mes copains.
10 Je regarde la télé.

Answers
1 P 2 F 3 F 4 F 5 P 6 F 7 F 8 P 9 F
10 P

6 Écris des phrases. (AT 4.5)

Writing. Using the picture prompts supplied, pupils write sentences saying what they normally do and what they are going to do this year. They should use the connective *mais* to join the two parts of each sentence, as shown in the example. When they have finished, pupils swap with a partner and underline any errors in each other's work. Pupils then correct their own work.

Answers
1 Normalement, je vais en Espagne, mais cette année, je vais aller en France.
2 Normalement, je fais du skate, mais cette année, je vais faire du VTT.
3 Normalement, je joue au foot(ball), mais cette année, je vais jouer au volley(ball).
4 Normalement, je mange au restaurant, mais cette année, je vais danser.
5 Normalement, je nage dans la mer, mais cette année, je vais faire de la planche à voile.
6 (Pupils' own answers)

PLTS R

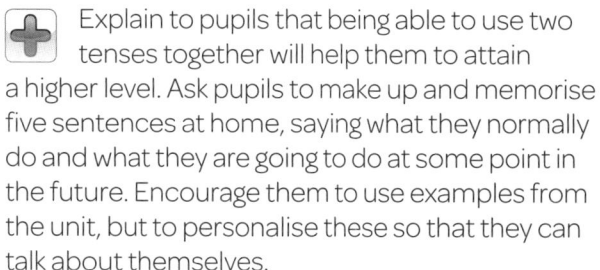

➕ Explain to pupils that being able to use two tenses together will help them to attain a higher level. Ask pupils to make up and memorise five sentences at home, saying what they normally do and what they are going to do at some point in the future. Encourage them to use examples from the unit, but to personalise these so that they can talk about themselves.

147

5 3…2…1 Partez!   4 Je vais aller en colo!

Plenary

Ask the class to summarise how the near future tense is formed and when it is used.

Then put the class into teams and get them to close their books. Give each team a piece of paper and a pen. Tell them they have three minutes to come up with as many different answers as they can to the question *Qu'est-ce que tu vas faire ce weekend?* All answers must feature the near future tense and a different activity. When they have finished they swap and correct another team's answers: two points for a completely correct sentence, one point if there's a minor error. The team with the most points wins.

Alternative Plenary:
Use ActiveTeach p. 096 Grammar practice to review and practise the near future tense.

Workbook A, page 45

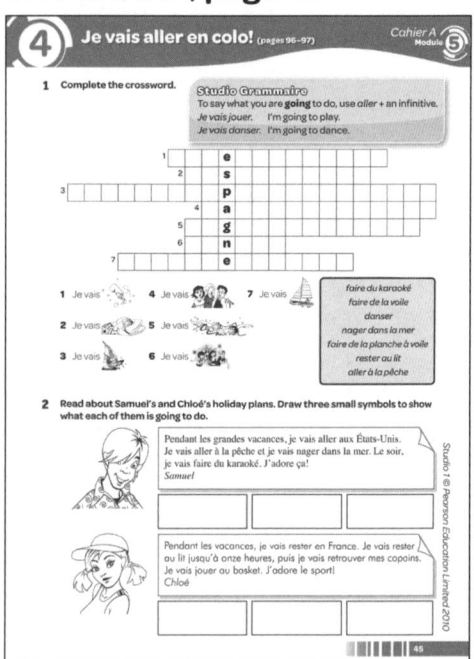

Answers
1 1 aller à la pêche   2 rester au lit
   3 faire de la planche à voile   4 faire du karaoké
   5 nager dans la mer   6 danser   7 faire de la voile
2 (Symbols for:)
   Samuel: fishing, swimming (in sea), karaoke
   Chloé: staying in bed, meeting friends, playing basketball

Workbook B, page 45

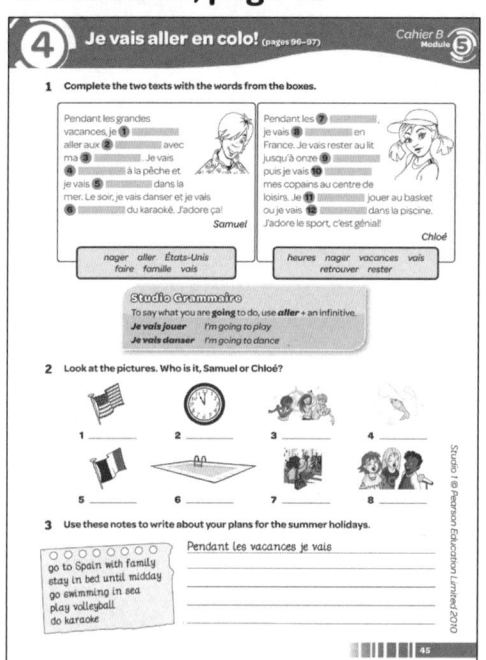

Answers
1 1 vais   2 États-Unis   3 famille   4 aller
   5 nager   6 faire   7 vacances   8 rester
   9 heures   10 retrouver   11 vais   12 nager
2 1 Samuel   2 Chloé   3 Samuel   4 Samuel
   5 Chloé   6 Chloé   7 Chloé   8 Samuel
3 (Example answer:)
   Pendant les vacances, je vais aller en Espagne avec ma famille. Je vais rester au lit jusqu'à midi. L'après-midi, je vais nager dans la mer et je vais jouer au volley. Le soir, je vais faire du karaoké. J'adore ça!

4 Je vais aller en colo! 3...2...1 Partez! 5

Worksheet 5.4 Logic puzzle

Answers
Marc va aller à Bordeaux du 1 au 31 août où il va visiter des vignobles.
Lucie va aller à la Martinique du 20 au 31 juillet où elle va faire du cyclisme.
Caroline va aller au Québec du 1 au 15 juillet où elle va aller aux restaurants.
Ahmed va aller à Paris du 1 au 15 août où il va visiter des musées.

Video

Episode 10: Fans d'accrobranche

For their next video StudioFR is at Cap Aventures, a treetop adventure park, where they are trying out 'accrobranche' for their viewers. Video worksheet 10 can be used in conjunction with this episode.

Answers to video worksheet (ActiveTeach)

1. **A** They indicate the level of difficulty.
   B No. They use the word 'tester' (to test).
   C [PLTS **T/E**] Hugo, who goes for the red level.
2. **A** She's talking about what she normally does in the holidays.
   B He uses the word 'challenge'.
   C She's worried it might be too high.
   D He's doing the filming.
3. **A** They are talking about what they are going to do in the future.
   B Because Marielle was saying 'Samira and Hugo are going to climb the ladder …', but she should have been saying '**we** are going to climb the ladder …'.
   C He has a go after all, despite saying he was going to do the filming.
   D Now she says green is too easy. Next time she will do red.
   E – It's too easy
   – We enjoy it!/We love it!
   – See you soon!
   F Superman!

5 Mes rêves (Pupil Book pp. 98–99)

Learning objectives
- Saying what you would like to do
- Using *je voudrais* + infinitive

Framework objectives
4.5/Y7 Language – (a) set phrases about the future: ex. 1

Grammar
- *je voudrais* + infinitive
- 'to'/'in' a place or country

Key language
Quels sont tes rêves?
Je voudrais aller ...
à Paris
en Australie
au Canada
aux États-Unis
Je voudrais ...
être footballeur professionnel
être danseuse professionnelle
habiter dans une grande maison
avoir une voiture très cool
faire le tour du monde
rencontrer mon acteur/actrice préféré(e)

PLTS
S Self-managers

Resources
CD 3, tracks 13–14
Cahier d'exercices A & B, page 46
ActiveTeach:
p.098 Flashcards
p.099 Grammar skills

Starter 1
Aim
To review the near future tense

Read out sentences from Unit 4, using a mixture of present tense and near future tense examples. Sometimes include *Normalement/Cette année* or *Ce weekend* as markers. Pupils sit down for sentences in the present and stand up for those in the near future.

Ask pupils to summarise how the near future tense is formed, giving their own examples. Explain that this unit covers another way of talking about the future: in it pupils will learn how to say what they would like to do in the future.

1 Écoute. C'est Olivia ou Samuel? Écris les bonnes lettres. (AT 1.4)

Listening. Pupils listen to two people talking about their dreams and identify what each person would like to do, writing the letters of the appropriate pictures.

Audioscript CD 3 track 13

- Bonjour. J'ai avec moi Olivia ...
- Bonjour!
- ... et Samuel.
- Salut!
- Ma question, c'est: Quels sont tes rêves? Samuel?
- J'adore le foot. Je voudrais être footballeur professionnel.
- Ah, bon? Footballeur professionnel!
- Et toi, Olivia?
- Moi, j'aime danser. Je voudrais être danseuse professionnelle!
- Danseuse professionnelle! Fantastique!
- Alors, Samuel, tu voudrais avoir beaucoup d'argent?
- Ah, oui! Je voudrais habiter dans une grande maison.
- Et toi, Olivia?
- Je voudrais avoir une voiture très cool – une Porsche, par exemple.
- Est-ce que tu voudrais voyager aussi?
- Oui. Je voudrais aller en Australie et aux États-Unis.
- Et toi, Samuel, tu voudrais voyager aussi?
- Oui, mais moi, je voudrais faire le tour du monde!
- Et finalement, Olivia, tu as un autre rêve, je crois!
- Ah, oui ... je voudrais rencontrer mon acteur préféré ...
- C'est qui, ton acteur préféré?
- C'est Robert Pattinson.
- Ah, oui. Il est beau, n'est-ce pas? Bon, merci, Olivia et Samuel, et au revoir.

Answers
Olivia: d, f, a, b, h
Samuel: c, e, g

Studio Grammaire: *je voudrais* + infinitive
Use the *Studio Grammaire* box to cover *je voudrais* + infinitive. There is more information and further practice on Pupil Book p. 105.

2 Écris dix phrases qui commencent par *Je voudrais*. (AT 4.3)
Writing. Pupils write ten sentences using *Je voudrais* and their own choice of the verbs and phrases supplied.

Answers
(Any ten of:)
Je voudrais …
avoir une Xbox 360/un vélo BMX.
aller à Paris/à Disneyland/en France/au Canada.
être chanteur/chanteuse professionnel(le).
faire du snowboard/de la planche à voile.
habiter à Paris/en France/au Canada.
rencontrer mon actrice préférée/mon sportif/ma sportive préféré(e)/mon groupe préféré.

R Write up sentences from exercise 1 (e.g. *Je voudrais avoir une voiture très cool.*), jumbling the order of the words. With books closed, pupils say the sentences in the correct order.

3 En tandem. Interviewe ton/ta camarade. (AT 2.4)
Speaking. In pairs: pupils take it in turn to ask about their dreams and to respond using *je voudrais*. A sample exchange is given.

Starter 2
Aim
To review *je voudrais* + infinitive

Put pupils into pairs. Tell them to imagine what their partner's dreams for the future are. Give them three minutes working individually to write three dreams for their partner using *je voudrais*. Check that everyone remembers that *je voudrais* is followed by the infinitive before they start.

Hear some answers. Ask partners to comment on the accuracy of the French and of the dreams chosen.

Alternative Starter 2:
Use ActiveTeach p. 098 Flashcards to review and practise *je voudrais* + infinitive.

4 Écoute et regarde les images. Qui parle? (1–4) (AT 1.4)
Listening. Pupils listen to four conversations, in which people talk about their dreams, and use the pictures to identify the speaker each time.

Audioscript   CD 3 track 14

1 *Je suis canadien, mais un jour, je voudrais aller en France. Je voudrais aller à Paris. Je voudrais visiter la tour Eiffel. Ensuite, je voudrais faire les magasins!*

2 *Moi, je voudrais aller en Angleterre parce que j'adore l'anglais! Je voudrais aller à Londres, la capitale. Je voudrais visiter Big Ben. Et le soir, je voudrais manger des fish and chips – du poisson avec des frites. Miam-miam!*

3 *Mon rêve, c'est d'aller aux États-Unis. Je voudrais aller à New York. Je voudrais visiter la Statue de la Liberté, je voudrais manger un hamburger-frites et je voudrais rencontrer le Président, Barack Obama!*

4 *Un jour, je voudrais habiter en Australie parce que j'adore le soleil! Je voudrais faire un barbecue sur la plage. Et je voudrais faire du surf et aller à la pêche.*

Answers
1 *Baptiste*   2 Emma   3 Morgane   4 Abdel

Studio Grammaire: 'to'/'in' a place or country
Use the *Studio Grammaire* box to cover the different ways of saying 'to' or 'in' a place/country.

5 Écris des textes pour les personnes de l'exercice 4. (AT 4.4)
Writing. Using the picture prompts in exercise 4 and the gap-fill versions supplied, pupils write a short text for each of the people in exercise 4. The missing words are supplied in random order.

Answers
Moi, je voudrais aller en **Angleterre**. Je voudrais aller à Londres. Je voudrais visiter **Big Ben**. Le soir, je voudrais manger **des fish and chips**.
Je voudrais aller en France. Je voudrais aller à **Paris**. Je voudrais visiter **la tour Eiffel**. Ensuite, je voudrais faire **les magasins**.
Un jour, je voudrais aller en **Australie**. Je voudrais faire un barbecue **sur la plage**. Je voudrais faire **du surf et aller à la pêche**.
Je voudrais aller aux **États-Unis**. Je voudrais aller à **New York**. Je voudrais manger **un hamburger-frites**. Je voudrais rencontrer **le Président, Barack Obama**.

6 Fais un mini exposé au sujet de tes rêves. (AT 2.4)
Speaking. Pupils prepare and give a short presentation about their own dreams for the future. A list of the details to include and a sample opening are supplied. Ask the rest of the class to give constructive feedback on content and pronunciation.

5 3...2...1 Partez! 5 Mes rêves

7 Écris un court paragraphe sur «Mes rêves». (AT 4.4)
Writing. Pupils write a short paragraph about their own dreams for the future, adapting their presentation from exercise 6.

PLTS S

Read together through the *Stratégie* on Pupil Book p. 107, covering letter and sound patterns. Set pupils the challenge of choosing and learning five pairs of words using this approach, either in the classroom or at home.

Plenary
Ask pupils to summarise how to talk about what they would like to do in the future using *je voudrais* + infinitive. Then ask them to give examples of the structure from their presentations in exercise 6. Reward the most imaginative ideas.

Workbook A, page 46

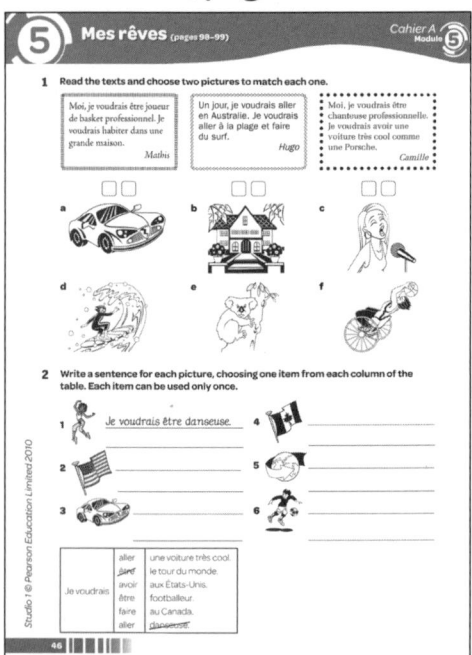

Answers
1 **1** f, b   **2** e, d   **3** c, a
2 **1** Je voudrais être danseuse.
   2 Je voudrais aller aux États-Unis.
   3 Je voudrais avoir une voiture très cool.
   4 Je voudrais aller au Canada.
   5 Je voudrais faire le tour du monde.
   6 Je voudrais être footballeur.

Workbook B, page 46

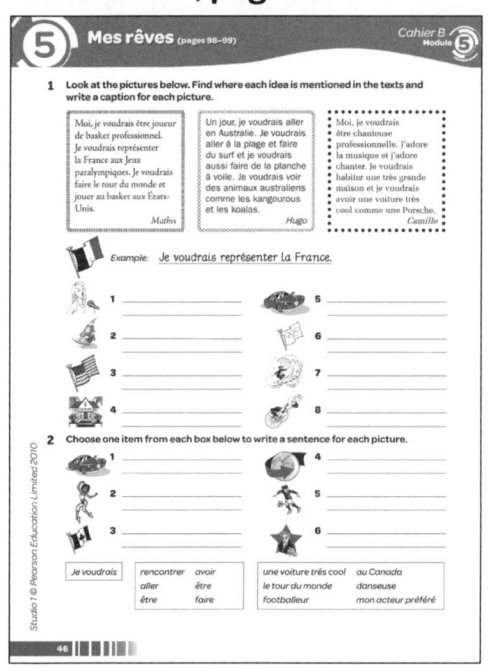

Answers
1 **1** Je voudrais être chanteuse professionnelle./J'adore chanter.
   2 Je voudrais aussi faire de la planche à voile.
   3 Je voudrais jouer au basket aux États-Unis.
   4 Je voudrais habiter dans une très grande maison.
   5 Je voudrais avoir une voiture très cool, comme une Porsche.
   6 Je voudrais représenter la France aux Jeux paralympiques.
   7 Je voudrais faire du surf.
   8 Moi, je voudrais être joueur de basket professionnel./Je voudrais jouer au basket aux États-Unis.
2 **1** Je voudrais avoir une voiture très cool.
   2 Je voudrais être danseuse.
   3 Je voudrais aller au Canada.
   4 Je voudrais faire le tour du monde.
   5 Je voudrais être footballeur.
   6 Je voudrais rencontrer mon acteur préféré.

Worksheet 5.5 Using two tenses together

Answers

A
1. Je vais aller en Grèce et je vais visiter des monuments. F
2. Je fais de la natation et je fais des activités sportives. P
3. Tu vas rester en France? F
4. Je nage dans la mer et quelquefois, nous visitons des monuments. P
5. Normalement, je vais en vacances avec ma famille. P
6. On va manger une pizza. F

B
1. Cette année, nous allons visiter des monuments.
2. Cette année, je vais aller au restaurant.
3. Cette année, il va faire du camping.
4. Cette année, on va faire de la rando.
5. Cette année, ils vont faire de la natation.

C
1. Je ne vais pas rester au lit.
2. Il ne va pas nager dans la mer.
3. Ils ne vont pas jouer au foot.
4. Vous n'allez pas danser.
5. Tu ne vas pas faire du karaoké.
6. Elle ne va pas faire de la planche à voile.

5 Bilan et Révisions (Pupil Book pp. 100–101)

Bilan
Pupils use this checklist to review language covered in the module, working on it in pairs in class or on their own at home. Encourage them to follow up any areas of weakness they identify. There are Target Setting Sheets included in the Assessment Pack, and an opportunity for pupils to record their own levels and targets on the *J'avance* page in the Workbook, p. 49. You can also use the *Bilan* checklist as an end-of-module plenary option.

Révisions
These revision exercises can be used for assessment purposes or for pupils to practise before tackling the assessment tasks in the Resource & Assessment File.

Resources
CD 3, tracks 15–16
Cahier d'exercices A & B, pages 47 & 48

1 Écoute et écris la bonne lettre. (1–5) (AT 1.3)
Listening. Pupils listen to five conversations, in which people order food and drinks in a café. They identify the picture for each order, writing the appropriate letter.

Audioscript CD 3 track 15

1 – Monsieur? Que désirez-vous?
– Je voudrais un coca et un croquemonsieur, s'il vous plaît.
– Voilà, monsieur. Un coca et un croquemonsieur.
– Merci. C'est combien, s'il vous plaît?
– 10,10€, s'il vous plaît.

2 – Mademoiselle? Que désirez-vous?
– Je voudrais une limonade et un sandwich au jambon, s'il vous plaît.
– Voilà, mademoiselle. Une limonade et un sandwich au jambon.
– Merci. C'est combien, s'il vous plaît?
– 5,00€, s'il vous plaît.

3 – Monsieur? Que désirez-vous?
– Je voudrais un jus d'orange et une glace au chocolat, s'il vous plaît.
– Voilà, monsieur. Un jus d'orange et une glace au chocolat.
– Merci. C'est combien, s'il vous plaît?
– 6,35€, s'il vous plaît.

4 – Mademoiselle? Que désirez-vous?
– Je voudrais un café-crème et un sandwich au fromage, s'il vous plaît.
– Voilà, mademoiselle. Un café-crème et un sandwich au fromage.
– Merci. C'est combien, s'il vous plaît?
– 4,50€, s'il vous plaît.

5 – Monsieur? Que désirez-vous?
– Je voudrais un thé au citron et une crêpe, s'il vous plaît.
– Voilà, monsieur. Un thé au citron et une crêpe.
– Merci. C'est combien, s'il vous plaît?
– 7,20€, s'il vous plaît.

Answers
1 d 2 e 3 b 4 a 5 c

2 Écoute à nouveau et note les prix. (1–5) (AT 1.4)
Listening. Pupils listen to the recording from exercise 1 again and note the prices using figures.

Audioscript CD 3 track 16

As for exercise 1

Answers
1 10,10€ 2 5,00€ 3 6,35€ 4 4,50€ 5 7,20€

3 Dis comment tu te prépares quand tu sors. Utilise les images ou tes propres idées. (AT 2.2–4)
Speaking. Pupils say how they get ready when they're going out, using either the picture prompts supplied or their own ideas.

4 Lis le texte et réponds aux questions en anglais. (AT 3.5)
Reading. Pupils read Candice's text and answer the questions on it in English.

Answers
1 Spain 2 go camping (in the countryside)
3 it's boring
4 (Any two of:) swim (in the sea), sailing, karaoke
5 Australia 6 surfing and fishing

5 Écris un court paragraphe sur les vacances. (AT 4.3–5)
Writing. Pupils write a short paragraph about their own holidays. Details of what to include are supplied. Draw pupils' attention to the tip box on how to attain a higher level by including details of what they are going to do this year and where they would like to go in the future.

Bilan et Révisions 3 ... 2 ... 1 Partez! **5**

Workbook A, page 47

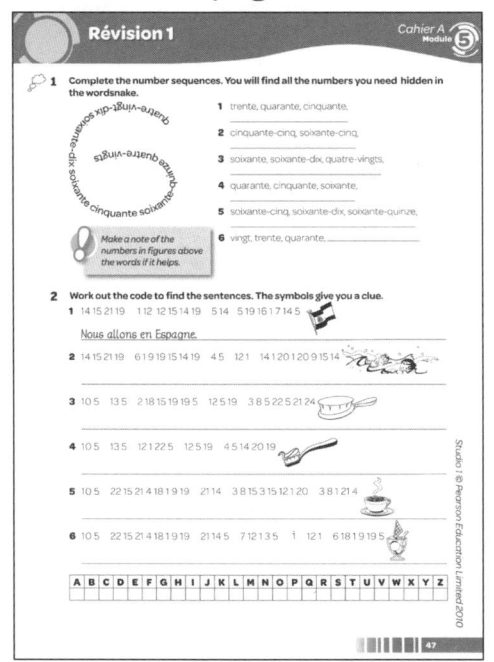

Workbook A, page 48

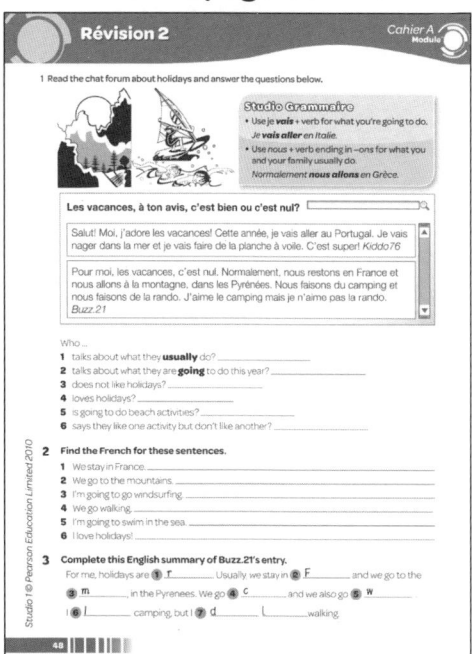

Answers

1 1 soixante 2 soixante-quinze 3 quatre-vingt-dix
   4 soixante-dix 5 quatre-vingts 6 cinquante
2 1 Nous allons en Espagne.
   2 Nous faisons de la natation.
   3 Je me brosse les cheveux.
   4 Je me lave les dents.
   5 Je voudrais un chocolat chaud.
   6 Je voudrais une glace à la fraise.

Answers

1 1 Buzz.21 2 Kiddo76 3 Buzz.21 4 Kiddo76
   5 Kiddo76 6 Buzz.21
2 1 Nous restons en France.
   2 Nous allons à la montagne.
   3 Je vais faire de la planche à voile.
   4 Nous faisons de la rando.
   5 Je vais nager dans la mer.
   6 J'adore les vacances!
3 1 rubbish 2 France 3 mountains 4 camping
   5 walking 6 like 7 don't like

155

5 3...2...1 Partez! Bilan et Révisions

Workbook B, page 47

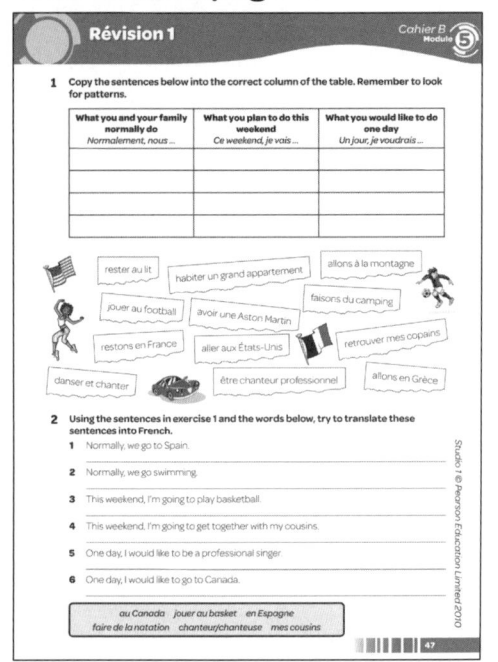

Answers

1

What you and your family normally do *Normalement, nous...*	What you plan to do this weekend *Ce weekend, je vais...*	What you would like to do one day *Un jour, je voudrais...*
allons à la montagne	rester au lit	habiter dans un grand appartement
faisons du camping	jouer au football	aller aux États-Unis
restons en France	danser et chanter	avoir une Aston Martin
allons en Grèce	retrouver mes copains	être chanteur professionnel

2
1. Normalement, nous allons en Espagne.
2. Normalement, nous faisons de la natation.
3. Ce weekend, je vais jouer au basket.
4. Ce weekend, je vais retrouver mes cousins.
5. Un jour, je voudrais être chanteur professionnel/chanteuse professionnelle.
6. Un jour, je voudrais aller au Canada.

Workbook B, page 48

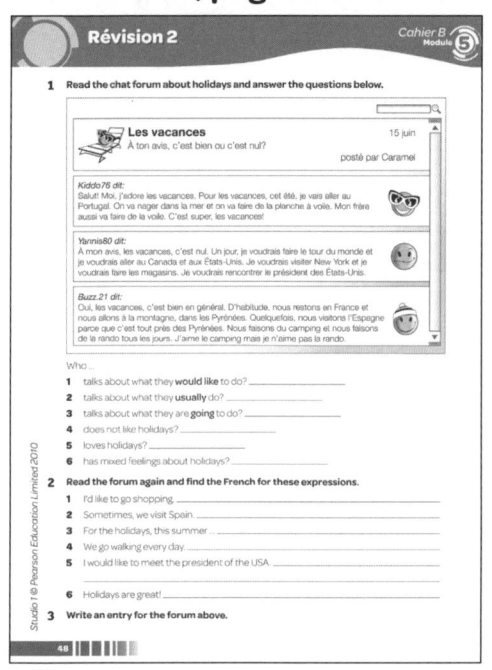

Answers

1 1 Yannis80 2 Buzz.21 3 Kiddo76 4 Yannis80
    5 Kiddo76 6 Buzz.21

2 1 Je voudrais faire les magasins.
    2 Quelquefois, nous visitons l'Espagne.
    3 Pour les vacances, cet été ...
    4 Nous faisons de la rando tous les jours.
    5 Je voudrais rencontrer le président des États-Unis.
    6 C'est super, les vacances!

5 Partez! En plus: Tu vas aller où? (Pupil Book pp. 102–103)

Learning objectives
- Talking about where people go on holiday
- Finding out about holidays in France

Framework objectives
2.2/Y7 Reading – (b) text selection: Plenary
5.5 Strategies – reference materials: ex. 2

Key language
Review of language from the module
le canoë-kayak, le surf, le ski nautique, le VTT, le tir à l'arc, le quad
la voile, la planche à voile, la plongée sous-marine, la spéléologie, la randonnée
l'accrobranche, l'escalade, l'équitation

PLTS
T Team workers

Cross-curricular
ICT: Internet research

Resources
CD 3, tracks 17–18
ActiveTeach:
p.103 Assignment 5
p.103 Assignment 5: prep

Starter
Aim
To use reading strategies

Give pupils three minutes working in pairs to translate into English the activities listed on the holiday camp website in exercise 1 (*voile, planche à voile*, etc.).

Check answers, asking pupils to explain how they worked them out (cognates, context or educated guesswork).

(Answers: **A** sailing, wind-surfing, kayaking, surfing, water-skiing, scuba diving, **B** horse-riding, mountain biking, treetop adventure, hiking, archery, quad biking, **C** climbing, hiking, kayaking, mountain biking, caving)

1 Écoute et regarde le texte. Où vont-ils – colo A, B ou C? (1–3) (AT 1.5)

Listening. Pupils listen to three conversations in which people talk about the holiday camp they are going to this year. For each person, they identify the holiday camp – A, B or C – using the information supplied on the website.

Audioscript CD 3 track 17

1 – *Bonjour, Flavie. Qu'est-ce que tu vas faire pendant les vacances?*
– *Cette année, je vais partir en colo.*
– *En colo? C'est top, ça! Qu'est-ce que tu vas faire en colo?*
– *Alors, je vais faire du VTT, de l'équitation, du tir à l'arc ...*
– *Du tir à l'arc? Super! Tu as de la chance!*
– *Je vais faire du quad aussi.*
– *Du quad! Moi aussi, je voudrais faire du quad.*
– *Oui, c'est génial, hein? Et je vais faire de l'accrobranche.*
– *De l'accrobranche? Cool! Alors, amuse-toi bien!*
– *Merci.*

2 – *Alors, Quentin. Qu'est-ce que tu vas faire pendant les vacances?*
– *Je vais partir en colo avec mon frère.*
– *Cool! Qu'est-ce que vous allez faire, comme activités?*
– *On va faire du canoë-kayak, de la voile, de la planche à voile ...*
– *C'est super, ça. Tu vas aussi faire de la plongée sous-marine?*
– *Oui, moi, je vais faire de la plongée sous-marine, mais mon frère n'aime pas ça. Il va faire du ski nautique.*
– *Je voudrais bien faire du ski nautique, moi. Tu as de la chance! Alors, bonnes vacances!*
– *Merci, au revoir.*

3 – *Salut, Aurélie. Qu'est-ce que tu vas faire pendant les vacances?*
– *Je vais partir en colo à la montagne.*
– *C'est fantastique. Tu vas faire de la randonnée?*
– *Oui, je vais faire de la randonnée. Je vais aussi faire du canoë-kayak, du VTT ...*
– *C'est top, ça! J'adore faire du VTT. Tu vas faire de l'escalade?*
– *Oui, je vais faire de l'escalade. Et je vais aussi faire de la spéléologie.*
– *De la spéléologie! Beurk! Je ne voudrais pas faire ça. Alors, amuse-toi bien!*
– *Merci. Et bonnes vacances!*

Answers
1 Flavie: B **2** Quentin: A **3** Aurélie: C

2 C'est quelle activité? (AT 4.4)

Writing. Pupils label the seven pictures with the correct activity. Draw their attention to the tip box on using a dictionary to find out the gender of a word.

5 3 … 2 … 1 Partez! En plus: Tu vas aller où?

Answers
1 le canoë-kayak 2 la plongée sous-marine
3 le ski nautique 4 l'accrobranche 5 le tir à l'arc
6 le quad 7 la spéléologie

3 Écoute à nouveau. On mentionne combien d'activités? Fais une liste. (1–3) (AT 1.5)

Listening. Pupils listen to the recording from exercise 1 again and note all the activities listed.

Audioscript CD 3 track 18

As for exercise 1

Answers
(13 activities are mentioned:)
1 VTT, équitation, tir à l'arc, quad, accrobranche
2 canoë-kayak, voile, planche à voile, plongée sous-marine, ski nautique
3 randonnée, (canoë-kayak), (VTT), escalade, spéléologie

4 En tandem. Choisis la colo A, B ou C et fais un dialogue. (AT 2.5)

Speaking. In pairs: pupils choose holiday camp A, B or C from exercise 1 and have a dialogue about it. A framework is supplied. Draw pupils' attention to the tip box on including opinions and reactions.

5 Regarde la carte et lis les textes. Ils vont aller où? (AT 3.5)

Reading. Pupils look at the map and photos, and read the texts. They identify where the people are going to go, writing a sentence for each person.

Answers
Albane: Je vais aller à Tours.
Frank: Je vais aller à Paris.
Leïla: Je vais aller à Marseille.
Clément: Je vais aller à Rouen.
Zoë: Je vais aller à Chamonix.
Damien: Je vais aller à Disneyland Paris.

6 Qu'est-ce que c'est en anglais? Explique comment tu as trouvé le sens. (AT 3.5)

Reading. Pupils work out the meanings of the six French expressions taken from the texts in exercise 5. They explain which reading strategies they used to work out each one.

Answers
1 a monument 2 seafood 3 cider
4 to meet my idol 5 to go skiing on grass 6 fondue

7 Imagine que tu vas aller en vacances en France. Fais des recherches sur Internet. Choisis une ville. Qu'est-ce que tu vas faire? (AT 4.3–5)

PLTS T

Writing. Pupils imagine that they are going to go on holiday in France and research a destination of their choice on the Internet. They then write a paragraph about what they are going to do there. A sample opening is given. Ask pupils in groups of three or four to read each other's work and decide individually which of the holidays sounds most appealing.

Pupils could use this task as an opportunity to exchange information with French pupils, if you have a partner school in France. In return for information about France, they could supply information in English about holiday areas of the UK. Pupils could also exchange details of what they typically do on holiday and what their future plans are.

Plenary

To review the near future tense, ask pupils round the class to talk about the place they researched in exercise 7, saying some of the things they are going to do there.

Alternative Plenary:

Give pupils three minutes to look through Module 6 and select a text that they are looking forward to reading. Ask them to say why in English.

Alternatively, you could bring in a range of short simple texts from French magazines, books or Internet sites on one of the topics already covered in the course and ask pupils to choose from these.

En plus: Tu vas aller où? 3 ... 2 ... 1 Partez! 5

Worksheet 5.6 Chanson pour l'Europe!

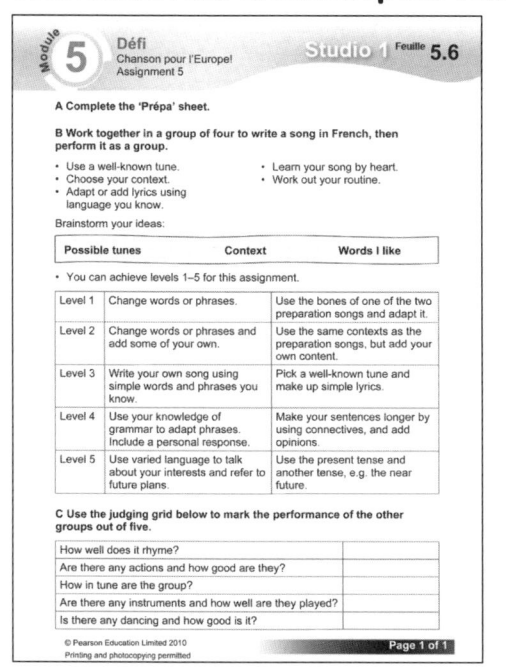

A Complete the 'Prépa' sheet.

B Work together in a group of four to write a song in French, then perform it as a group.
- Use a well-known tune.
- Choose your context.
- Adapt or add lyrics using language you know.
- Learn your song by heart.
- Work out your routine.

Brainstorm your ideas:

Possible tunes	Context	Words I like

- You can achieve levels 1–5 for this assignment.

Level 1	Change words or phrases.	Use the bones of one of the two preparation songs and adapt it.
Level 2	Change words or phrases and add some of your own.	Use the same contexts as the preparation songs, but add your own content.
Level 3	Write your own song using simple words and phrases you know.	Pick a well-known tune and make up simple lyrics.
Level 4	Use your knowledge of grammar to adapt phrases. Include a personal response.	Make your sentences longer by using connectives, and add opinions.
Level 5	Use varied language to talk about your interests and refer to future plans.	Use the present tense and another tense, e.g. the near future.

C Use the judging grid below to mark the performance of the other groups out of five.

How well does it rhyme?	
Are there any actions and how good are they?	
How in tune are the group?	
Are there any instruments and how well are they played?	
Is there any dancing and how good is it?	

Worksheet 5.7 Chanson pour l'Europe! Prépa

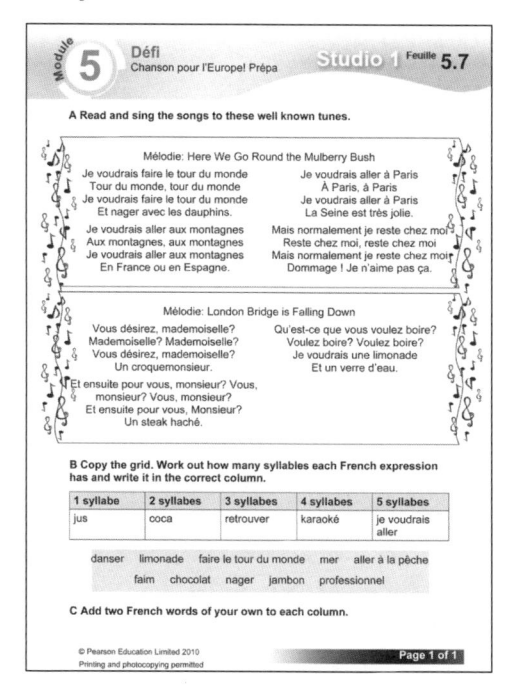

A Read and sing the songs to these well known tunes.

Mélodie: Here We Go Round the Mulberry Bush

Je voudrais faire le tour du monde
Tour du monde, tour du monde
Je voudrais faire le tour du monde
Et nager avec les dauphins.

Je voudrais aller aux montagnes
Aux montagnes, aux montagnes
Je voudrais aller aux montagnes
En France ou en Espagne.

Je voudrais aller à Paris
À Paris, à Paris
Je voudrais aller à Paris
La Seine est très jolie.

Mais normalement je reste chez moi
Reste chez moi, reste chez moi
Mais normalement je reste chez moi
Dommage ! Je n'aime pas ça.

Mélodie: London Bridge is Falling Down

Vous désirez, mademoiselle?
Mademoiselle? Mademoiselle?
Vous désirez, mademoiselle?
Un croquemonsieur.

Et ensuite pour vous, monsieur? Vous, monsieur? Vous, monsieur?
Et ensuite pour vous, Monsieur?
Un steak haché.

Qu'est-ce que vous voulez boire?
Voulez boire? Voulez boire?
Je voudrais une limonade
Et un verre d'eau.

B Copy the grid. Work out how many syllables each French expression has and write it in the correct column.

1 syllabe	2 syllabes	3 syllabes	4 syllabes	5 syllabes
jus	coca	retrouver	karaoké	je voudrais aller

danser   limonade   faire le tour du monde   mer   aller à la pêche
faim   chocolat   nager   jambon   professionnel

C Add two French words of your own to each column.

Answers

A (Answers will vary.)

B

1 syllabes	2 syllabes	3 syllabes	4 syllabes	5 syllabes
jus	coca	retrouver	karaoké	je voudrais aller
mer	danser	limonade		faire le tour du monde
faim	nager	chocolat		aller à la pêche
	jambon			professionnel

C (Answers will vary.)

Studio Grammaire (Pupil Book pp. 104–105)

Partez! 5

The *Studio Grammaire* section provides a more detailed summary of the key grammar covered in the module, along with further exercises to practise these points.

Grammar topics
- regular *-er* verbs in the present tense
- using *nous* in the present tense
- reflexive verbs
- *je voudrais* + infinitive
- the near future tense

Regular *-er* verbs in the present tense

1 Find all the parts of *jouer* (to play) and match them with the English.
Pupils identify all the parts of *jouer* in the word snake and match them with the English versions listed.

Answers
ils jouent   tu joues   il joue   nous jouons   on joue
je joue   vous jouez   elles jouent   elle joue
1 *je joue*   2 tu joues   3 il joue   4 elle joue
5 nous jouons, on joue   6 vous jouez   7 ils jouent
8 elles jouent

2 Complete each sentence by selecting the correct form of the verb.
Pupils write the completed sentences, choosing the correct verb form from the two options given each time.

Answers
1 Il **mange** un sandwich.
2 J'**écoute** de la musique.
3 Vous **désirez**?
4 Tu **restes** au lit.
5 Elles **dansent**.
6 Elle **aime** les vacances.
7 Nous **jouons** au volley.
8 On **adore** le reggae.

Using *nous* in the present tense

3 Replace the verbs in brackets with the correct form.
Pupils complete the gap-fill text, replacing each infinitive with the *nous* form of the verb.

Answers
1 *allons*   2 allons   3 aimons   4 allons   5 visitons
6 faisons

Reflexive verbs

4 Translate into French (*se réveiller* – to wake up).
Pupils translate the verb forms into French using *se réveiller*.

Answers
1 *il se réveille*   2 tu te réveilles   3 elle se réveille
4 je me réveille   5 on se réveille

5 Describe these morning routines.
Pupils use the picture prompts to write descriptions of Rémy and Mia's morning routines.

Answers
Rémy se réveille. Il se douche. Il s'habille. Il se lave les dents. Il se rase.
Mia se réveille. Elle se lave les dents. Elle se maquille. Elle se parfume. Elle s'habille.

Je voudrais + infinitive

6 Translate the sentences into French.
Pupils translate the sentences into French using *je voudrais* + infinitive.

Answers
1 Je voudrais visiter la France.
2 Je voudrais aller aux États-Unis.
3 Je voudrais jouer au tennis.
4 Je voudrais nager dans la mer.
5 Je voudrais faire le tour du monde.
6 Je voudrais rencontrer Johnny Depp.

The near future tense

7 Copy and complete the text using the correct forms of the near future tense.
Pupils copy and complete the gap-fill text, using the picture prompts and the near future tense.

Answers
1 vais nager   2 vais faire de la planche à voile
3 allons danser   4 allons faire du karaoké
5 vont faire de la rando(nnée)   6 vont aller à la pêche
7 va faire du rafting   8 vas faire

Studio Grammaire 3…2…1 Partez! 5

8 Translate the text in exercise 7 into English.

Pupils translate the completed text from exercise 7 into English.

> **Answers**
> It's the holidays soon and I can't wait. I'm going to swim in the sea and I'm going to go windsurfing. In the evening we're going to dance and we're going to do karaoke. My friends/mates are going to go to the mountains. They're going to go hiking and they're going to go fishing. My sister is going to go to holiday camp. She's going to do white water rafting. What are you going to do?

5 À toi (Pupil Book pages 126–127)

Self-access reading and writing

A Reinforcement

1 Décode les mots en gras et copie les phrases. (AT 3.2)

Reading. Pupils use the code supplied to decode the words in bold and copy out the sentences.

Answers
1 Nous allons en **Espagne**.
2 Nous allons en **France**.
3 Nous allons à la **montagne**.
4 Nous faisons du **camping**.
5 Nous faisons de la **natation**.
6 Nous allons au **restaurant**.

2 Associe chaque phrase de l'exercice 1 à la bonne image. (AT 3.2)

Reading. Pupils match the sentences in exercise 1 to the correct pictures.

Answers
1 d 2 c 3 a 4 e 5 b 6 f

3 Regarde les images. C'est Ronan le clown ou Zahra la gymnaste? (AT 3.2)

Reading. Pupils look at the pictures and read the texts. They decide whether the items pictured belong to Ronan the clown or Zahra the gymnast.

Answers
a Zahra b Ronan c Ronan d Zahra e Ronan
f Zahra

4 Tu as combien d'argent? Écris des phrases. (AT 4.2–3)

Writing. Pupils add up each group of notes and coins and write a sentence in French saying how much money they have.

Answers
1 J'ai dix euros cinquante.
2 J'ai deux euros soixante.
3 J'ai vingt euros soixante-dix.
4 J'ai cinq euros quarante.
5 J'ai dix euros quatre-vingts.

B Extension

1 Cherche l'intrus à chaque ligne et explique pourquoi en anglais. (AT 3.4)

Reading. Pupils find the odd one out in each line and explain why in English. The tip box points out that they are looking for grammatical differences here.

Answers
(The following are suggested answers. Other answers which have a valid explanation may also be possible.)
1 b – because the noun is masculine
2 a – because the others are reflexive verbs
3 c – because *me* is shortened to *m'*
4 b – because the noun is feminine
5 a – because the others are in the near future tense
6 c – because the others use *je voudrais*

2 Lis le texte et réponds aux questions pour Colette. (AT 3.5)

Reading. Pupils read the text and answer the questions for Colette. The tip box gives support in using the appropriate tense.

Answers
1 Non, nous ne partons pas en vacances./Non, nous restons en France.
2 Non, je déteste ça parce que c'est ennuyeux.
3 Je fais du vélo, je vais à la piscine et j'écoute de la musique.
4 Je vais aller en Grèce.
5 Je vais aller à la plage, je vais nager dans la mer, je vais faire du jet-ski, je vais manger au restaurant et je vais danser. (Answers using 'on va' can also be accepted.)
6 Je voudrais être danseuse professionnelle.

3 Écris tes réponses aux questions de l'exercice 2. Écris un paragraphe. (AT 4.5)

Writing. Pupils write a paragraph giving their own answers to the questions in exercise 2.

Module 6: Studio découverte
(Pupil Book pp. 108–117)

Unit & Learning objectives	PoS & Framework objectives	Key language	Grammar and other language features
1 Animaux (pp. 110–111) Talking about animals	**2.1e** use reference materials **2.2i** reuse language they have met **4a** use language in the classroom, etc. **4c** use more complex language **4e** use a range of resources **4g** language for a range of purposes	J'ai choisi (le zèbre). J'ai étudié son habitat. J'ai recherché son alimentation. etc.	**G** the perfect tense – giving feedback on a presentation
2 Poésie (pp. 112–113) Writing a poem	**2.2g** write clearly and coherently **2.2j** adapt previously learned language **3d** use a range of vocab/structures **4c** use more complex language **4f** language for interest/enjoyment **4g** language for a range of purposes	Review of language from throughout the course Il est né … Il a travaillé … Il a écrit … Il est allé … etc.	**G** the perfect tense – giving feedback on pronunciation – writing skills: adapting a model text; using language and structures you know
3 Peintures (pp. 114–115) Describing a painting	**2.1d** previous knowledge **2.2j** adapt previously learned language **4b** communicate in pairs, etc. **4c** use more complex language **4f** language for interest/enjoyment **4g** language for a range of purposes	Review of language for expressing opinions J'ai choisi … J'ai bien regardé. J'ai identifié (douze) couleurs différentes. etc. au centre, sur la gauche/droite, devant, derrière	**G** the perfect tense
Studio Grammaire (pp. 116–117) Detailed grammar summary and practice exercises			**G** the perfect tense – using the perfect tense in other contexts – attaining Level 5: using the present tense and one other tense – attaining Level 6: using the present tense and two other tenses

1 Animaux (Pupil Book pp. 110–111)

Studio découverte 6

Learning objective
- Talking about animals

Grammar
- the perfect tense

Key language
J'ai choisi (le zèbre).
On peut trouver (des tigres) en …
J'ai étudié son habitat.
(Le loup) habite …
J'ai examiné son caractère.
J'ai observé son aspect physique.
Il/Elle est …
Il/Elle aime/n'aime pas …
J'ai recherché son alimentation.
En général, il/elle mange …
J'ai trouvé son ennemi.
Ses prédateurs sont …

PLTS
E Effective participators

Cross-curricular
Science: animals and their habitats
English: vocabulary groups (animal sounds)

Resources
CD 3, track 19
Accès Studio pages 18–19
Cahier d'exercices A & B, pages 52–53
ActiveTeach:
p.111 Thinking skills

Accès Studio Unit 8 (pp. 18–19) can be used with this unit to review or introduce vocabulary to talk about animals.

Starter 1
Aim
To review verb structures; To use grammatical knowledge to work out connections

Write up the following, jumbling the order of the second column. Give pupils three minutes to match the sentence halves.

1 *Je veux aller au*   a *cinéma.*
2 *Il adore traîner*   b *avec ses copains.*
3 *On*   c *peut manger au restaurant.*
4 *Amélie n'aime*   d *pas jouer au football.*
5 *Je vais*   e *faire du karaoké.*

Check answers, asking pupils to explain how they worked them out. Pupils then translate the sentences into English.

1 Lis les textes. Copie et remplis la carte d'identité pour chaque animal. (AT 3.3)
Reading. Pupils read the two texts, then copy and complete the identity card for each animal. Some vocabulary is glossed for support.

Answers
Animal: tigre
Habitat: la forêt
Caractère: solitaire, nocturne; n'aime pas partager son habitat
Aspect physique: orange avec des rayures noires et un peu de blanc sur la poitrine
Alimentation: carnivore – mange les herbivores
Ennemi: l'homme

Animal: loup
Habitat: la montagne, dans la forêt
Caractère: intelligent, pas solitaire – habite dans un groupe/une meute
Aspect physique: fauve avec un peu de gris et un peu de noir, les yeux jaunes
Alimentation: carnivore
Ennemi: l'homme

2 Associe les animaux et leurs cris. Traduis les phrases en anglais. (AT 3.2)
Reading. Pupils complete the sentences by matching the animals with the sounds they make, then translate the sentences into English. You may want to draw their attention to the strategies listed in exercise 3 for support.

Answers
1 *Le tigre rugit.*   A tiger roars.
2 *Le loup hurle.*   A wolf howls.
3 *L'éléphant barrit.*   An elephant trumpets.
4 *Le serpent siffle.*   A snake hisses.
5 *Le zèbre hennit.*   A zebra neighs.
6 *L'hippopotame grogne.*   A hippopotamus grunts.
7 *La girafe meugle.*   A giraffe moos.
8 *La hyène ricane.*   A hyena laughs.
9 *Le singe crie.*   A monkey shouts (chatters/gibbers in English).

1 Animaux Studio découverte 6

3 À trois. Discute et décide.
Speaking. In threes: pupils compare their answers to exercises 1 and 2 and decide who is right. They then discuss how they tackled exercises 1 and 2, referring to the list of strategies supplied.

Starter 2
Aim
To review language for talking about animals

Write up the headings from the identity card in exercise 1 on p. 110 of the Pupil Book. Give pupils three minutes working in pairs to remember as many of the facts as they can for either the tiger or the wolf. Pupils can answer in French or English, depending on the level of the class.

4 Lis l'exposé de Yanis et complète les phrases en anglais. (AT 3.5)
Reading. Pupils read Yanis's presentation on zebras and complete the sentences summarising it in English.

Answers
1 You can find zebras in **Africa**.
2 They live on **the plains** and in **the mountains**.
3 Zebras are sociable – they live together in **a group**.
4 Zebras don't like **predators**.
5 Zebras eat **grass and plants**.
6 Their predators are **hyenas, lions and crocodiles**.

5 Trouve les verbes dans le texte. (AT 3.5)
Reading. Pupils re-read the text in exercise 4 and find the French versions of the six English verbs listed.

Answers
1 j'ai choisi   2 j'ai étudié   3 j'ai examiné
4 j'ai observé   5 j'ai recherché   6 j'ai trouvé

➕ Explain how to form the perfect tense of regular –er verbs which take *avoir* (singular forms). Pupils write out the *je* and *il* forms of the perfect tense of the following verbs: *manger, jouer, regarder, surfer, télécharger, envoyer*. Explain that the perfect tense is covered in detail in *Studio 2*.

6 Écoute. C'est quel animal? (AT 1.5)
Listening. Pupils listen to a presentation and identify the animal being described.

Audioscript CD 3 track 19

J'ai choisi (…). J'ai étudié son habitat.
On peut trouver cet animal dans l'hémisphère sud, dans l'Antarctique. C'est un oiseau. Il habite au bord de la mer.
J'ai examiné son caractère. Il est drôle. Il aime rester en groupe: une colonie.
J'ai observé son aspect physique. Il est grand. Il est noir et blanc. Il a un bec et des ailes. Il nage, mais il ne vole pas.
J'ai recherché son alimentation. En général, il mange des poissons. Ses prédateurs sont l'orque et le phoque.

Answer
le pingouin (penguin)

7 Choisis un animal. Fais des recherches. Prépare un exposé sur ton animal. (AT 2.1–5)
PLTS E

Speaking. Pupils research an animal of their choice, then prepare and give a presentation on it. Key language is supplied.

When pupils are ready to do their presentations, they should work in groups of four. They take it in turn to present to the rest of the group, then vote on which of the four presentations they liked best, giving reasons for their preference.

Plenary
Make up a presentation on an imaginary animal as a class, using the presentation topics outlined in exercise 7 (animal name, country, habitat, character, likes/dislikes, physical appearance, food, enemy). Encourage the class to be imaginative. Note the details on the board, then get pupils to use the details to say a sentence each about the animal.

6 Studio découverte 1 Animaux

Workbook A, pages 52–53

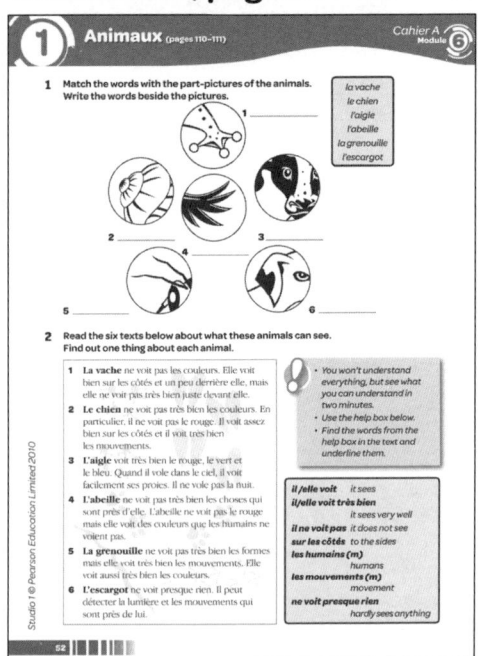

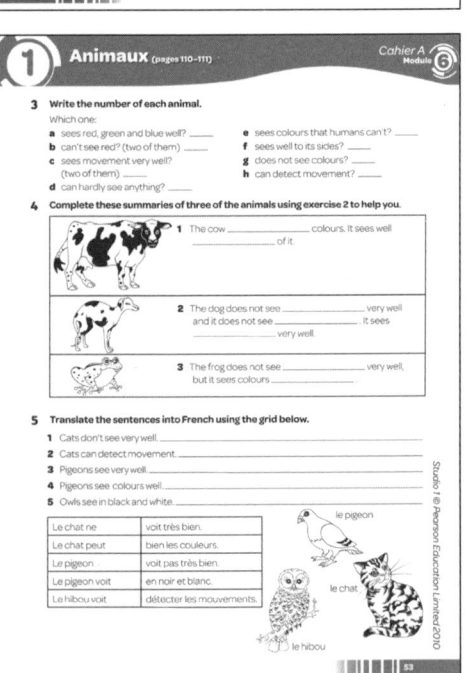

Answers

1 1 la grenouille 2 l'escargot 3 la vache
   4 l'aigle 5 l'abeille 6 le chien
2 (Accept any one fact for each animal:)
   1 Cow: can't see colours, sees well to the sides and slightly behind, doesn't see very well close up
   2 Dog: can't see colours very well, can't see red, sees quite well to the sides, sees movement very well
   3 Eagle: sees red, blue and green very well. When flying, it sees prey easily, does not fly at night
   4 Bee: doesn't see things that are near it very well, can't see red, but sees colours that humans can't see
   5 Frog: doesn't see shapes very well but sees movement very well, can see colours very well
   6 Snail: can hardly see anything, can detect movement and light which are near to it
3 a 3 b 2, 4 c 2, 5 d 6 e 4 f 1 g 1 h 6
4 1 doesn't see; to the sides
   2 colours; red; movement 3 shapes; very well
5 (Example answers:)
   1 Le chat ne voit pas très bien.
   2 Le chat peut détecter les mouvements.
   3 Le pigeon voit très bien.
   4 Le pigeon voit bien les couleurs.
   5 Le hibou voit en noir et blanc.

1 Animaux Studio découverte 6

Workbook B, pages 52–53

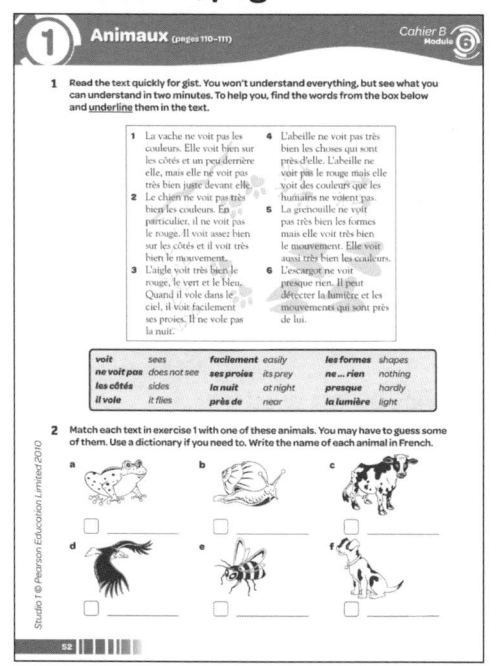

Worksheet 6.1 Les animaux

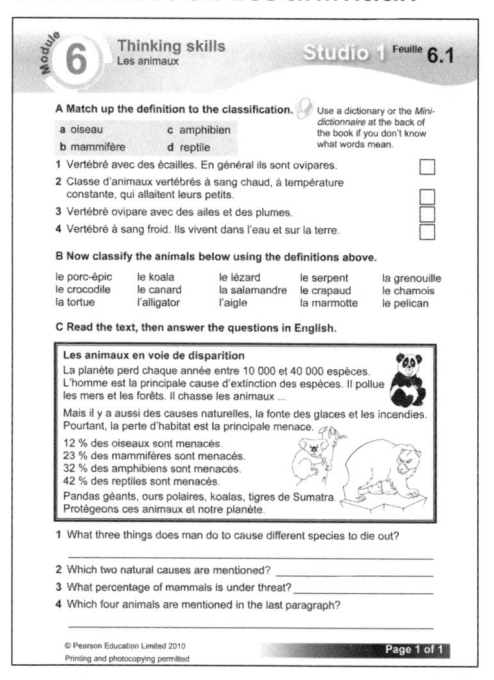

Answers
A 1 d 2 b 3 a 4 c

B

oiseau	mammifère	amphibien	reptile
le canard	le porc-épic	la grenouille	le lézard
l'aigle	le koala	la salamandre	le serpent
le pélican	le chamois	le crapaud	le crocodile
	la marmotte		la torture
			l'alligator

C 1 Pollutes the seas, pollutes the forests, hunts animals.
   2 Ice melting and fires.
   3 23%
   4 Giant pandas, polar bears, koalas, (Sumatran) tigers.

Answers
2 a 5 (la grenouille) b 6 (l'escargot) c 1 (la vache)
   d 3 (l'aigle) e 4 (l'abeille) f 2 (le chien)
3 a 2,4 b 5 c 3 d 1 e 3 f 6 g 4 h 2
   i 1 j 6
4 1 does not see 2 to the sides 3 behind it
   4 does not see 5 colours 6 does not see
   7 sees quite well 8 movement 9 shapes
   10 movement 11 sees 12 very well

2 Poésie (Pupil Book pp. 112–113)

Learning objective
- Writing a poem

Grammar
- the perfect tense

Key language
Review of language from throughout the course
Il est né …
Il a travaillé …
Il a écrit …
Il est allé …
Il est décédé …

PLTS
C Creative thinkers

Cross-curricular
English: discussing and writing poetry

Resources
CD 3, tracks 20–21
Cahier d'exercices A & B, pages 54–55
ActiveTeach:
p.113 Learning skills
p.116 Grammar
p.116 Grammar practice

Starter 1
Aim
To introduce the topic of poetry

Ask the class what poetry they have read. Do they have any favourite poems? Ask what makes a poem, prompting as necessary to cover rhyme, rhythm, repetition and linguistic features such as alliteration. Point out that poems don't need to contain all of these elements.

1 Écoute et mets les images dans l'ordre du poème. (AT 1.4, AT 3.4)
Listening. Pupils listen to the poem, reading the text at the same time. They then put the pictures in the order they are mentioned. Some vocabulary is glossed for support.

Audioscript CD 3 track 20

La fourmi (par Robert Desnos)
Une fourmi de dix-huit mètres
Avec un chapeau sur la tête,
Ça n'existe pas, ça n'existe pas.

Une fourmi traînant un char
Plein de pingouins et de canards,
Ça n'existe pas, ça n'existe pas.

Une fourmi parlant français,
Parlant latin et javanais,
Ça n'existe pas, ça n'existe pas.
Et pourquoi pas?

Answers
c, a, b

2 En tandem. Lis le poème à voix haute. Commente la prononciation de ton/ta camarade. (AT 2.4)
Speaking. In pairs: pupils take it in turn to read the poem in exercise 1 aloud and to comment on their partner's pronunciation. A tip box with expressions to use in giving this feedback is supplied.

3 Écoute et écris les mots qui manquent. (1–6) (AT 1.3, AT 3.3)
Listening. Pupils listen to and read another poem and complete the gap-fill version of the text.

Audioscript CD 3 track 21

Un **éléphant** de quarante mètres
Avec des **lunettes** sur la tête,
Ça n'existe pas, ça n'existe pas.

Un éléphant jouant au **flipper**
Avec un tigre et un **lion** vert,
Ça n'existe pas, ça n'existe pas.

Un éléphant faisant du **vélo**,
Regardant la **télé** et des vidéos,
Ça n'existe pas, ça n'existe pas.
Et pourquoi pas?

Answers
(Also in bold in the audioscript.)
1 éléphant 2 lunettes 3 flipper 4 lion 5 vélo 6 télé

Starter 2
Aim
To review the features of poems; To look at a poem critically

Ask pupils to read the poem in exercise 1 on p. 112 of the Pupil Book aloud. Then ask the class questions about the poem. Is it a good poem? Which features can they spot? Prompt as necessary to cover repetition (*Une fourmi, Ça n'existe pas*), humour, rhythm, surprise ending, etc. Ask pupils if they like the poem.

4 Lis le texte. Copie et remplis la fiche d'identité. (AT 3.5)
Reading. Pupils read the text about the poet Robert Desnos and complete the identity card about him. *il a été arrêté* is glossed for support.

2 Poésie Studio découverte 6

Answers
Date of birth: 4/7/1900
Profession: journalist
Other interests: poetry
Wartime activity: went to war, then worked for the Resistance, then was arrested
Cause of death: typhoid

➕ Explain that the text contains three verbs in the perfect tense which don't use *avoir* as the auxiliary. Ask pupils to find the verbs and, if possible, to identify the verb used *(il est né, il est allé, il est décédé – être)*. Explain that most verbs use *avoir* in the perfect tense, but some common verbs (mainly verbs of movement) use *être*. Introduce *je suis allé(e)* and *je suis sorti(e)* as two of the most useful forms. The *je* form of the perfect tense (for both *avoir* and *être* verbs) is summarised and practised on p. 116.

5 Compose un poème suivant le modèle de *La fourmi*. Puis dessine trois images pour illustrer ton poème. (AT 4.4)
PLTS C

Writing. Pupils write a poem using 'La fourmi' as a model and draw three pictures to illustrate their poem. A spidergram that they can use as a model to prepare what they will write is supplied for support. Draw pupils' attention to the tip box on adapting a written model.

Plenary
Ask some pupils to read their poems aloud, with the rest of the class giving constructive feedback.

Alternative Plenary:
Use ActiveTeach p. 116 Grammar practice activities to review and practise the perfect tense.

Workbook A, pages 54–55

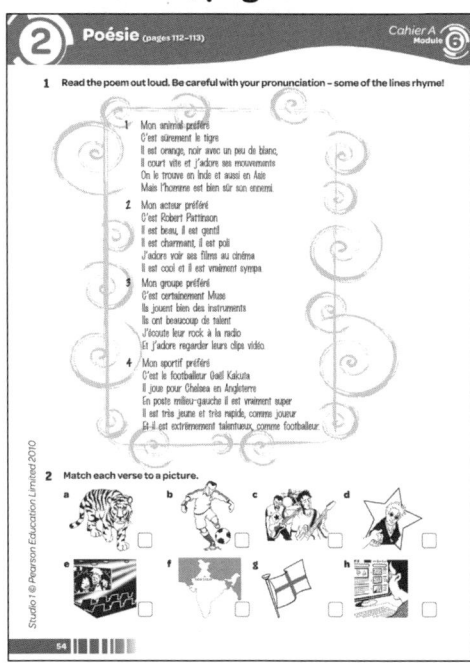

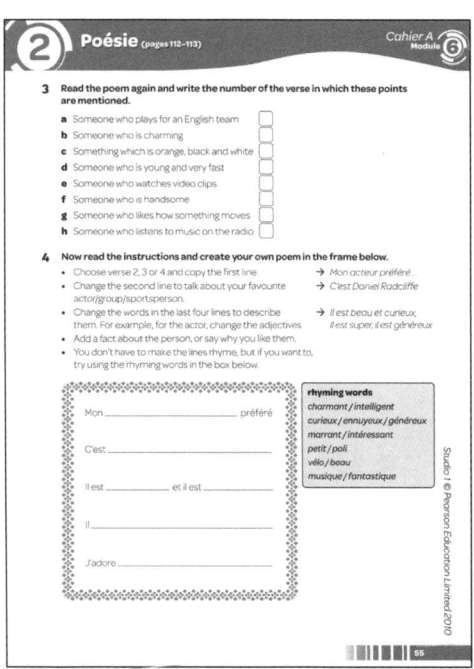

Answers
2 a 1 b 4 c 3 d 2 e 2 f 1 g 4 h 3
3 a 4 b 2 c 1 d 4 e 3 f 2 g 1 h 3

6 Studio découverte 2 Poésie

Workbook B, pages 54–55

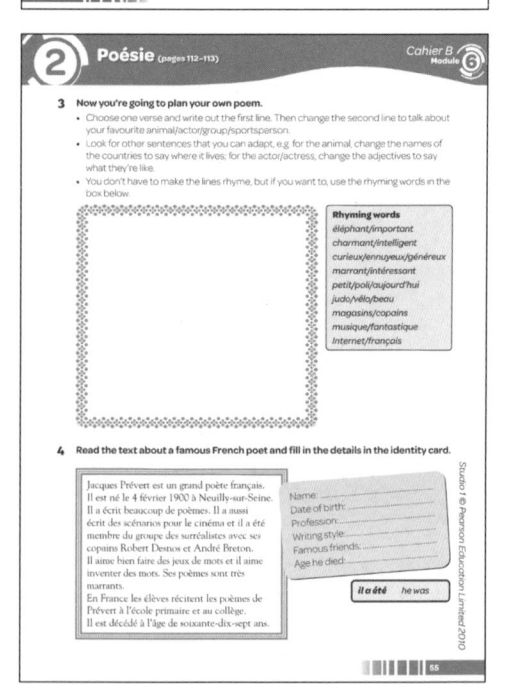

2 Poésie (pages 112–113)

1 Read the poem out loud. Be careful with your pronunciation – some of the lines rhyme!

1 Mon animal préféré
   C'est sûrement le tigre
   Il est orange, noir avec un peu de blanc,
   Il court vite et j'adore ses mouvements
   On le trouve en Inde et aussi en Asie
   Mais l'homme est bien sûr son ennemi.

2 Mon acteur préféré
   C'est Robert Pattinson
   Il est beau, il est gentil
   Il est charmant, il est poli
   J'adore voir ses films au cinéma
   Il est cool et il est vraiment sympa.

3 Mon groupe préféré
   C'est certainement Muse
   Ils jouent bien des instruments
   Ils ont beaucoup de talent
   J'écoute leur rock à la radio
   Et j'adore regarder leurs clips vidéo.

4 Mon sportif préféré
   C'est le footballeur Gaël Kakuta
   Il joue pour Chelsea en Angleterre
   En poste milieu-gauche il est vraiment super
   Il est très jeune et très rapide, comme joueur
   Et il est extrêmement talentueux, comme footballeur.

2 Read the poem again and answer these questions.

1 What is said about the tiger? (2 things) _____
2 Where can you find the tiger? _____
3 How is Robert Pattinson described? (4 things) _____
4 How does the writer listen to and watch Muse? _____
5 Who is Gaël Kakuta? _____
6 How is he described? (2 things) _____

3 Now you're going to plan your own poem.

- Choose one verse and write out the first line. Then change the second line to talk about your favourite animal/actor/group/sportsperson.
- Look for other sentences that you can adapt, e.g. for the animal, change the names of the countries to say where it lives; for the actor/actress, change the adjectives to say what they're like.
- You don't have to make the lines rhyme, but if you want to, use the rhyming words in the box below.

Rhyming words
éléphant/important
charmant/intelligent
curieux/ennuyeux/généreux
marrant/intéressant
petit/poli/aujourd'hui
judo/vélo/beau
magasins/copains
musique/fantastique
Internet/français

4 Read the text about a famous French poet and fill in the details in the identity card.

Jacques Prévert est un grand poète français.
Il est né le 4 février 1900 à Neuilly-sur-Seine.
Il a écrit beaucoup de poèmes. Il a aussi écrit des scénarios pour le cinéma et il a été membre du groupe des surréalistes avec ses copains Robert Desnos et André Breton.
Il aime bien faire des jeux de mots et il aime inventer des mots. Ses poèmes sont très marrants.
En France les élèves récitent les poèmes de Prévert à l'école primaire et au collège.
Il est décédé à l'âge de soixante-dix-sept ans.

Name:
Date of birth:
Profession:
Writing style:
Famous friends:
Age he died:

il a été — he was

Worksheet 6.2 Les poèmes

A Choose the right word from the box to fill in the gaps.

Sept couleurs magiques

Rouge comme un _____ du Mexique
Orangé _____ comme le sable d'Afrique
Jaune comme les girafes _____
Vert _____ comme un sorbet de Jamaïque
Bleu comme les vagues du _____
Indigo _____ un papillon des tropiques
Violet comme les _____ de Martinique
Qui donc est aussi fantastique
Est-ce un rêve ou est-ce véridique?
C'est dans le ciel magnifique
L'arc aux sept couleurs magiques

comme
chics
volcans
fruit
Vert
Pacifique
Orangé

Mymi Doinet
Mon premier livre de devinettes,
Poèmes et dessins inédits réunis
par Jacques Charpentreau,
Édition de l'Atelier

B Read the poem aloud.

C Find the French for these nouns in the poem.

1 volcanoes _____   2 sand _____   3 waves _____
4 giraffes _____   5 butterfly _____

D Use a dictionary to write your own version of this poem.

Rouge comme _____   Violet comme _____
Orangé comme _____   Qui donc est aussi fantastique
Jaune comme _____   Est-ce un rêve ou est-ce véridique?
Vert comme _____   C'est dans le ciel magnifique
Bleu comme _____   L'arc aux sept couleurs magique
Indigo comme _____

Answers

A Rouge comme un **fruit** du Mexique
   Orangé comme le sable d'Afrique
   Jaune comme les girafes **chics**
   Vert comme un sorbet de Jamaïque
   Bleu comme les vagues du **Pacifique**
   Indigo **comme** un papillon des tropiques
   Violet comme les **volcans** de Martinique
   Qui donc est aussi fantastique
   Est-ce un rêve ou est-ce véridique?
   C'est dans le ciel magnifique
   L'arc aux sept couleurs magiques

C 1 volcanoes   les volcans
   2 sand   le sable
   3 waves   les vagues
   4 giraffes   les girafes
   5 butterfly   un papillon

D (Answers will vary.)

Answers

2 1 (Any two of:) orange and black with a bit of white, runs quickly; man is its enemy
   2 India and Asia
   3 (Any four of:) handsome, kind, charming, polite, cool, really nice
   4 listens to music on the radio and watches their videos
   5 footballer who plays for Chelsea
   6 (Any two of:) great, very young, very quick, extremely talented

4 Name: Jacques Prévert
   Date of birth: 4 February 1900
   Profession: Poet and scriptwriter
   Writing style: He writes funny poems
   Famous friends: Robert Desnos and André Breton (surrealist people)
   Age he died: 77

3 Peintures (Pupil Book pp. 114–115)

Studio découverte 6

Learning objective
- Describing a painting

Grammar
- the perfect tense

Key language
Review of language for expressing opinions
J'ai fait des recherches sur …
J'ai choisi un tableau qui s'appelle …
J'ai bien regardé.
J'ai identifié (douze) couleurs différentes.
J'ai trouvé …
au centre
sur la gauche/droite
devant
derrière
il y a …/on peut voir …

PLTS
I Independent enquirers

Cross-curricular
Art: famous painters
ICT: Internet research

Resources
CD 3, tracks 22–24
Accès Studio pages 16–17
Cahier d'exercices A & B, pages 56–57
ActiveTeach:
p.115 Learning skills

Accès Studio Unit 7 (pp. 16–17) can be used with this unit to review colours and adjective agreement.

Starter 1
Aim
To review adjectives

Give pupils three minutes working in pairs to list as many adjectives in French as they can.

Check answers, asking pupils to translate them into English. Write up: *bleu, un livre, une fleur*. Ask the class the French for 'a blue book' and 'a blue flower' to review agreement and position of adjectives.

1 Écoute et lis. (AT 1.4)
Listening. Pupils listen to the description of a painting by Henri 'le Douanier' Rousseau, reading the text at the same time. Explain that his nickname, *le Douanier*, came from the fact that he used to work as a customs officer before he became an artist. Some vocabulary is glossed for support.

Audioscript — CD 3 track 22

Au centre, on peut voir le peintre. Il s'appelle Henri «le Douanier» Rousseau. Il a les cheveux blancs. Il porte un béret et il a une moustache. Il est assis sur un tigre et il joue de la guitare.
Le tigre est superbe. Il est de couleur orange avec des rayures noires. Il a aussi un peu de blanc. Il a de grandes dents.
Sur la gauche et sur la droite du tableau, il y a des fleurs roses, blanches et bleues.
Sur la gauche, on peut voir un lion parmi les fleurs. Derrière, on peut voir la lune. Devant, il y a des plantes.

2 Trouve ces phrases en français dans le texte. (AT 3.4)
Reading. Pupils re-read the text in exercise 1 and identify in it the French versions of the English phrases listed.

Answers
1 au centre 2 sur la gauche 3 sur la droite
4 on peut voir 5 il y a 6 derrière 7 devant
8 sur

R Reinforce the prepositions in exercise 2 by using a soft toy or classroom item as a prompt.

3 Écoute. Qui dit quoi? Écris le bon nom. (1–6) (AT 1.4)
Listening. Pupils listen to three people discussing the painting shown in exercise 1. They read the six comments on the painting and identify who said each one.

Audioscript — CD 3 track 23

– Décris ce tableau, Alyzée.
– Eh bien, au centre il y a un oiseau. Il est bleu et rouge.
Sur la gauche, il y a un singe dans un arbre. Il est drôle! Il y a aussi des fleurs blanches et des oranges. Sur la droite, il y a une fleur bleue et, en haut du tableau, des fleurs roses. Devant, il y a un groupe de singes avec des oranges. Derrière, on peut voir le soleil orange.
– Quelle est ton opinion sur le tableau, Lucie?
– Moi, j'aime les singes et j'aime les couleurs. J'adore, surtout les fleurs et les plantes. J'adore le tableau. À mon avis, c'est très intéressant et amusant. Tu es d'accord, Florian?

6 Studio découverte 3 Peintures

– Non, je ne suis pas du tout d'accord. À mon avis, c'est bizarre. Je n'aime pas les fleurs et je n'aime pas les plantes non plus. Est-ce qu'on trouve des oranges dans la jungle? Je ne sais pas, moi. Je n'aime pas du tout le tableau. Pour moi, c'est nul. Et toi, Alyzée? Tu aimes ce tableau?

– Oui, j'aime bien. J'aime les plantes et les couleurs, mais je n'aime pas beaucoup les singes. Ils sont un peu bizarres. Moi, personnellement, je préfère les tableaux de Monet.

Answers
1 Florian 2 Alyzée 3 Lucie 4 Lucie 5 Alyzée
6 Florian

Starter 2
Aim
To review language for expressing opinions;
To use grammatical knowledge to work out connections

Write up the following, jumbling the order of the second column. Give pupils three minutes to match the sentence halves.

1 J'aime le   a tableau.
2 Je n'aime   b pas les couleurs.
3 À mon   c avis, c'est amusant.
4 C'est   d très intéressant.
5 Surtout, j'adore   e le tigre.
6 Je préfère les   f tableaux de Picasso.
7 Pour moi,   g c'est nul.

Check answers, asking pupils to explain how they worked them out. Pupils then translate the sentences into English.

4 Écoute à nouveau. Identifie l'attitude de chaque personne. (AT 1.4)
Listening. Pupils listen to the recording from exercise 3 again and answer the questions on it, identifying the attitude of the three speakers towards the painting.

Audioscript CD 3 track 24

As for exercise 3

Answers
1 Lucie 2 Alyzée 3 Florian

5 En tandem. Décris le tableau de Rousseau et donne ton opinion. Adapte les phrases de Florian, d'Alyzée et de Lucie. Utilise les mots à droite. (AT 2.4)
Speaking. In pairs: pupils describe another painting by Rousseau, shown on the page, and give their opinion of it.

6 Lis le texte et trouve les phrases en français. (AT 3.5)
Reading. Pupils read the text and identify in it the French versions of the English verbs listed. This involves the perfect tense. *une montgolfière* is glossed for support.

Answers
1 j'ai observé 2 j'ai fait des recherches sur
3 j'ai trouvé 4 j'ai choisi 5 j'ai identifié
6 j'ai (bien) regardé

7 Choisis un tableau. Écris une description. (AT 4.5)

PLTS

Writing. Pupils research a painting of their own choice, either using books or the Internet. The painting can be by any artist. They then write a description of the painting, using the perfect tense. A framework is supplied.

8 Crée un tableau dans le style d'Henri Rousseau. Présente le tableau à la classe. (AT 2.4)
Speaking. Pupils draw or paint a scene in the style of Henri Rousseau, then present their drawing/painting to the class.

Plenary
Challenge pupils to remember the six verbs in the perfect tense that they found in exercise 6. Then ask pupils to tell the class which picture they chose to research in exercise 7 and to say one thing about it using one of the perfect tense verbs.

3 Peintures   Studio découverte   6

Workbook A, pages 56–57

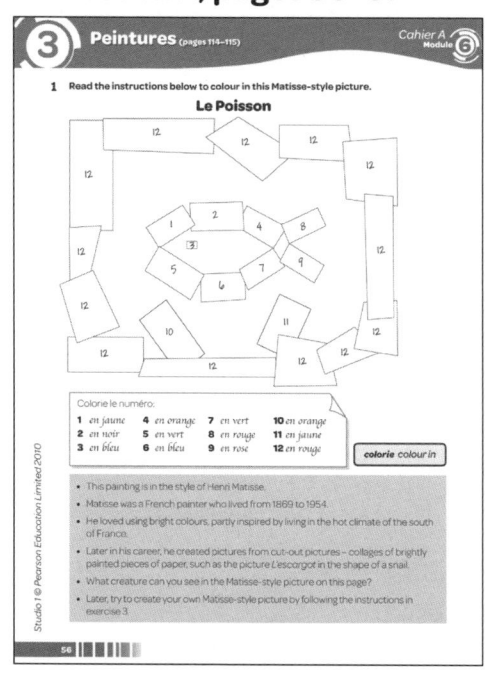

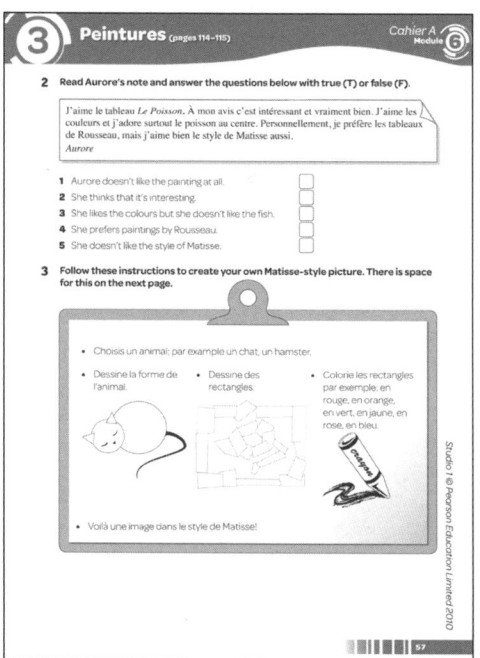

Workbook B, pages 56–57

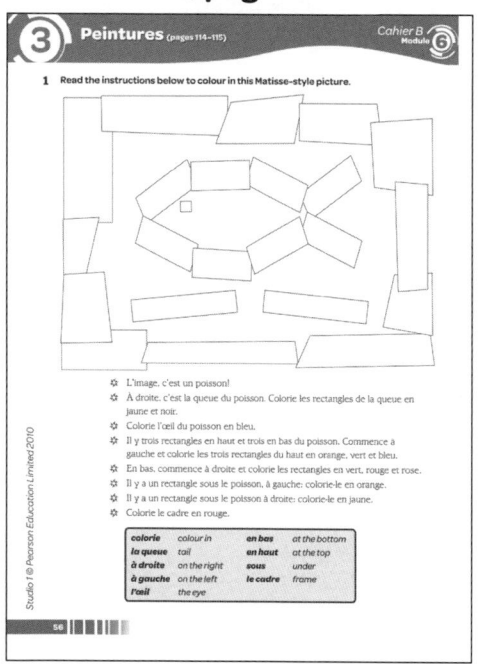

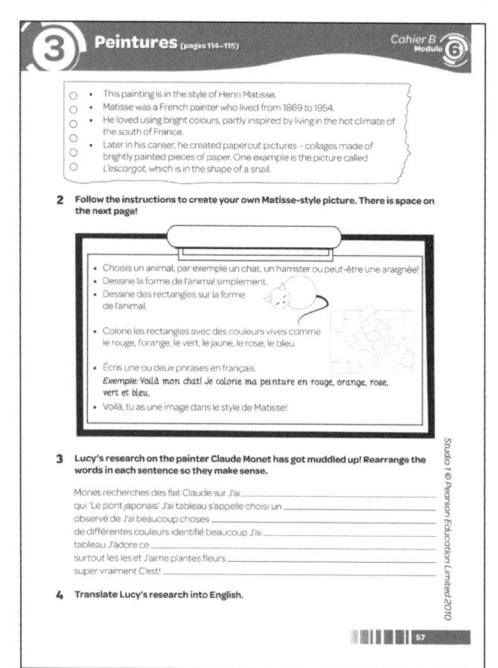

Answers
1 (The picture should be coloured as follows:)
   1 yellow **2** black **3** blue **4** orange **5** green
   6 blue **7** green **8** red **9** pink **10** orange
   11 yellow **12** red
2 **1** F **2** T **3** F **4** T **5** F

6 Studio découverte 3 Peintures

Answers

1 (The picture should be coloured as follows:)
- two rectangles of tail: yellow and black
- eye: blue
- three rectangles forming top of fish, starting at the left: orange, green and blue
- three rectangles forming bottom of fish, starting on the right; green, red and pink
- rectangle under the fish on the left: orange
- rectangle under the fish on the right: yellow
- frame: red

3 J'ai fait des recherches sur Claude Monet.
J'ai choisi un tableau qui s'appelle 'Le pont japonais'.
J'ai observé beaucoup de choses.
J'ai identifié beaucoup de couleurs différentes.
J'adore ce tableau.
J'aime surtout les plantes et les fleurs.
C'est vraiment super!

Worksheet 6.3 La peinture

Answers

A Au centre du tableau, il y a une **table**. Sur la table, on peut voir une **cage**. Dans la cage, il y a un oiseau. Il y a aussi une lampe **sur** la table. **Entre** la cage et la lampe, on peut voir des fruits. Il y a une **chaise** derrière la table et **sous** la table, on peut voir un petit chat.

B (Answers will vary.)

C (Answers will vary.)

Studio Grammaire (Pupil Book pp. 116–117)

Studio découverte 6

The *Studio Grammaire* section provides a more detailed summary of the key grammar covered in the module, along with further exercises to practise these points.

Grammar topic
- the perfect tense

Resources
ActiveTeach:
p.117 Grammar skills

The perfect tense

1 How would you say the following in French?
Pupils look in the summary of the perfect tense on this page, to find the French versions of the English verbs listed.

Answers
1 j'ai choisi   2 j'ai examiné   3 j'ai fait
4 je suis allé(e)   5 je suis sorti(e)   6 j'ai regardé
7 j'ai rencontré   8 j'ai aimé   9 j'ai mangé
10 j'ai étudié

2 Read the text, then complete the sentences in English, as though you were Rebecca.
Pupils read Rebecca's text, then complete the sentences summarising it in English as if they were her.

Answers
1 I chose **the coral snake**.
2 I studied **its habitat**.
3 I examined **its character**.
4 I observed **what it looks like/its physical appearance**.
5 I researched **its food**.
6 I found **its enemy**.

3 Make a list of the six verbs in the perfect tense in the text.
Pupils re-read the text in exercise 2 and list the six verbs in the perfect tense that are used in it.

Answers
j'ai choisi   j'ai étudié   j'ai examiné   j'ai observé
j'ai recherché   j'ai trouvé

4 Write out the past participles of the verbs.
Pupils write the past participles of the infinitives listed. Draw pupils' attention to the tip box, which explains that learning how the perfect tense is formed will help them to apply it in other contexts, and achieve a higher level.

Answers
surfé   partagé   regardé   dansé   travaillé   nagé
téléchargé   fini

5 Ryan has made six mistakes in the perfect tense. Can you correct them for him?
Pupils read Ryan's text and correct the six errors he has made in using perfect tense verbs.

Answers
Hier soir, j'ai **fait** mes devoirs et ensuite, j'**ai** surfé sur Internet.
J'ai **regardé** des clips vidéo et j'ai aussi **téléchargé** de la musique.
Plus tard, **j'ai** regardé la télévision et j'ai **envoyé** des e-mails à mes copains.

6 Read these sentences. Copy out and fill in the grid.
Pupils copy out the grid. They read the five sentences and complete the grid with the verbs used, separating them into present tense and perfect tense. The tip box points out that pupils need to show they can use the present tense plus another tense in order to attain Level 5.

Answers

Normally, during the holidays ... (present tense)	but this summer ... (perfect tense)
je visite	j'ai visité
je fais	j'ai joué
je vais	je suis allé
je vais	je suis allée
je nage	j'ai nagé

7 Write out these sentences to show you can use the present tense and the perfect tense together.
Pupils use the phrases supplied to write sentences using a combination of the present tense and the perfect tense. Draw pupils' attention to the tip box on using the present tense plus two other tenses to attain Level 6.

175

6 Studio découverte Studio Grammaire

Answers

1. Normalement, pendant les vacances, **je danse**, mais cet été, **j'ai fait du karaoké**.
2. Normalement, pendant les vacances, **je fais de la voile**, mais cet été, **j'ai fait de la planche à voile**.
3. Normalement, pendant les vacances, **je joue au volley**, mais cet été, **j'ai joué au football**.
4. Normalement, pendant les vacances, **je vais à la campagne**, mais cet été, **je suis allé(e) à la mer**.
5. Normalement, pendant les vacances, **je vais en Grèce**, mais cet été, **je suis allé(e) en Italie**.

Worksheet 6.4 The perfect tense

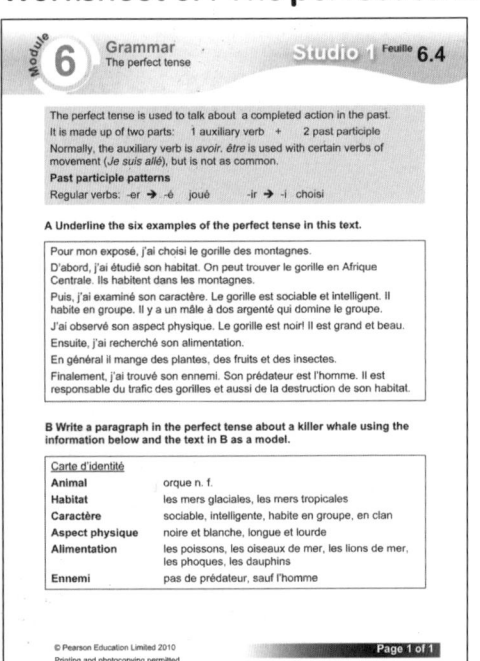

Answers

A Pour mon exposé, j'ai choisi le gorille des montagnes.
D'abord, j'ai étudié son habitat. On peut trouver le gorille en Afrique Centrale. Ils habitent dans les montagnes.
Puis, j'ai examiné son caractère. Le gorille est sociable et intelligent. Il habite en groupe. Il y a un mâle à dos argenté qui domine le groupe.
J'ai observé son aspect physique. Le gorille est noir! Il est grand et beau.
Ensuite, j'ai recherché son alimentation. En général, il mange des plantes, des fruits et des insectes.
Finalement, j'ai trouvé son ennemi. Son prédateur est l'homme. Il est responsable du trafic des gorilles et aussi de la destruction de son habitat.

B (Example answer:)
Pour mon exposé, j'ai choisi l'orque.
D'abord, j'ai étudié son habitat. On peut trouver l'orque dans les mers glaciales et les mers tropicales.
Puis, j'ai examiné son caractère. L'orque est sociable et intelligente. Elle habite en groupe, en clan.
J'ai observé son aspect physique. L'orque est noire et blanche! Elle est longue et lourde.
Ensuite, j'ai recherché son alimentation.
En général, elle mange des poissons, des oiseaux de mer, des lions de mer, des phoques et des dauphins.
Finalement, j'ai trouvé son ennemi. Elle n'a pas de prédateur sauf l'homme.